A Dictionary of
Social Science Methods

A Dictionary of
Social Science Methods

P. McC. Miller
*Medical Research Council Epidemiology Unit,
Royal Edinburgh Hospital*

and

M. J. Wilson
*Faculty of Social Sciences
The Open University*

JOHN WILEY & SONS
Chichester . New York . Brisbane . Toronto . Singapore

H
41
.M54
1983

Library of Congress Cataloging in Publication Data:

Miller, P. McC.
  A dictionary of social science methods.

  Includes index.
  1. Social sciences—Methodology—Dictionaries.
I. Wilson, M. J. (Michael John), 1939– . II. Title.
H41.M54 1983   300'.1'8   82–13681

ISBN 0 471 90035 4 (cloth)
ISBN 0 471 90036 2 (paper)

British Library Cataloguing in Publication Data:

Miller, P.McC.
  A dictionary of social science methods.
  1. Social sciences—Methodology—Dictionaries
  2. Social sicences—Fieldwork—Dictionaries
  I. Title   II. Wilson, M. J.
  300'.72   H61

ISBN 0 471 90035 4 (cloth)
ISBN 0 471 90036 2 (paper)

Typeset by Activity, New Canal, Salisbury.
Printed by Page Bros. (Norwich) Ltd.

Acknowledgements

The idea for this dictionary first arose from our work in preparing materials for a course on research methods in the social sciences for The Open University. We are grateful to the University for allowing us to re-use a small part of that material and to those colleagues with whom we worked in preparing the course. We should emphasize that neither the University nor our colleagues are in any way responsible for this book and our thanks to them are due for what we learnt in our collaboration. Especial thanks to: Martin Bulmer, John Bynner, Judith Calder, Peter Coxhead, Jim Davis, Jeff Evans, Martyn Hammersley, Cathie Marsh, Desmond Nuttall, Bram Oppenheim, Albert Pilliner, and Betty Swift.

We are grateful to Tiiu Miller and Glen McDougall who both gave sustained and thoughtful advice throughout the preparation of the dictionary and to Aillinn Wilson for editorial help in the planning of a long and complex work.

Yvonne Honeywell at The Open University, Caroline Urquhart and Joyce Greig at the MRC Unit have all helped with the lengthy and difficult typing which the manuscript required and we are in their debt.

Finally, our families deserve our particular thanks for their forbearance and help during the dictionary's preparation.

P.McC.M.
M.J.W.
April 1982

Preface

The major purpose of this dictionary is to collect in one convenient source accounts of the current methods of inquiry which the empirical social sciences share in common, together with accounts of methods peculiar to particular disciplines and which are (or ought to be) of wider interest. Mere definitions have a limited usefulness since they may give the essence of a term or method but lose sight of the controversies, plural meanings, and above all of the context which surrounds its use in the social sciences. It is, then, a second important purpose of this book to extend beyond definition only and to try to explain, illustrate, and to set in context the majority of the terms which this book contains. Setting in context has been achieved in two ways: within the entries themselves, although the extent to which this has been done depends on the length of the entry, and by a system of internal cross-referencing which indicates to the reader where to find terms relevant to a particular term under discussion. The system of cross-referencing is fully explained in 'How to use this Dictionary' (page ix).

The selection of terms for a dictionary of methods is doubly difficult because of the indistinct line to be drawn between methods as such and substantive theory, and again between methodological issues and philosophical terms and debates. We have resolved these choices as well as we can and kept the book to a reasonable length by excluding for the most part substantive theories and techniques for intervention. There is no coverage, for example, of concepts drawn from learning theory or from behaviour therapy.

We have also left out terms which are commonly confined to discourse within the philosophy of science but we have thought it best to include as entries those terms and concepts which, though philosophical, frequently enter into debates about research practice or the interpretation of research. Thus, we include a full entry on CAUSATION as a question actively debated in the findings of substantive research but we exclude any reference to primitive terms on the grounds that the problems which they raise are still of concern mainly to philosophers of theory construction.

The large body of statistical models and terms which readers will expect to find in a work such as this has been kept to manageable proportions by omitting the more obscure statistics and concentrating on the more commonly used ones. Although, doubtless, our choices on what to include and what to exclude will offend some, we hope to have reflected the general practice of research in the social sciences. When in doubt as to whether to include a term or not we have used the criterion of its relevance to the current practice of research rather than its potential theoretical importance.

We have dealt with statistical theory as far as possible from the practitioners' point of view and we have made no attempt to be mathematically rigorous or to derive expressions strictly. We have, however, given formulae and equations where useful (as is the usual case) and all the symbols used are fully explained. Note that we have adopted the convention of using greek symbols for population statistics and roman ones for sample statistics.

Lastly, we are certainly aware that a work such as this will contain errors; some in the choice of what to include and what to leave out in the way of entries, and some in what we write about particular concepts and methods. We leave it to the reader to judge.

P.McC. MILLER
Medical Research Council Epidemiology Unit
Royal Edinburgh Hospital

M.J. WILSON
Faculty of Social Sciences,
The Open University

How to use this Dictionary

The headings of entries in the text are of three different kinds, each of which is shown by a distinct typeface. Bold capitals (e.g. **FACTOR ANALYSIS**) signify a long entry which defines a method or term of central importance in the methodology of the social sciences. Such entries place a term in context, list and explain the vocabulary associated with it, discuss its uses in the literature, and assess its relative strengths and weaknesses. Under **FACTOR ANALYSIS** will be found a general account of the logic of the method followed by a briefer one of the different types of factor analysis and their specific terms, and ending with a discussion of the main uses and limitations of the technique.

Ordinary bold type (e.g. **Anchor Definition**) signifies an entry which has more or less a standard dictionary definition, although usually more expansive in form and frequently containing an illustrative example.

Bold italics (e.g. *Biassed Estimator*) represent an entry which is simply a heading cross-referenced to another entry where it will be found to be explained as part of a discussion of related terms.

The *Dictionary* has been written on a system of internal cross-referencing in order to avoid excessive repetition. In an entry, terms which are defined elsewhere in the book are shown by the corresponding typeface so that the reader will know at a glance how long an entry to expect if he or she chooses to look it up. The reader is invited to follow up such cross-references until satisfied that no more useful knowledge is to be gained.

For example, under **ESTIMATION** will be found in part:

'... estimation of **regression weights** or coefficients in simple or multiple **REGRESSION ANALYSIS** follows the principles above but ...'

The reader who is unsure of either or both of the cross-referenced terms will know that a long entry for regression analysis and a short one for regression weights will be found in the appropriate place and may be quickly consulted if desired.

A

Abscissa The horizontal axis in a two-dimensional graph. The vertical axis is the *ordinate*. More modern usage is to call the horizontal axis the X-axis and the vertical one the Y-axis. See also **Graphic Presentation**

Absolute Difference The difference between two quantities taken irrespective of the sign, so that both negative and positive differences are treated as if positive. The absolute difference between two quantities x and y is symbolized as $|x - y|$.

Access Legitimate entry to a research field with reasonable freedom of action within it.

Achievement Test A test which measures how much has been learnt or is known by a subject, as distinct from an *aptitude test* which measures *ability to learn*. Achievement tests are published commercially. Many of them have **norms** relative to other people rather than to an absolute standard.

Acquiescence Response Set A tendency to agree with any statement put, regardless of its content. The effects of possible acquiescence in questionnaires may be controlled — usually by keying items in opposing directions so that agreement sometimes scores and sometimes does not score on the dimension being measured.

Action Research Research where instead of minimizing the impact of the investigations on the subjects or individuals under study, changes are purposefully introduced in order to study what, if any, effects occur.
Examples of action research include the use of intensive reading development programmes in classrooms, treatments for alcoholism, new types of penal institutions, and community development programmes in inner city districts. Ideally, changes (the 'action') should not be introduced before the existing field of study has been fully investigated so that some accurate 'baseline' is available against which to measure the results of the planned intervention. This intervention itself should be carefully designed so that unknown factors (or variables) are not brought into play accidentally and the changes may be attributed

unequivocally to the researchers' deliberate manipulations. If these points are adequately met then action research becomes a form of **field experiment**, but with the reservation that historical or **maturational** changes are not allowed for. That is to say, the field of study may have changed because of the elapse of time whether or not 'action' or intervention by the researchers had taken place. In reading development programmes, for example, the fact that the group under study may be significantly older after the programmes has been applied might well, in itself, lead to improvements in reading attainment.
Action research reports frequently show a gulf between the researchers who design the study and the practitioners who put it into effect. Such a lack of co-ordination between the two central tasks of action research may weaken its validity.

Additivity In MULTIPLE REGRESSION analysis, if the value of the **dependent variable** can be accurately estimated by summing the particular values of the **independent variables** (each weighted by a **regression coefficient**) and the constant term then the equation is an additive one.
The converse of additivity is **interaction** where the value of the dependent variable will depend on how the value of one independent variable may interact with the value of another. More generally, if an effect is produced by several variables acting simultaneously, then the statistical model is additive if and only if the portion of the effect contributed by an independent variable does not depend on the value of any other independent variable. In Mendelian genetics, for example, the contribution of father's height to offspring's height will not depend on mother's height and vice versa, and offspring's height can be estimated simply by $H_0 = \alpha + \beta (H_f + H_m)$.
Additivity may be an asumption (which can be tested) of models or a requirement of a test or analytical technique.

Adjusted Mean A mean which has been adjusted, using the technique of **covariance analysis**, in order to allow for the effects of an extraneous uncontrolled variable.

Age-Cohort-Survival Method Forecast of the future size and composition (age and sex) of a

1

human population, either national or regional, based on assumptions about future rates of fertility, mortality, and migration.

The projection starts from a base year (*t*) whose *age-specific fertility* and *death-rates* are known and are applied to age cohorts of the current population in order to calculate survivors (from death-rates) who will pass into the next age cohort, and live births (fertility) who will progress through the age cohorts and be subjected to successive death-rates and fertility-rates. The effect of in- and out-migration on both the size of the population and on its fertility and death-rates is also added to the forecast. Forecasts may be made for successive time-intervals ahead of the base year (*t* + 1, *t* + 2, ..., *t* + *n*) allowing for age cohorts changing through migration and ageing steadily and thus requiring different age-specific rates. Projection errors are cumulative and systematic because rates are fixed in the last year of observation (*t*) and may change, particularly in the case of fertility rates. Population forecasts are continually revised to use the most recent rates of death, birth, and migration, as they are incresingly prone to error the further ahead a projection is made.

Age-specific Death-rate   See under **Death-Rate**

Age-specific Fertility-Rate   See under **Birth-Rate**

Age-specific Sex Ratio   See **Sex Ratio**

Agreement Coefficient   An agreement coefficient measures not only the extent to which two variables are correlated or associated but also the extent to which they have the same values in correspondence. Agreement in this sense implies correlation, but correlation does not imply agreement. Agreement is, therefore, much the more demanding concept of the two. Fisher used an agreement coefficient for his analysis of data from sets of twins, where the theoretical demands of the study required twins to show identical measurements in mental and physical traits.

Various agreement coefficients are available depending on the level of measurement — in the **nominal** case **Scott's** π, in the **ordinal** case **Kendall's Tau**, and in the **interval** case, Fisher's **Intra-class correlation** coefficient.

AGGREGATION

The placing of discrete observations on individuals (companies, subjects, etc.) into groups so that individual observations can no longer be recovered except by going back to the original sources of data. This is frequently not practicable or possible in the case of official

statistics or in any case where the original data before aggregation have been lost or have been withheld. *Disaggregation* is either re-partitioning the aggregated groups into new and smaller groups, or at the extreme, recovering data at the individual level.

All official statistics aggregate data. This leads to clarity of presentation (by removing excessive detail) especially in tabulated forms, protection of individuals from possible identification, and to easier analysis. Unfortunately, in many cases, the aggregated groups do not match the investigator's theoretical objectives. The **Standard Industrial Classification** (SIC), for example, is widely used in the social sciences where it forms the variable of the industrial sector in a number of statistical series, but it reports data for very large aggregates of companies or sections of the labour-force. SIC data has high **variances** on useful variables such as size of work-force, capital intensity, and technological level both within and between aggregate sectors. Thus, comparison of sectors on a variable such as man-days lost in industrial disputes (from the **Employment Gazette**) will be difficult because extraneous variables such as company size will be confounded with industrial sector.

Aggregation may be a source of special difficulties in economic analysis over and above the general problems noted above. Many economic theories are based on models of microeconomic behaviour and yet can be tested only on data which is highly aggregated and which has to 'represent' microeconomic activity, perhaps not accurately if the aggregate group is not a homogeneous one with respect to the variable or variables under study.

AH5 Test   A **group-administered** intelligence test devised for use with highly intelligent people. It aims to discriminate amongst these more precisely than other intelligence tests would. It can be used from age 13 years and there are **norms** for several groups including university students, grammar school children, and engineering apprentice applicants.

Alpha Coefficient (Cronbach's Alpha)   The mean value of all possible **split half reliability** coefficients for a test. It is given by

$$\alpha = \frac{n}{n-1}\left(1 - \frac{\text{sum of variances of question scores}}{\text{variance of total scores}}\right)$$

where *n* is the number of questions in the test. See also RELIABILITY

Alpha (α) *Probability of Type I Error*   See **Type I Error**

2

Alternate Forms Reliability RELIABILITY assessed using two equivalent forms of a test on different occasions.

Alternative Hypothesis An hypothesis which is 'alternative' to the **null hypothesis** and states that differences will be found between two or more groups on some particular variable. A second meaning is an hypothesis which explains results equally as well as the hypothesis being tested.

Ambiguity of Testing When an hypothesis is tested it is generally possible that the results obtained may be explained at least in part by some hypothesis other than the one tested. This is ambiguity of testing.

ANALYSIS OF VARIANCE (ANOVA)

A flexible technique which has many uses. Two of the most important are to test whether there are significant differences between the means of several different groups of observations, and to test the significance of simple and MULTIPLE CORRELATION coefficients. The test is particularly useful where there are several means or correlations to test at the same time. Testing each separately by means of a **Z-test** or a **t-test** would increase the probability of falsely rejecting the **null hypothesis** (probabilities of error sum across tests, and with twenty tests and a 5 per cent significance level it is virtually certain that a spuriously significant result will be reported); analysis of variance helps to overcome this problem.

An analysis of variance is termed simple or one-way if only one independent variable is involved, e.g. if one wished to see whether reading ability (**dependent variable**) was different for pupils of high, middle, and low socio-economic status (**independent variable**). It is said to be multiple or complex if there is more than one independent variable, e.g. if it was desired to test whether both sex and socio-economic status affected reading ability. In multiple analysis of variance, **interactions** may arise. That is to say, the various levels of one independent variable may not affect the dependent variable in the same way within all the levels of another independent variable. For example, in the two-way analysis cited above socio-economic status might affect the reading ability of girls and boys in different ways. Interactions are tested after the **main effects** (i.e. overall effects) of the independent variables have been assessed.

Theoretically, analysis of variance is a special case of the general **linear model** which also underlies MULTIPLE REGRESSION ANALYSIS. The first step in an analysis of variance is to obtain *sums of squares*. The *total sum of squares* (TSS) is the sum of the squares of the deviations of all the measurements from the mean of all the measurements (the grand mean). The TSS may be split into components, the most basic of which are an *explained sum of squares* (ESS) (also known as the *between-groups sum of squares*) and a *residual* or *within-groups sum of squares* (RSS). ESS is the proportion of TSS which may be explained by a small number of factors/variables such as sex, socio-economic status, etc. in which a researcher may be interested. RSS is the proportion of TSS which may not be so explained. TSS = ESS - + RSS (and ESS/TSS = R^2, the square of the multiple correlation coefficient for predicting the dependent variable from the explanatory variables). ESS can often, if desired, be split up into further parts corresponding to each single explanatory variable and/or the interaction(s) between the explanatory variables. To each sum of squares there is a corresponding *mean square* obtained by dividing the sum of squares by the appropriate **degrees of freedom**. There is thus an *explained mean square* (EMS) and a *residual mean square* (RMS), and, if desired, mean squares corresponding to single variables or interactions. The point of computing mean squares is that they are **variance** estimates and, as variance estimates, they may be compared using the **F-ratio**. The RMS is taken as the standard of comparison and if any of the other mean squares are shown to be significantly greater than the RMS then the variables corresponding to these mean squares explain a significant proportion of the total variance.

When this is so, such conclusions may be drawn as that there *are* differences between group means, that a multiple correlation is significant, etc.

Once it is established that differences between means are significant, the researcher may wish to know which means differ from the rest (e.g. whether it is the high socio-economic status pupils which differ from the middle and low status pupils or whether it is the middle group that is different, etc.). There are several techniques available for this purpose, and which one to use depends on whether it was hypothesized in advance that a particular difference would exist, i.e. there was a *planned comparison* or whether the researcher was simply exploring the data, i.e. making **unplanned comparisons**. For the planned comparison situation a modified form of the t-test is appropriate. Examples of procedures for use in unplanned comparisons are the **least significant difference test**, the **Tukey test**, the **Scheffé method**, the **Newman–Keuls test**, and the **Duncan multiple range test**.

Analytic Categories

Analysis of variance makes powerful assumptions about **interval scale** measurement, NORMALITY OF DISTRIBUTION of scores, and homogeneity of certain variances (**homoscedasticity**). Furthermore, complex analyses of variance become tricky to perform and require special procedures if the numbers of cases in all the cells are not equal or if there are missing values. The normality of distribution problem may sometimes be overcome by an appropriate TRANSFORMATION of the scores, and, in any case, it has been shown that analysis of variance is robust to violations of its basic assumptions, and particularly so when cell numbers are equal. It is uniquely appropriate to analysing EXPERIMENTS, where the experimenter can control the conditions, randomly assign cases, arrange equal numbers in the cells, and make useful and accurate measurements. Survey data, where such direct manipulation is impossible, are usually more easily and appropriately analysed using multiple regression directly.

Analytic Categories In PARTICIPANT OBSERVATION, analytic categories are categories referring to the structure of the field developed by the observer during the course of field-work.

Analytic Concept A concept developed by a researcher to assimilate some phenomenon to a structure. It is to be distinguished from 'a members' concept', i.e. one employed by the people studied. In social science there is always some danger that analytic concepts bear no relationship to ordinary peoples' consciousness. Therefore one of the major requirements of ethnography is that analytic concepts be explicitly related to members' concepts.

Analytic Induction See under PARTICIPANT OBSERVATION

Anchor Definition In order to improve reliability of a rating scale some points on it may be given brief descriptions or **anchor definitions**. For instance, on a 10-point rating scale of intelligence, scale point 10 might be described as 'very intelligent indeed — a genius', point 7 might be called 'highly intelligent', point 3 'below average', and point 2 'extremely unintelligent'.

Anonymity If a research subject is promised anonymity, it means that the researcher has promised that the research is to be conducted in such a way that the identity of the subject is unknown, even to the researcher.

Aptitude Test See under **Achievement Test**

Arcsine Transformation A TRANSFORMATION which may be applied to proportions (fractions, percentages, cases per thousand population, etc.).

The DISTRIBUTION of a proportion (P) tends to be very bunched at the extreme values and its **variance**, i.e. $P(1 - P)$ depends on the value of P. The **arcsine transformation** spreads out the extreme values giving an approximately normal sampling distribution and usually renders the variance of the scores approximately constant, no matter what the original value of P.

The arcsine transformation is given by:
$A = 2 \arcsine \sqrt{P}$,
i.e. twice the angle (measured in radians) whose trigonometric sine is the square root of the proportion being transformed.

It has little effect and may not need to be applied if the proportions being measured all lie between 0.25 and 0.75.

Area Sampling See under SAMPLING THEORY AND METHODS

Arithmetic Mean The sum of values of a variable for all the observations in a data set divided by the total number of observations, i.e.

$$\frac{\sum_{i=1}^{n} x_i}{n}$$

As a **measure of central tendency** the arithmetic mean takes into account all the observations in the set and can be influenced by atypical extreme values. It is appropriate only when measurement is at least on an **interval** or **ratio scale.** The sum of deviations of all observations from the mean is zero; from the knowledge of the mean and the number of observations, the total of all the observations may be found.

Array All the values in a set of data set out together. An *array mean*, in the context of a **joint distribution**, is the mean of a set of data for one variable for a constant value of the other.

Artefact The result of human activity rather than of natural processes. In the social sciences the term most commonly denotes a spurious result, which arises purely or at least partly, out of some feature of the design of a study.

Artificiality Artificiality enters into experiments and surveys which rely on the use of artificial contexts, laboratory situations, and *structured interviews* when collecting data. Since these contexts are established and controlled by the researcher they may be unrepresentative of everyday life.

Association   See under RELATIONSHIP

Asymmetric Measure of Association   Some measures of association give different numerical results depending on which variable is taken as the **independent variable**. These are known as **asymmetric measures of association** — an example being the *d-statistic*. A **symmetric measure of association** (e.g. the **Pearson** *r*) gives the same numerical result no matter which variable is chosen as the independent variable.

Asymmetric Relation   A relation which holds strongly in one direction only. Causation is an example. To say 'smoking causes lung cancer' does not imply that 'lung cancer causes smoking'.

Asymptotically Unbiased Estimator   See under ESTIMATION

Atomism (Social)   The assumption that discrete elements in the field of investigation may be joined together into larger wholes, these larger wholes being describable in terms of the discrete elements and nothing else.
See also **Gestalt**

Attenuation   The correlation between two variables is always somewhat lessened or **attenuated** by the errors of measurement in both. When it may be assumed that the **error scores** are uncorrelated with the **true scores** or with each other a correction for attenuation is sometimes made, given by:

$$r_{tt} = \frac{r_{xy}}{\sqrt{r_{xx}}\sqrt{r_{yy}}}$$

where r_{tt} is the corrected correlation, r_{xy} is the observed correlation, and r_{xx}, r_{yy} are the reliabilities of the tests. Corrected correlations cannot be used in REGRESSION ANALYSIS and the technique requires caution as corrected correlations can sometimes exceed unity.

Attitude Dimension   A unitary and continuous **dimension** along which it is postulated that an attitude may vary. An **attitude scale** is a set of items designed to assign scores to individuals on this dimension.

Attitude Scale   A scale which assigns a numerical score to a person on an underlying **attitude dimension** and thus makes comparisons between people possible. There are several

established procedures for setting up attitude scales including the **Thurstone, Likert**, and **Guttman** methods and the McKennell procedure (alpha scaling).
See also ATTITUDE SCALING

ATTITUDE SCALING
The process of empirically constructing a method for measuring a particular concept, attitude, or trait within an individual. There are several properties which are desirable in an ideal scale. It should be **unidimensional**, measuring only one concept and not influenced by others. In particular, there should be no **response bias**. It should be graduated into a number of equal intervals and thus be linear. It should be RELIABLE, giving the same answer when applied to the same individual on different occasions, unless the concept being measured has itself altered. It should be VALID, measuring exactly what it is intended to measure, and it should be *reproducible*, that is, there should be only one way of obtaining a given score.
In the social sciences such ideal scales are virtually unobtainable for a number of reasons. There are three common methods of scale construction.
The *Thurstone Scaling Method* produces a set of items with which the subject is invited to agree or disagree. There may be, perhaps, 20 or 30 of these items in a typical scale and each one has been assigned a score showing its position on the scale. The subject scores on the item only if he agrees with it. The **median score** of the items to which the subject agrees is taken as his score on the whole scale. The steps in establishing a Thurstone scale are as follows: first, a large pool of items, perhaps 100–150, are written reflecting the whole range of the concept to be scaled; secondly, a number of judges, preferably people similar to the subjects on whom the scale will be used, are asked to order the statements or items into a number of categories, usually eleven. The judgements for each item are then examined and the median rating is taken as the item score. A small number of items on which there is good rating agreement between judges and which together cover all the eleven categories is then chosen to constitute the final scale.
In the *Likert Scaling Method* the subjects have to register their responses to each item on a five (or seven) point scale, ranging from strongly agree to strongly disagree. Each point of the item-scale carries a numerical value. The score on the whole scale is the sum of the scores on each of the items. The scale is constructed by trying out a large number of items on a sample of individuals similar to the ones on whom the final scale is to be used. **Item**

analysis, usually in the form of correlating the grouped scores on each item with the total score for the individual on all the trial items, is then used to select the best items, i.e. those with the highest correlation coefficients.

The *Guttman Scaling method* results in a series of items arranged in a hierarchy or cumulative scale such that agreement with an item implies agreement with all the items below it in the hierarchy. An individual's score is the number of items with which he agrees. Suitable items for a concept are selected by scalogram analysis on a large pool of items which have been tried out on a sample of respondents. The items do not have to be dichotomous but, if they are not, a cut-off point is usually established to make them so. It is uncommon to find a set of items which form a perfect Guttman scale and the *coefficient of reproducibility (R)* is an indication of how good the final scale is. It is given by:

$$R = 1 - \frac{\text{number of errors}}{\text{number of items} \times \text{number of respondents}}$$

An error is a deviation from the ideal Guttman pattern of a perfect hierarchy of items. (See under **Guttman Scale**.) A perfect Guttman scale is necessarily unidimensional in scaling the concept. It is desirable to establish a scale on at least one sample of 100 or more respondents and the minimum criterion for satisfactory reproducibility is usually taken as $R = 0.9$

Thurstone scales on the whole tend to be only moderately good at meeting the desirable criteria for an ideal scale and they need considerable labour to construct, unlike Likert scales which are much easier to construct and which often have higher reliability. However, Likert scales may not always be unidimensional and they have no reproducibility — the same score on a Likert scale may be obtained in a large number of different ways. Guttman scales have excellent reproducibility and unidimensionality but this is often to be attained only by severely limiting the content area which the items cover. There is no guarantee in advance that a Guttman scale to measure a certain attitude can be constructed. If it can, its construction tends to be long and laborious.

There are many modifications to these basic methods of scale construction. In particular, FACTOR ANALYSIS may be used to construct several scales simultaneously from a large pool of items, and there are many types of precaution which may be taken against response bias. Items may be keyed so that for about half of them a 'yes' answer (and for the other half a 'no' answer) indicates presence of the attitude

being measured. *Buffer items*, which have nothing to do with the attitude being measured but are there to camouflage the purpose of the questionnaire, may be included. There may also be *lie-detector* or *social desirability items* included which, if scored too often, mean that the respondent is answering so as to leave a good impression on the tester. This type of bias may also be reduced by using *a forced choice format* in which items have two or more alternative answers each of which is equal on social desirability but for which the respondent has to say which is most and which least characteristic of himself. One relatively new technique, the *M'Kennell procedure* takes as its starting point the opinions/attitudes of a sample of people interviewed freely in a preliminary study. A large pool of Likert-type items is then written and this is administered to a new sample. **Elementary linkage analysis** is applied to determine how many CLUSTERS there are in the responses. This is followed by **principal components analysis** to extract as many components as the number of clusters which have been found and rotating by the **varimax method**. This sets up a number of **orthogonal** attitude dimensions. The final step is for the researcher to decide on the minimum level of reliability which is acceptable and is measured by **Cronbach's alpha**. The researcher then chooses a small number of items which together will attain the desired level of alpha. This method meets many, but not all, of the criteria for an ideal scale.

Attitude Survey   A study, on a properly drawn sample of a specified population, designed to find out what people in that population feel about some particular issue. Attitude surveys usually use carefully constructed, well STANDARDIZED questionnaires.
See also **Sample Survey**

Attitudinal Item   See **Item**

Attribute   A qualitative measurement assigned to objects or to individuals. Useage of the term varies greatly. **Nominal categories** are certainly attributes, e.g. religious affiliation classified as Protestant, Catholic, and Jew is a set of attributes without any imputation of scaling. Some regard even **ordinal measures** as attributes, e.g. examination grades. Any set of categories which implies an ordering is an **ordered attribute. Interval** and **ratio scales** are unquestionably true variables rather than attributes.
See also SCALE OF MEASUREMENT, **Categorical Variable**

Auto-correlation   See under ESTIMATION

Auxiliary Hypothesis   An hypothesis which may afford an alternative explanation of some phenomenon and which needs to be ruled out before conclusions are reached about the main hypothesis under test.
See also **Ambiguity of Testing**

Average   Often another term for **arithmetic** **mean**, but is more generally an undefined **measure of central tendency** of the values in a data set or **frequency distribution.**

Average Deviation   See **Mean Deviation**

Axis   See under **Graphic Presentation**

B

Slope of Least Squares Regression Line See **Regression Coefficient**

Bales Interaction Analysis A system which enables an observer to classify the behaviour of people in groups. Each social interaction between group members is clasified into one or more of twelve categories grouped into four broad areas — social–emotional area positive, social–emotional area negative, task area attempted answers, and task area questions. Examples of the twelve categories are: 'Shows tension release, jokes, laughs, shows satisfaction' (social–emotional area positive) and 'asks for orientation, information, repetition, confirmation' (task area questions).

Bar Chart A diagram for displaying **nominal scale** data. For each category in the data a bar is drawn from the axis, usually the horizontal axis, to a height proportional to the number of observations in the category. The bars are all made the same width, are separated from each other along the horizontal axis, and may be placed in any order along the axis.

Base Data A set of data, e.g. retail prices for a particular month in a particular year, which serves as a baseline against which changes can be measured.

Baseline A standard of performance which exists prior to an experimental treatment and against which that treatment may be measured.

BAYESIAN STATISTICS

Classical statistics are basically concerned with describing and comparing samples of data and making valid inferences about the underlying population parameters. Bayesian statistics afford a means for combining new information with other information already known in order to refine the conclusion to be drawn.

The backbone of Bayesian statistics is Bayes theorem. This takes various forms according to the nature of the problem. The simplest is:

$$P(A/B) = \frac{P(B/A)P(A)}{P(B/A)P(A) + P(B/\bar{A})P(\bar{A})},$$

where

$P(A/B)$ is the probability that A is true given that B has occurred,

$P(B/A)$ is the probability that B will occur given that A is true,

$P(A)$ is the probability that A is true before knowing whether or not B occurred,

$P(B/\bar{A})$ is the probability that B will occur if A is *not* true,

$P(\bar{A})$ is the probability that A is not true before knowing about B.

For example, suppose political party A has a chance of 0.5 of winning the next election $[P(A)]$. If they win, the probability of tax increases $[P(B/A)]$ is 0.8. If they lose, the probability of tax increases $[P(B/\bar{A})]$ is 0.5. A few months later taxes *have*, in fact, gone up. The probability that party A won is now

$$\frac{(0.8)(0.5)}{(0.8)(0.5) + (0.5)(0.5)}$$

$$= 0.62$$

That is, the probability that party A won should be revised from 0.5 to 0.62, given the information that taxes have gone up.

The original probability estimate $[P(A)]$, before the addition of new information, is known as the *prior probability* of event A. The conditional probabilities of event B depending on A, $[P(B/A)$ and $P(B/\bar{A})]$ are known as *likelihoods*. The final probability estimate that A has occurred $[P(A/B)]$ is termed the *posterior probability* of event A.

Both the prior and the posterior probabilities sum to one over all possible event outcomes. The likelihoods, however, do not.

Bayes theorem may be extended to cover more complex cases, e.g. where there are several different discrete outcomes (several parties with a chance of winning an election) and many separate pieces of information to be used in refining the prior probability. It may also be generalized to the case where all the variables are measured on **continuous** scales.

Bayesian statistics are useful in situations where the prior probabilities and the likelihoods are easily inferred or even approximated. In these cases, use of Bayesian methods to update existing information may be much preferred to the trouble and expense of data collection on a new **random sample**. Furthermore, it has been shown that these methods are much sounder than informal subjective refining of the prior probabilities. In most situations informal refinement tends to be much too conservative.

Beck Depression Inventory (BDI)   An inventory developed to measure the severity of a depression.

There are 21 items each scored from 0 to 3. Each item consists of a series of statements related to depression, one of which is to be chosen. These alternatives are usually read out to the patient who then indicates his response. The BDI has satisfactory RELIABILITY and VALIDITY and has been widely used. There is a short form available.

Before–after Study   A study which aims to assess the effects of some given **treatment**, e.g. a propaganda exercise or training programme, by taking measurements before and after its occurrence. Often the study will include a **control group** measured at the same time as the **experimental group** but not exposed to the treatment.

See also EXPERIMENT

Best Linear Unbiased Estimator (BLUE)   See under ESTIMATION

Beta Coefficient   See **Standardized Regresion Coefficient**

Beta (β) Probability of Type II Error   See **Type II Error**

Beta Weight   See **Standardized Regression Coefficient**

Between-Groups Variance   The variance of a group of mean values about the mean of these means. In the ANALYSIS OF VARIANCE technique the between-groups variance is compared to the *within-groups variance*, i.e. the average variance of the observations about their group means, in order to determine whether there are significant differences between any of the means.

Between-Groups Sum of Squares   See under ANALYSIS OF VARIANCE

BIAS

Deviation from a correct conclusion because of a flaw in the procedures which led to it.

The main identified sources of bias in social science research lie in the researcher, in the data-gathering methods, and in the sampling procedures.

The researcher may be biased in the ordinary sense of the term. He or she may, often quite unconsciously, hold tenaciously and unreasonably to erroneous attitudes and beliefs. These may influence the hypotheses selected for testing, the manner in which the research is conducted, and the interpretation of the findings. In particular, bias may be transmitted in various ways during the testing procedures. In the *experimenter bias effect*, in knowing the hypothesis to be tested the experimenter (perhaps quite unconsciously) uses subtle influences, such as extra encouragement, tone of voice, or selective probing, to extract answers from the subject which confirm the hypothesis. Where global judgements are to be made there may be a *halo effect* in which the rater's general attitude dictates the ratings for particular items — for example, the prettiest girl is rated the most intelligent. When a survey is being done *interviewer bias* will occur when the interviewer's social class (perhaps effected through his or her manner of speaking) influences what the respondent says. Where the researcher is a participant-observer there may be *over-rapport*, in which case he or she identifies so much with the subject that he or she adopts a particular perspective as obvious and beyond question.

Research procedures in themselves may often introduce bias. In general, people who know that they are being observed may not behave in their normal manner. In the *Hawthorne effect* the extra attention which is given by the researcher has an effect quite distinct from that predicted by the experimental manipulation. More specifically, the interview as a technique affords many opportunities of introducing bias, e.g. by the use of leading questions or selective coverage of the field. There are a number of systematic ways in which the answers to questionnaires may be biased (*response biases*). *Social desirability responding* occurs when answers are altered to show the subject in a more favourable light *vis-à-vis* the interviewer. *Acquiescence* is where 'yes' is the answer no matter what the question. In *extreme responding* the subject exaggerates his or her answers by always choosing the extreme amongst alternatives. There may also be an *order effect* in which the order of the items making up a test or questionnaire influences the responses to the items taken as individual elements of the test.

Finally, bias may occur because of faulty sampling. A *biased sample* is one which fails to reflect adequately the population it is meant to reflect. This may occur because proper sampling procedures have not been followed or

9

because certain types of people refuse to be interviewed, i.e. where the non-respondents are not a crosssection of the population.
Available methods to combat bias include:

(i)   having people who do not know the hypothesis under test conduct the data-gathering,

(ii)   having **ratings** made by several different judges,

(iii)   careful STANDARDIZATION of interviews,

(iv)   the inclusion of suitable **control groups**,

(v)   **counterbalancing** the item order,

(vi)   keying responses to items so that the answers which indicate a particular attitude or trait are sometimes 'yes' and sometimes 'no',

(vii)   using **forced choice items** in which the items have equal social desirability,

(viii)   vigorously searching for respondents who have been selected in the sample but are not easy to contact.

Biased Estimator   See under ESTIMATION

Biased Sample   A sample which fails to reflect adequately the characteristics of the population it is meant to reflect.
See also BIAS

Bimodal Distribution   A distribution which has two different values around which observations tend to cluster. When plotted it exhibits a characteristic double hump shape thus:

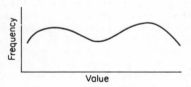

See also DISTRIBUTION

Binomial Distribution   A distribution which describes the frequencies of outcome for an event which is limited to occurring with a known probability (p). For instance, if an unbiased six-sided die is rolled 30 times the event 'a six' will occur about five times. If the 30 rolls are now repeated an infinite number of times the binominal distribution will describe the frequency of the event 'a six' — occasionally there will be no sixes at all and occasionally many more than five sixes, but usually about five. The binomial distribution has a mean Np

and a standard deviation $\sqrt{Npq}$, where N = sample size (number of die rolls), p = probability that the event will occur, and $q = 1 - p$ = probability the event will not occur.
It has a similar shape to the NORMAL DISTRIBUTION but is skewed — particularly when p differs markedly from 0.5 and N is small. As N becomes large the binomial distribution becomes indistinguishable from the normal distribution.
See also DISTRIBUTION

Binomial Test   When a sample can be divided into two discrete classes (e.g. men and women, rich and poor, achievers and non-achievers) the binomial test is appropriate for seeing whether the proportion in one of the classes corresponds to some expected proportion. This is done using the binomial theorem. For example, supposing it is known that one-third of a population are high achievers and in a sample of 20 low status people only two high achievers are observed, then, according to the binomial theorem, the chances of observing no high achievers is:

$$\frac{20!}{0!20!} \cdot \left(\frac{2}{3}\right)^{20} ;$$

the chances of observing one high achiever is:

$$\frac{20!}{1!19!} \left(\frac{1}{3}\right)^{1} \cdot \left(\frac{2}{3}\right)^{19} ;$$

the chances of observing two high achievers is:

$$\frac{20!}{2!18!} \left(\frac{1}{3}\right)^{2} \cdot \left(\frac{2}{3}\right)^{18} .$$

Therefore the probability of observing two *or less* high achievers by chance is the sum of all these, i.e. 0.0176 or 1.76 per cent. Thus, it may be concluded that those of low social status tend to be low achievers. As sample size increases, working out the probabilities by the binomial theorem becomes cumbersome and the normal approximation

$$Z = \frac{x - NP}{\sqrt{NPQ}}$$

may be used where N = sample size, x = observed number with a given outcome, P = probability of this outcome, and $Q = 1 - p$ is the probability of the other outcome. $\sqrt{NPQ}$ should be at least 9 before the approximation is used.

Bipolar Factor   See under FACTOR ANALYSIS

Birth-Rate   The crude birth-rate is the total of

live births in a year divided by the total population, estimated at the mid-year point. Birth-rate is expressed per 1,000 of a defined population (e.g. England and Wales) of all ages and both sexes. Crude birth-rates may be usefully compared to crude **death-rates** in estimating short-term changes in population. They may be subdivided by geographical region.

Longer term projections of population trends require *age-specific fertility rates*, i.e. *standardized birth-rates* calculated for particular age-groups of women in the child-bearing range of 15–44 years.

The *general fertility rate* is the total yearly live births per 1,000 women in the whole 15–44 years range.

Biserial Correlation Coefficient When one variable is measured on a **continuous** scale and another is a **dichotomy** which reflects a continuous variable, the **biserial correlation coefficient** is an estimate of what the **Pearson product-moment correlation** would have been had the dichotomy been measured on a continuous scale.

It is given by

$$r_b = \frac{(\bar{Y}_1 - \bar{Y}_2)pq}{hs_Y}$$

where $\bar{Y}_1$ and $\bar{Y}_2$ are the means on the continuous scale for categories 1 and 2 of the dichotomy, p and q are the proportions of scores in the dichotomy, S_Y is the **standard deviation** of the continuous variable, and h is the height of the standard **unit normal curve** at the point where its area is divided into p and q portions.

r_b is numerically greater than the **point biserial correlation** which is the product moment correlation actually observed in the data.

See also CORRELATION

Bivariate Distribution See under DISTRIBUTION

Bivariate Normal Distribution The **joint distribution** of two variables which are unrelated to each other, and both of which are NORMALLY DISTRIBUTED.

The scores on each variable may be transformed into **Z-scores** (i.e. the mean value is subtracted from each score and the result divided by the **standard deviation**), and the joint frequency distribution shown as a three-dimensional graph. For the ideal case, the result will be a symmetrical flat-topped hill shape, with the highest frequency (*modal value*) at the point (0,0) on both variables.

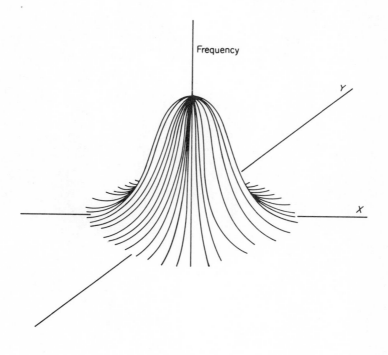

Frequency

Buffer Item An item on an **attitude scale** which does not itself directly measure the attitude, but is there for some other purpose, for example to mask what is really being measured, or to make it easier to choose answers from a set of alternatives, or to allay the respondent's anxieties.

C

Calibration   The graduation of a measurement scale in terms of some definite meaningful units — as when a degree centigrade is calibrated as one hundredth of the temperature difference between the boiling and freezing points of water.

In model-building the term is also used for the process of estimating **parameters** for the equations defining the MODEL.

California F-scale   See **F-(Fascism) Scale**

Canonical Correlation Analysis   A generalization of MULTIPLE REGRESSION ANALYSIS which seeks to discover and to describe the relationship between a set of **independent variables** and a set of **dependent variables**. Note that in both cases sets of variables are at issue rather than individual variables. For example, a set of demographic variables such as father's occupation, number of people in the family, and family income, might be used to predict overall school performance as represented by a set of variables consisting of the pupil's marks in different school subjects. Canonical correlation analysis derives a single variable to represent each set of variables (in a manner exactly analogous to FACTOR ANALYSIS). The two variables so derived — one for each set of variables — are known as the first *canonical variates*. Each separate variable (e.g. father's occupation, mark in English in the example above) receives a **regression weight** and a *structure coefficient* which is analogous to a **factor loading**, showing what part it plays in predicting the first canonical variate. Further pairs of canonical variates may be extracted (analogous to *orthogonal factors*) describing different aspects of the relationship between the two sets of scores. The *total redundancy index* is a measure of the total degree of relationship between the two sets of variables. It is the proportion of the total **variance** of one of the sets which may be explained by the other set via all the canonical variates extracted.

Canonical Variate   See under **Canonical Correlation Analysis**

Cartesian Co-ordinates   The location of any point on a graph may be specified by two numbers known as co-ordinates. In the Cartesian system, two axes are drawn at right angles

and a scale of measurement is marked off along each, the zero point being placed where they cross (the *origin*). The Cartesian co-ordinates of any point in the space so defined are the distance from the origin along the horizontal axis (given first) and the distance from the origin along the vertical axis. For example, co-ordinates $(1, -3)$ define the point shown:

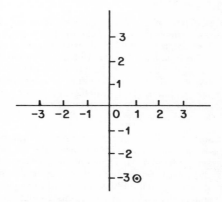

The system may be extended to three dimensions by adding a third co-ordinate.
See also **Graphic Presentation**

Case Study   A more or less intensive investigation of one particular individual, group, organization, or locale.

Catego   See under **Present State Examination**

Categorical Data   See **Categorical Variable**

Categorical Variable   A variable which may be classified only into discrete mutually exclusive categories. Usually there are only a few of these and it may or may not be possible to place them in an ordered series. Examples are sex, religious affiliation, and military ranks. Only the last example may reasonably form an ordered series of categories.

Categorization   A particular classification in a set of data to which some of the data clearly belong and the rest unequivocally do not. Category boundaries may be more or less obvious in the data — as when people are

13

categorized according to nationality; or they may be imposed in a fairly arbitrary manner — as when people are placed in high or low income categories with the researcher choosing a cut-off point.

Category See **Categorization**

Causal Hierarchy A sequence of variables such that ones higher up the hierarchy may cause lower ones, but lower ones are unlikely to cause higher ones.
See also MODEL

Causal Hypothesis An hypothesis that one or more variables are causally related to a **dependent variable** rather than simply covarying with it.
See also **Hypothesis**

Causal Inference An inference that variation on one variable is *caused* by variation on another. Such inferences must be drawn with care: e.g. tall people have a slight tendency to be more intelligent than short people. It would be a (clearly false) causal inference to assert that tallness *causes* greater intelligence. Other factors in fact underly both variables.
See also CAUSATION

Causal Model An integrated system of hypotheses put forward to explain a particular limited set of phenomena. The emphasis is on setting out causal connections rather than on simply describing relationships or predicting one phenomenon from another. Such models may vary in complexity, in the precision with which they specify the causal connections, and in their amenability to scientific testing.
See also MODEL, PATH ANALYSIS

Causal Path Analysis See PATH ANALYSIS

Causal Relationship A relationship in which the occurrence of certain values on a variable led directly to the occurrence of certain values on another variable.
See under RELATIONSHIP

CAUSATION

Causation is the necessary production of an event — an *effect* — by the prior occurrence of one or more other events — a *cause* or causes.

In the strictest interpretation of the concept, causation is a relationship between events or phenomena which is characterized by properties of *asymmetry, invariance*, and *temporal sequence*.

Asymmetry means that causal flow is unidirectional and for any proven causal relationship this direction is determined and cannot be reversed; this has been called the arrow of time.

In contrast, relationships of covariation or CORRELATION are *symmetric*, two variables or events may move together without one being the cause of the other.

If event *a* is a sufficient cause of event *b* then, whenever *a* occurs, *b* will *invariably* occur. Thus, a strict causal relationship cannot be a probabilistic one for it is not strict causation to demonstrate that 'if event *a*, then event *b* with a probability of (say) 0.6 A sufficient cause is one which, without the occurrence of other prior conditions, will produce or cause an effect.

Temporal sequence means that a cause must precede an effect. If two events occur simultaneously then they cannot be in a causal relationship.

Each of the requirements of strict causation raises problems in social science. Some social scientists are willing to accept a less stringent definition of causation in which probabilistic relations may be satisfactory, others deny that the concept of causation is necessary in the social sciences at all.

The difficulties of applying strict causation in the social sciences revolve around the issues of the temporal order of variables, multiple causation and indeterminacy, circular causation, and teleological causation. These issues will be considered in turn. The position in time of variables in non-experimental research is usually unclear and whether one variable precedes another and may be a cause of it is determined, if it can be determined at all, by an inspection of the nature of the variables themselves. In cross-sectional surveys, where the data is collected at the same point in time, background variables such as social class or age are regarded as historical variables whose values for individuals crystallized at some past time and are assumed to be relatively unchangeable. Background variables are thus considered to be potential causes of differences of attitudes or behaviour in the sample. The latter type of variable are often assumed to be both transient and of recent formation and a temporal sequence of background variables preceding behavioural or attitudinal variables is assumed to have been demonstrated. If a strong correlation between a background variable and a behavioural variable is found, then a causal relationship may be claimed.

Where experiment is possible in social science the demonstration of causal relationships is on firmer ground since the experimenter manipulates the **independent variable** in real time and the priority of the independent variable and its sufficiency to produce an effect is testable provided that adequate experimental controls have been used so that the possibility of extraneous independent variables producing the same effect can be ruled out. Nevertheless, since the major part of social science is non-experimental and will remain so, the temporal order of variables remains a serious problem facing proofs of causal relationships.

Models or theories which propose a single absolute cause of a phenomenon are now completely discredited in the social sciences because of their weak explanatory power. A single absolute cause is one which invariably produces a well-defined effect. Recognition that events are the consequence of multiple causes is now firmly established together with an understanding of the indeterminacy of causal models. For example, criminal behaviour is regarded as the product of several independent causes, all of which have to occur for an individual to commit crimes; relative poverty, mental deficiency, broken homes, personality defects, learning of criminal skills, membership of a criminal subculture are amongst the cited causes of crime which act multiply. Indeterminacy is of two kinds in theories based on multiple causation: effects may be produced when some specific causes are absent (e.g. not all criminals come from broken homes) and secondly, the form in which causes may combine is uncertain in non-experimental studies. At the simplest, multiple causes may be linearly additive and at the complex level there may be strong **interaction** effects. In the first case, the probability of criminal behaviour may increase in quantum steps as each cause occurs, and in the second case the combination of two specific causes (e.g. criminal subculture and relative poverty) may increase the probability of criminal behaviour by more than the simple addition of the increases in probability for each cause taken separately (statistical interaction).

This means that prediction of effects by MULTIPLE REGRESSION models will always be subject to some degree of uncertainty. It is rare, for example, for multiple regression models to explain more than 60 per cent of the **variance** of a **dependent variable** and the addition of more independent variables (additional causes) usually adds diminishingly to the variance explained. There appears to be some inherent upper limit to the amount of determinism which can be built into causal models no matter how complex they become and even the substitution of statistical determinism for strict causation does not result in the invariability which causation requires. The requirement in strict causation of asymmetry between cause and effect is often inapplicable in the social sciences. For example, a fall in aggregate demand will, other things equal, cause a fall in employment which in turn will cause a further fall in aggregate demand. Both variables are systemically related and both can act as causes of each other. The phenomenon of 'causal loops', together with philosophical doubts about the nature of causation, has led to a position which asserts that models should not be causal but functionally-dependent systems defined by a network of relations between variables. Such systems have properties which are not deducible from the specific relationships in them but only from the whole network; the system may be in equilibrium in which the current values of each variable sustain the current states of all other variables or they might oscillate so that a change in one or more variables will produce changes in all other variables which will react throughout the system until a new equilibrium is reached. Systems may oscillate because of endogenous variables, i.e. the relationships between variables are such that only dynamic equilibria are possible or because of exogenous shocks from changes outside the system which force it to move to a new equilibrium where it will remain until new exogenous changes occur.

Whether oscillating or in stable equilibrium such models are not causal in the sense of strict causation and they are constructed and evaluated not with reference to causal adequacy but by their ability to predict accurately. Although the language of independent and dependent variables may still be used in such models it is not to be confused with a causal interpretation of relationships.

The investigation of causal relationships in **nomothetic** social science necessarily involves the search for regularities between categories of events which are abstractions of large numbers of unique and specific events. In the process of abstraction the sequence of concrete events which generate a particular outcome at the level of the individual is purposively neglected in favour of models which have generality; that is, they can explain a large number of both present and past events. If a complete causal account of an event is required, then the intermediate steps or links between initial causes and final effect must be examined. A complete determinism of a cause—effect sequence requires an alternative approach to the application of causation in the social sciences. In this, a *causal narrative* is constructed to follow the chain of small causal links which lead to a final outcome. The causal connection between relative poverty and criminal behaviour, for example, is not an obvious one but requires interpretation by a scheme of action which could take a specific individual from an experience of poverty to eventually criminal behaviour. This scheme or causal narrative must involve individual motives and meanings as necessary elements.

Such an account would be completely deterministic, but only for an individual not for a class of individuals. Some generalization is possible if sufficient cases are investigated for the common elements of comparable instances to be drawn out, but it is the converse method of investigation to the nomothetic one which begins with a conjectured general relationship and explains individual cases as instances of the general form.

Ideographic methods, such as the causal narrative, answer many of the objections to strict causation in the social sciences but at the expense of an inability to frame general explanations of phenomena which may be used to predict future events.

Cell Frequency   A cell in a table is a category defined by specific values on several variables simultaneously, e.g. men, of social class one, who went to comprehensive schools. The cell frequency is the number in that cell.

See also TABULATION

CENSUS

A census is the collection and analysis of basic social, demographic, and economic data for the entire population of a country, i.e. a complete enumeration or 100 per cent sample. In Britain, as in most countries, completing census forms is a legal requirement.

The British Census began in 1801 in a simple form and has been repeated at ten-yearly intervals since with the exception of 1941. There was a 10 per cent sample census in 1966 (despite the contradiction in terms) using the 1961 census records as a **sampling frame**.

The British Census is a *de facto* one where individuals are enumerated at the actual place of residence on census night, usually one night in April to minimize absences because of holidays. Other censuses, notably that of the U.S.A. enumerate individuals at their normal place of residence, i.e. *de jure* residence. Censuses of the *de facto* type are thought to be more accurate. The British Census now takes the form of a self-administered questionnaire distributed and checked after completion by specially recruited enumerators who are also trained to locate each separate household (the basic unit of data collection) in an *enumeration district* of about 250 households.

Census forms are usually short because of the high marginal cost of additional questions and the high cost of the whole census. Census questions have to be approved in advance by Parliament and there is great difficulty in obtaining permission to include questions on sensitive topics such as racial classification or individual incomes.

The 1971 British Census contained 36 questions of a strictly factual rather than attitudinal nature dealing with housing tenure, household amenities, demographic characteristics, county of birth (used as a surrogate for race), residential mobility, occupation, educational

and professional qualifications, travel to work, access to different modes of transport, and economic activity. The specific questions change from census to census but in modern times always concentrate on basic personal data.

Tabulations are now mainly based on 1 per cent samples of the census forms for speed and cheapness of processing. Some 100 per cent enumerations both of individuals (population) and of households are also published. Tabulations are for major regions with national totals, for local authority districts, and by small areas, i.e. political wards, within a local authority and by enumeration district by special request — the smallest possible unit of analysis.

Although the census as such is not liable to probabilistic **sampling error**, those tabulations based on samples are and **standard error** estimates for statistics are available. Sampling error in the census is a poorly known quantity but vagrants and the very lowest socio-economic groups and new Commonwealth immigrants are thought to be under-represented. Heads of households who have the legal responsibility for completing the census form are a source of **non-sampling error** and enumerators are usually unable to check inaccurate information as contrasted with missing information.

Census data is widely used by central and local government for social and economic planning and for demographic checks on the continuous registration of births, deaths, and marriages, by market researchers and by academics. Standard tabulations are virtually free to the user and special tabulations may be obtained at cost from the Office of Population Census and Surveys.

Census of Production   An enquiry (first performed in 1948, and annual since 1970) of most industrial and some commercial enterprises in the United Kingdom, with the purpose of collecting information on the industrial structure of the economy. Firms with less than 25 employees are excluded, as are all enterprises in agriculture, fishing, forestry, construction, transport, distribution, insurance and banking, public administration, and defence; other sources are used for these sectors of the economy.

Completion of the census return is legally required of all qualifying establishments but there is suspicion that some information supplied by firms is inaccurate.

Basic information collected is wage and salary bill, value of stocks, capital expenditure, payments for transport, purchase of materials and fuel, and sales. Calculations of net output (i.e. value of outputs minus value of inputs) or of value added in production are made and tabulated by industrial group (from the **Standard Industrial Classification**) and for the whole economy in the National Income Statistics.

The central purpose of the Census of Production is estimation of national product from the output side (rather than by summing factor incomes or expenditure, which are also used). The data is also used to construct weights for estimating changes in the index of national product and for constructing input–output tables for particular industry groups.

Census Tract See **Enumeration District**

Central Limit Theorem A theorem which states that statistics such as the **mean** and **standard deviation** of a **sample** of n values drawn from *any* distribution will be NORMALLY DISTRIBUTED provided n is large enough and provided the distribution in question has a finite **variance**.

Centroid Method See under FACTOR ANALYSIS

Chance Variation See **Random Error**

Checklist A checklist is a list of items which may be selected by the respondent, e.g. the Mood Adjective Checklist allows the respondent to describe his mood of the moment by underlining those adjectives in the list which best describe it.

Chi-square (χ^2) A frequently used test of whether a particular pattern of entries in a table conforms to that expected on some basis which must be stated by the tester. For example, a pattern of entries in the cells of the table can be tested against the expectancy that they do not differ significantly from that to be expected on a chance basis, or a basis of normal distribution, or against any other expectation. The commonest expectancy to test against using chi-square is that there is no association between the variables in a table. Note that some expectation must be explicitly stated in order to use the test and in order to generate expected rather than observed entries for the cells of the table.

χ^2 is a **two-tailed test** (the observed entries may differ from the expected entries in either direction) and is appropriate even for **nominal level** data provided that there are sufficient observations in the cells of the table. A minimum of five observed entries per cell is the norm. A further requirement of the test is that all the observations are independent of one another.

The most general formula for χ^2 is:

$$\chi^2 = \sum_1^n \frac{(O - E)^2}{E}$$

where n is the number of cells in the table, O is the observed frequency in each cell, and E is the expected frequency in each cell.

A correction known as the **Yates' correction for continuity** may be applied in calculating a value of χ^2 for **two by two tables**. This is only important when the expected frequencies in such tables are small. Chi-square values are read from standard tables which consist of a number of different **critical values** at or beyond which to reject the **null hypothesis** depending on the **degrees of freedom** for a particular table. Chi-square values may depend (undesirably) on the total number of observations in the table and for this reason various derivatives of chi-square are often preferred for practical use.

See also **Goodness of Fit**

Class Boundary The boundary between two **class intervals**.

Class Interval When data measured on a scale is to be summarized, particularly in the form of **frequency distributions** or **histograms**, it is convenient to reduce the number of scale points to just a few categories. This is done by dividing the scale into class intervals. These are ranges of mutually exclusive scale values, of equal size except for intervals at the two extremes of the scale. These latter are designated to be all values above and below certain levels on the scale. The class intervals are made mutually exclusive by placing the boundaries between them (**class boundaries**) where no observations can possibly fall.

As an example, income measured to the nearest £ might be divided into: up to 2,000, 2,001–5,000, 5,001–7,000, 7,001–9,000, 9,001 upwards.

(N.B. *not* 2,000–5,000, 5,000–7,000, etc. Certain values, e.g. 5,000, would fall in two different intervals.)

There is no hard-and-fast rule about the number of class intervals into which a scale should be divided. Twenty is sufficient for most purposes and the number is often much fewer. Too many class intervals may result in insufficient observations within each class for statistical testing. Too few may lead to loss of valuable information about distribution shape.

See also TABULATION

Classical Test Theory Model A model which postulates that an individual's score on a test on any given occasion is made up of his *true score* plus his *error score*. The true score is the average score he would have obtained over a very large number of testings. The error score is the result of the extraneous effects which acted on that particular occasion and made the score deviate from the true score. To make use of the model, several assumptions have to be made, a major one being that the error scores are unrelated to the true scores.

See also RELIABILITY

Classification Function See under DISCRIMINANT ANALYSIS

Closed Question A question where the respondents' answers are restricted to a list of alternatives, each of which has usually been assigned a code in advance. Synonymous with structured question.

Clumping Technique A method of CLUSTER ANALYSIS which separates data into groups, or 'clumps', having facets in common. These clumps are not necessarily mutually exclusive, and this is the distinction from other methods of cluster analysis.

CLUSTER ANALYSIS

Cluster analysis seeks to select from a large number of individuals (or other entities), measured on several different variables, groups of individuals who are like each other. For example, if 100 people were measured on intelligence, creativity, and occupational status a cluster analysis might assign 20 people to cluster one, characterized by high intelligence, high creativity, and high occupational status and the rest to cluster two. The majority of cluster analytic techniques yield mutually exclusive groups — an individual is assigned to only one cluster. However, this is not always the case, and when there is overlap between the groups finally obtained the technique is often termed **clumping**. Other terms sometimes used to describe cluster analysis are *Q-analysis, typology, grouping*, and *classification*. In the most usual useage cluster analysis differs from FACTOR ANALYSIS in that the former seeks to group together individuals while the latter seeks to group together dimensions.

There are four broad types of cluster analysis. *Hierarchical types* involve a step-by-step process. Clusters are formed by successively joining individuals together, or alternatively by successively dividing the total group, according to some mathematical criterion such as the least distance between the cores. Techniques which successively join together are termed *agglomerative* while those which successively divide are termed *divisive*. The steps in either type may be described by a diagram

known as a *dendrogram*. For example, suppose that five individuals are being clustered in an agglomerative manner using the minimum distance between individuals. The process might be represented by the following dendrogram:

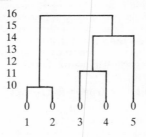

The first step was the fusion of individuals 1 and 2 who were 10 units apart. In the second step, 3 and 4 were joined at 11 units apart. In the third step, 5 was added to 3 and 4 and 5's distance from either 3 or 4 was 14 units. Finally, 1 and 2 were added to 3, 4, and 5, the minimum distance between these groups being 16 units. In practice the clustering would be stopped before all the individuals were joined into the same cluster. For example, if it stopped after stage two there would be two clusters 1, 2 and 3, 4.

There are several hierarchical methods of cluster analysis which differ in the mathematical criterion used to determine which individuals are closest (or most distant). McQuitty's **elementary linkage analysis** is a well-known example.

Partitioning techniques again proceed on a step-by-step basis. The main difference from hierarchical techniques is that the clusters initially formed are tentative, and some method is incorporated of allocating individuals from their initial clusters to others in order to improve the solution.

Density search techniques search for parts of the k-dimensional space which contain a high density of individuals and other parts which contain a low density — e.g. the average density over the whole space might be computed, the space might be divided up into smaller portions, and the density of points within each determined. Where this is significantly higher than average there is a cluster.

Finally, *clumping techniques* partition the data into clusters which may overlap. One method of doing this proceeds in three stages. First, a similarity matrix is computed. Secondly, starting with a particular observation a step-by-step hierarchical agglomerative process is followed. This is repeated several times starting from a different observation each time, yielding a large number of clusters some of which are duplicates. The third step is to prune this yield down into clusters of interest.

Problems of cluster analysis include: what shall constitute a cluster, which variables shall be chosen for analysis, how many clusters shall be sought and on which measure of similarity (or distance) between individuals the analysis is to be based. As with factor analysis, there is no one ideal solution to these problems and the choice must depend on the type of data and the purpose of the investigation.

Cluster Sampling The population is viewed as being divided into groups (e.g. school children into school classes, bank workers into bank branches) and these groups are then sampled. This method may often save time and money but at the expense of statistical precision. In *single-stage cluster sampling* the process stops with the selection of the whole groups. In *multi-stage cluster sampling* further subsamples may be selected from within the whole groups, e.g. if one wanted to select a national sample of doctors one might (a) sample area health boards (b) sample practices within these boards.

See also SAMPLING THEORY AND METHODS

Coding The assignment of responses (or other data) into predetermined categories, e.g. when a university vice-chancellor is coded as belonging to social class one. Ideally a survey (or any other method of collecting data) should be designed so that coding is easy and unambiguous.

Coding Frame The full set of categories into which survey data may be classified. Every variable is represented by a set of (usually numeric) codes, and all data are degraded to fit these categories if they do not already do so. For example, exact ages are recoded as age ranges. The term may legitimately be applied to a pre-coded questionnaire, but is more often used in connection with surveys employing *office coding* or coding by interviewers of responses to **open questions.**

Coefficient of Determination The square of the Pearson correlation coefficient (r^2). This represents **variance** explained in one variable by another. The *coefficient of non-determination* is $1 - r^2$, or the variance which is unexplained.

Coefficient of Non-determination See under **Coefficient of Determination**

Coefficient of Reliability A measure of the RELIABILITY of a set of data. There are many such coefficients applicable to different aspects of reliability.

Coefficient of Reproducibility A measure applied to a **Guttman scale** indicating to what extent it has been possible to obtain a valid hierarchy of items to constitute the scale. It is given by

$$R = 1 - \frac{\text{no. of deviations from ideal scalogram pattern}}{\text{no. of items} \times \text{no. of respondents}}$$

See also ATTITUDE SCALING

Coefficient of Variation A simple standardized measure of the **dispersion** of a DISTRIBUTION given by the **standard deviation** divided by the **mean** and expressed as a percentage.

Cohort See under COHORT ANALYSIS

COHORT ANALYSIS

The term cohort usually refers to a complete group of people who are together passing through a similar stage in their life-cycle or career and who may be followed by other such groups — a class of schoolchildren or all babies born in a certain week. Another common use of the term is in describing a group of identical twins with something in common — e.g. criminality or accident proneness. This group can be seen as an 'experimental' cohort while the group made up of their twins constitutes the 'control' cohort.

In a basic cohort study an experimental treatment is given to one cohort and not to another. Many extraneous factors will be at least partly controlled. Successive classes of primary children, for instance, are likely to be drawn from the same area, will have nearly the same mean age, and will be taught by the same teacher in the same environment. Furthermore, where a cohort is of this close-knit character, it is often particularly easy to gather data on possible **extraneous variables** or to look up relevant records. There are three common difficulties with cohort designs. First, there may be systematic bias due to some identifiable extraneous variable which happens to affect one cohort rather than another. For instance, with two successive cohorts of schoolchildren, school policy may have changed or a 'flu epidemic may have struck one and not the other. Secondly, it may happen, quite by chance, that one of the cohorts is particularly good or bad at the task being assessed. Thirdly, where testing is involved, it could be that the tests or testing conditions are not comparable for all cohorts, or, in some designs, that there is a bias due to one cohort being compared on their second time of testing with another on their first time.

Ways of countering these problems include (a) using several control and/or experimental cohorts, (b) finding another control group of the same year as the experimental cohort, and (c) partitioning the experimental treatment into several levels. The last of these may be particularly effective because if the level of performance in the experimental cohort varies directly with level of treatment and there is an overall effect as judged against a control cohort, then it is usually difficult to see how a spurious result can arise.

Collapse To join together two or more adjacent categories. This may be desirable for clear presentation of the data but also almost inevitably leads to a loss of data. Some statistical tests, notably χ^2, require certain minimum cell frequencies before they are valid, and collapsing of categories is often performed to achieve these. The term is also used to describe the process of constructing a **two by two table** from a large one.

Column A vertical line of entries in a table.
See also TABULATION

Communality In FACTOR ANALYSIS, the communality of a test or other measure is that part of its variance which may be considered to be shared in common with other tests. Its *specificity* is that part of its variance which is not **error variance** and which is specific to the test itself, i.e. not shared in common with other tests.

Comparability of Responses Responses are comparable when the questions asked and the total situation in which they are asked have the same meaning to all the respondents. One attempt to achieve this (unattainable) ideal is to standardize the wording of all the questions. Another is for the interviewer to take pains to establish rapport, to make sure that he is understood, and to obtain a clear picture of the meaning of the subjects' responses.
See also BIAS

Comparative Method The selection for study of situations which are similar in most respects but which differ in known ways, thus allowing dimensions of interest to the researcher to be tested. The method may be used to test the generality of an hypothesis, to decide between hypotheses, or to generate and develop theories as in **theoretical sampling**.
See also EXPERIMENT

COMPOSITE MEASUREMENT

The combination of several smaller measures (items, test scores, etc.) into one valid and reliable index of some underlying construct.
The process of achieving composite measurement usually commences with the assembly of a large pool of items which seem to measure the desired construct — e.g. a **personality trait**, an attitude, or an ability. A variety of methods may then be applied to reduce the item pool to a small number of items constituting the final scale. These methods include FACTOR ANALYSIS, CLUSTER ANALYSIS, **item analysis** and specific scaling methods for attitudes such as the **Thurstone, Likert**, and **Guttman** methods. (For these latter see ATTITUDE SCALING.)

Cluster and factor analytic methods are applied in situations where the items in the pool may be measuring more than one underlying construct. They are used to determine how many such constructs or dimensions may be present, which items measure these dimensions, and how these items should be weighted. Factor analysis may be followed by some form of item analysis which aims to reduce the number of items (and therefore the time required for completion of the test) while maintaining RELIABILITY and VALIDITY.

The term **item analysis** covers a broad range of techniques for examining the usefulness of items tentatively included in a composite measure. The extent to which an item correlates with other items or with the total score may be assessed. Different combinations of items may be tried to see how some criterion of reliability may be obtained most economically. For attainment tests, a **facility index** and/or a **discrimination index** may be computed for each item. The facility index measures how hard or easy the item is, and is the proportion of some trial sample who pass it. A discrimination index measures the power of the item to discriminate between high and low achievers, as assessed in reference to their overall performance on a test. Discrimination depends to some extent on facility — very easy items, which everybody passes, cannot discriminate. Neither, clearly, can extremely difficult items. A good attainment test is therefore likely to contain many items of moderate difficulty which discriminate well, with a few hard and easy items in order to extend the range of application of the test.

Two further steps which may be necessary are the elimination of **response biases** and the establishment of **norms**.

Responses biases are particularly likely to affect personality and attitude measures. **Social desirability** responding involves the subject toning down his responses to appear in a more favourable light. **Acquiescence** is always answering 'yes', no matter what the question. **Extreme responding** is exaggeration by choosing the most extreme response categories for most items. **Order effects** occur when the answer to an early item has an effect on the answer to a later item. There are many methods for attempting to combat response biases. Social desirability may be tackled by the **forced choice method** where the subject must choose between responses of equal social desirability, by including 'lie scale' items which aim to detect whether a subject is answering in a manner too good to be true, or by including **buffer items** which have nothing to do with the construct being measured but may help to conceal the purpose of the test. To eliminate acquiescence, items may be keyed so that a 'yes' response sometimes scores positive and sometimes negative on the construct. For extreme responding the remedy may be to give equal weight to extreme and less extreme item alternatives, and (rarely) order effects may be controlled by having different versions of the test with the items in different orders.

Norms are established by giving the final version of the test to large random samples of the populations of interest and computing such statistics as the **means** and **standard deviations**. Any individual subsequently tested can then be compared with these norms for the group to which he or she belongs.

Composite Variable A variable constructed from two or more other variables, e.g. a composite variable called 'mathematical ability' might be the sum of the scores on two different maths tests or perhaps the score on one of them and twice the score on the other, etc. Special statistical methods (e.g. FACTOR ANALYSIS) exist for deriving the best possible composite variables from a set of single variables thus allowing them to be summarized and simplified.

See also COMPOSITE MEASUREMENT

Concept A mental construct which selects and summarizes an aspect of the observable world for theoretical attention. Concepts are the fundamental terms in theoretical relationships.

Concepts as such are non-observable entities, being pure thought constructs, e.g. social mobility, intelligence, suicide, clan, demand, and they must be interpreted by **indicators** in order to be used empirically.

Concepts may be simple or complex and they may denote properties which can be scaled as **variables**, e.g. intelligence, or denote **attributes** which are either present or absent, e.g. suicide. They may also be capable of denoting variables or attributes depending on the particular indicator which is used.

Concepts are linked to observation by indicators which are potential observations made under defined rules; for example, an indicator of intelligence is 'standardized score on the progressive matrices test' which embodies

both rules for the subject taking the test and rules for interpreting the score in relation to a large sample of subjects. An indicator, together with rules for using and interpreting it, is an **operational definition** of a concept.
See also **Operationalization**

Concomitant Variation The parallel variation of two or more variables without there necessarily being a direct causal relationship between them.

Concordance See **Kendall Coefficient of Concordance**

Concordant Rankings Several rank order measures of association (e.g. **Kendall's tau, Somer's** d_{YX} and Kruskall–Wallis's **gamma**) require calculation of the numbers of *concordant* and *discordant* rankings. The idea is best illustrated by an example.

Suppose two judges have each made ratings of the rank order of five essays. There will be five pairs of ranks:

	judge 1	judge 2
A	1	2
B	2	3
C	3	1
D	4.5	5
E	4.5	4

Judge 1's ranks are arranged in order highest to lowest. Every pair of ranks may now be compared to every other pair to see whether both judges agree or disagree on the ordering. For instance, pair B is concordant to pair A because both judges rank B lower than A. Pair B is discordant to pair C because judge 1 ranks C lower than B and judge 2 ranks C higher than B. The total number of concordant ranks is often designated P, and the number of discordant ranks Q.

If there are ties on either variable the pairs involved are ignored. For example, judge 1 has scored essays D and E as equal or *tied* (both getting rank 4.5). The comparison of pair D to pair E is therefore ignored. Some measures of association make allowance for the number of ties, others do not.

Concurrent Validity A test or questionnaire is said to have concurrent validity if it correlates well with other measures of the same concept.
See VALIDITY

Conditional Table A table showing the distribution of a variable (or variables) for a particular value of another variable, e.g. a table showing the income level × years of education classification for people who are manual workers.

Confidence Interval See under ESTIMATION, STATISTICAL INFERENCE

Confounded Variable Two variables are said to be confounded if they vary with each other in a systematic way so that it is difficult to tell which of the two is affecting some third variable, e.g. height and weight are largely confounded — there would not be many tall light-weights or short heavy-weights and this would make it difficult to sort out their effects unequivocally on a third variable such as boxing ability.

Conservatism Scale (C-scale) A 50-item scale measuring conservatism. The items consist of single words or phrases and the respondent is asked which one he favours or believes in. The response alternatives are 'yes', 'no', or 'doubtful'. To avoid **acquiescence responding** the items are keyed alternately for 'yes' and 'no' on conservatism. Two points are given for each response in the conservative direction and one for each 'doubtful' response, the scale range therefore being 0–100. The C-scale has excellent internal consistency, is strongly unidimensional and virtually acquiescence free.
See also **F-(fascism) Scale**

Consistent Estimator See under ESTIMATION

Constant Comparative Method A term for the process of continually comparing segments of qualitative data with each other (e.g. specific incidents of death in nursing experience). This allows important dimensions and hypotheses to emerge (e.g. that social loss is related to nurses' professional composure during the death).

Constant Sampling Fraction In **stratified sampling**, a constant proportion of individuals to be taken from each stratum.

Construct Validity A test or questionnaire is said to have construct validity if it conforms to predictions made about it from theory.
See VALIDITY

Content Validity A test or questionnaire is said to have content validity if it samples adequately the domain it is supposed to measure.
See VALIDITY

Context of Discovery The formulation of ideas and the inductive procedures by which new concepts are created belong to the context of discovery. The deductive testing of hypotheses and theories, perhaps employing new concepts, belongs to the **context of justification**.

Context of Justification The context of justification covers the procedures by which **hypotheses** and THEORIES are tested and either *corroborated* or not. It contrasts with the *context of discovery* which deals with the creation of new hypotheses and **concepts**.

Contingency Coefficient A measure of association applicable to **contingency tables** of any size. It is given by

$$C = \sqrt{\frac{\chi^2}{N + \chi^2}}$$

where χ^2 = chi-square value for the table, and N is the total number of observations.
It is not an estimate of the **Pearson r**, and can never be negative. Its uppermost value may exceed one and depends on the size of the table.
See also CORRELATION, **Cramers' V**

Contingency Table A table of joint frequencies of occurrence of two variables classified into categories. For example, a contingency table for a sample of right- and left-handed boys and girls would show the number of right-handed boys, right-handed girls, left-handed boys, and left-handed girls, together with the sex and handedness totals (sometimes called **marginals**). It could be laid out thus:

	Boys	Girls	Total
Right-handed			
Left-handed			
Total			

This example is of a two by two contingency table — each variable is divided into two categories. A three by two table would have three categories on one variable, two on the other, and, in general, a $k \times l$ table has k on one and l on the other. The categories may be **nominal categories**, points on a scale, or **class intervals**, and besides the frequencies in each cell the percentages of the total may be given.
See also TABULATION

Continuous Random Variable See under RANDOM VARIABLE

Continuous Variable A continuous variable may assume any value between two extremes, whereas a **discrete variable** is limited to values at certain points on a dimension. For example, height is continuous, family size is discrete. Continuous variable is virtually synonymous with *continuum*, except that the latter term implies an underlying theoretical dimension.

Continuum See **Continuous Variable**

Control The attempt to eliminate the effects of **extraneous variables** so that one may be sure that any results found are due only to the **independent variables** being tested. Methods of 'physical control' include using the same subjects under all experimental conditions, using **matched pairs**, keeping an extraneous variable constant (e.g. by using only men), and randomly allocating subjects to the different groups. Methods of 'statistical control' (i.e. control at the analysis stage) include seeing if a result holds good for all groups in a sample (e.g. if the result holds good for boys and girls, then the extraneous variable sex can be having no effect), and making allowance for extraneous variables by special statistical methods, e.g. **Partialling out** or **Covariance Analysis.**
See also EXPERIMENT

Control Group A group of people as similar as possible to an experimental group and treated in exactly the same way, except that they are not given the experimental treatment. The control group thus furnishes a baseline against which the effects of this treatment may be measured.
See also EXPERIMENT

Convergent Validity A test or questionnaire is said to have convergent validity when several dissimilar measures of the same concept correlate well with it.
See VALIDITY

Co-ordinates Numbers indicating where points on a graph should lie. In two-dimensional graphs Cartesian co-ordinates are written (X, Y) where the first figure locates the point on the horizontal axis, the second on the vertical axis. For three-dimensional location, a third co-ordinate (Z) is used.
See also **Graphic Presentation**

CORRELATION

The extent to which two variables vary together. Correlation is positive when high values on one variable go with high values on the other, and low values with low values. It is negative when high values on one variable go with low values on the other and vice versa. Correlation is measured by a statistic called the correlation coefficient (often abbreviated to correlation) of which there are many types. Nearly all these make the assumption that the relationship between the two variables is

linear, and nearly all may only take values from $+1.0$, indicating perfect positive correlation, through zero, indicating no relationship at all, to -1.0 indicating perfect negative correlation. A value of ± 1.0 means, that given the score (X) on one variable the score (Y) on the other may be predicted with absolute certainty. Put another way the proportional reduction in error (PRE) of the estimate of Y given X over the estimate of Y without being given X is unity. For values between $+1$ and -1 prediction is less certain and the closer the value approaches to zero the less good it is. At zero, there is no reduction in error and the two variables are said to be **independent** of each other.

Correlation does not necessarily imply causation. The correlation between A and B may be high because A causes B or because B causes A, or because other variables underlie both A and B.

The most common correlation coefficient is the *Pearson product moment correlation (r)*. It is given, quite equivalently, by any of the following three formulae:

$$r = \frac{\text{covariance}(xy)}{S_x S_y}, \tag{1}$$

$$r = \frac{\Sigma Z x_i Z y_i}{n}, \tag{2}$$

$$r = \frac{n\Sigma x_i y_i - \Sigma x_i \Sigma y_i}{\sqrt{[n\Sigma x_i^2 - (\Sigma x_i)^2][n\Sigma y_i^2 - (\Sigma y_i)^2]}}, \tag{3}$$

where

covariance $(xy) = 1/n\,[\Sigma\,(x_i - \bar{X})\,[y_i - \bar{Y})]$,

S_x, S_y are the *standard deviations* of x and y,
x_i, y_i are individual scores on the two variables,
n is the number of pairs of scores,
$\bar{X}, \bar{Y}$ are the mean scores,
Zx_i, Zy_i are the individual *standardized scores* (deviations of the individual scores from their mean divided by their standard deviation).

The first two formulae have theoretical interpretations. The covariance (xy) is a measure of the tendency for x and y to vary together, as measured in their original units. Dividing the covariance by the standard deviation of the two variables has the effect of limiting r to values between ± 1 and making it independent of the original units of measurement. In the second formula it is seen that r is quite equivalently interpreted as the average product of the standard scores of the two variables.

Correlation Matrix

The third formula has no theoretical significance but is the easiest for hand computation (and will give exactly the same numerical result as the other two).

Another important theoretical interpretation concerns the square of r. It may be shown that r^2 is the proportion of the **variance** in one of the variables which may be predicted from the other.

The Pearson r is intended for use in situations where both variables are continuous, have been measured on **interval** or **ratio scales**, and are NORMALLY DISTRIBUTED. When the data are all in the form of ranks, or when one or both variables are dichotomous, the computation of r may be simplified and a special name is given to r in these three situations.

For data in the form of ranks, the *Spearman rank order correlation coefficient* (r_s) is given by

$$r_s = 1 - \frac{6 \Sigma d_i^2}{n(n^2 - 1)},$$

where n is the number of pairs of observations and d_i is the difference in rank between members of a given pair.

When one variable is a dichotomy and the other is continuous, the *point biserial correlation coefficient* (r_{pb}) is given by

$$r_{pb} = \frac{\bar{Y}_1 - \bar{Y}}{S_Y} \sqrt{\frac{n_1}{n_2}},$$

where n_1 is the number of observations in category 1 of the dichotomy and n_2 the number in category 2, $\bar{Y}_1$ is the mean on the continuous variable of those cases in dichotomy category 1, $\bar{Y}$ is the overall mean of the continuous variable, and S_Y its standard deviation.

When both variables are dichotomous the ϕ *(phi) coefficient* r_ϕ is given by

$$r_\phi = \frac{BC - AD}{\sqrt{(A + B)(C + D)(A + C)(A + D)}},$$

where A, B, C, and D are the numbers in the cells of the two by two **contingency table**.

r_{pb} and r_ϕ can sometimes be restricted in value when the proportions of cases in the dichotomies differ from 50:50, that is, it may be impossible to obtain values of r_{pb} or r_ϕ as extreme as ± 1. If it may be assumed that the dichotomous variables really reflect normally distributed continuous variables (e.g. if arithmetical ability is measured in terms of passing or failing an exam), then an estimate of what the product moment r would have been had the dichotomies been measured on an interval scale may be obtained. For a dichotomy and a continuous variable this estimate is the *biserial correlation coefficient* (r_b). In the case of two dichotomies it is the *tetrachoric correlation coefficient* (r_t). r_b is given by

$$r_b = \frac{(\bar{Y}_1 - \bar{Y}_2)pq}{h \cdot S_y},$$

where $\bar{Y}_1$ and $\bar{Y}_2$ are the means on the continuous variables for categories 1 and 2 of the dichotomy, p and q are the proportions of cases in the categories of the dichotomy, S_Y is the standard deviation of the continuous variable, and h is the height of the standard **unit normal curve** where its area is divided into p and q portions.

The formula for r_t involves an infinite series and its exact valuation is therefore laborious. However, there are diagrams from which it may be read off given the proportions in the two by two contingency table.

r_b and r_t are greater than their counterparts r_{pb} and r_ϕ but do not represent observed correlations in the data. Rather, they are hypothetical estimates of what would be if continuity and normality of distribution of the dichotomous variable(s) may be assumed; and, for most purposes, r_{pb} and r_ϕ are sufficiently accurate.

Two other commonly encountered correlation coefficients are the **contingency coefficient (C)** and the **Kendall tau** (τ). Neither of these is an estimate of the product moment r. The contingency coefficient is applicable to contingency tables of any size (i.e. not just two by two). It can never be negative. Its uppermost value may be greater than one and depends on the size of the table. It is given by

$$C = \sqrt{\frac{\chi^2}{N + \chi^2}},$$

where χ^2 is the **chi-square** value for the table and N the number of observations. Kendall's τ is an alternative to r_s for data in the form of ranks. Its numerical values are usually smaller than those of r_s and it contains a correction for ties. For the formula and computation of tau see **Kendall's rank correlation coefficient (tau).** See also **Regression Coefficient, Coefficient of Reliability, Partial Correlation, MULTIPLE REGRESSION, Z-transformation,** and **Cramer's** *V*.

Correlation Matrix A table of all the possible correlations between a number of variables. The variables are listed in the same order across the top and down the side of the table, and this leads to the rows and columns being interchangeable. Any given correlation appears twice in the matrix (e.g. the correla-

24

tion between variables 1 and 2 is entered in row 1, column 2, and in column 1, row 2). The diagonal running from top left to bottom right contains the correlations of each variable with itself. These are all unity and are often omitted. Decimal points also are frequently omitted.

Correlation Ratio (η)   See **Eta**

Corollary   See under THEORY

Corroboration   See under **Hypothesis**

Cost-of-Living Index   See **Retail Price Index**

Counterbalance the Order   A method of controlling for the effects of the order of presentation of two or more experimental treatments (e.g. *A*, *B*, and *C*) given to the same subjects. The subjects are randomly split into groups of equal size, each group receiving one of the possible orderings (e.g. *ABC, ACB, BAC, BCA, CAB, CBA*). In this way unwanted effects such as improvement with practice or deterioration due to fatigue or boredom are controlled out.
See also **Randomize the Order, Order Effct**

Covariance   Covariance is an abbreviation for common variance. Like CORRELATION it indicates (by means of a numerical value) the extent to which two variables covary, i.e. either high values on one variable correspond to high values on the other variable (and low values with low values) or high values on one variable correspond with low values on the other. Again, like correlation, the statistical measure of covariance is designed to show the extent of covariation between two variables. The formula is:

$$\text{cov} = \frac{1}{n} \Sigma (X_i - \bar{X})(Y_i - \bar{Y}),$$

here n = number of observations, and $\bar{X}$ and $\bar{Y}$ are the means of the two variables. X_i and Y_i are individual scores.
Unlike correlation coefficients, however, values of covariance are not limited to the range of -1 to $+1$ and do depend on the units of measurement of the two variables. This is because the deviation of an observation from the mean of the set of observations of which it forms an element is not entered into the covariance formula in standardized units. Without standardization of units of measurement of the variables X and Y, covariance is of no use as a summary measure of correlation between two variables. Such standardization is achieved by dividing cov by the standard

deviations of both variables and results in the **Pearson correlation coefficient (*r*)**. Covariance has applications, e.g. in some forms of ANALYSIS OF VARIANCE (ANOVA).

Covariance Adjustment   An adjustment made to the **'between'** and **'within'-groups variance** estimates in an ANALYSIS OF VARIANCE to allow for the contaminating effects of an extraneous uncontrolled variable.
See also **Covariance Analysis**

Covariance Analysis   When two or more groups are being compared and these groups are unfortunately not equal on some **extraneous variable(s)** which may affect the comparison, **analysis of covariance** affords a means of allowing for the unwanted variable(s). For instance, suppose a sample of boys and a sample of girls are to be compared on mechanical aptitude (dependent variables) and the two samples differ substantially on IQ (an extraneous variable which may have an effect of mechanical aptitude). Analysis of covariance enables the comparison to be made allowing for IQ.
This covariance technique may be regarded as a special case of multiple REGRESSION ANALYSIS. It is often preferable to trying to match out an extraneous variable by eliminating subjects, but it makes several important assumptions. The **dependent variable** should be at least approximately NORMALLY DISTRIBUTED, and its **variances** in the separate groups roughly equal. Also, it is assumed that the relationship between the extraneous variable(s) and the dependent variable are the same within all the groups being compared.

Covary   Two variables are said to covary if the scores on them go together, i.e. if high scores on one variable occur with high scores on the other and low scores with low scores they covary *positively*, and if high scores on one variable occur with low scores on the other and vice versa they covary *negatively*.

Covering Law   Synonymous with *Hypothetico-deductive Method*. See under EXPLANATION

Cramer's *V*   A useful coefficient of association for **contingency tables** of any number of rows or columns:

$$V = \sqrt{\frac{\chi^2}{N(k-1)}}$$

where N = total number subjects in the tables (i.e. the grand total) and k is either the number of columns or the number of rows in the table, whichever is the smaller. **Chi-square (χ^2)** is calculated in the usual manner.

V has the advantage over *C* (the **contingency coefficient**) as a statistic of association that its value is reasonably invariant with respect to the number of rows or columns. *C*, however, can have a maximum value less than 1 because it is influenced by the size of the table (rows multiplied by columns), so that even with maximal association, *C* may underestimate the true value where *V* would not.

Criterion Analysis A method of rotation in FACTOR ANALYSIS in which factors are rotated to distinguish maximally between two opposite groups of people — e.g. known neurotics and known non-neurotics.

Criterion and Criterion Validity **Criterion** is often used as synonymous with **dependent variable** but is more correctly a standard against which performance may be assessed. Criterion-related validity covers all those methods of assessing VALIDITY which rely on evaluating a test or questionnaire against some other measure(s) known or assumed to be valid.

Criterion Referenced Test A test aiming to demonstrate mastery of a particular skill to at least some given level of competence — e.g. a driving test or accounting examination.

Critical Case Analysis The deliberate examination of an atypical (e.g. extreme) setting in order to test the limits of applicability of one's **hypotheses**, or, by spotlighting what has usually been taken for granted, to suggest new hypotheses.

Critical Value A borderline value which may be specified for a given statistical test, dividing the region of acceptance from the region of rejection of the **null hypothesis.**
See also STATISTICAL INFERENCE

Cronbach's Alpha See **Alpha Coefficient**

Cross-Lagged Coefficients See under LONGITU-DINAL STUDY

Cross Products Given two sets of observations (*A* and *B*) which may be matched in some way — e.g. the scores in a single test on two different occasions, or two different measures taken on the same subjects — the term cross product refers to a score from one set multiplied by the corresponding score from the other set; that is, $A_1.B_1$ or $A_2.B_2$.
Another useage refers to two by two (fourfold) **contingency tables**, where the term signifies the products of or proportions lying on the same diagonal. In the diagram, cross-

product *ad* represents the observations which contribute to positive association and cross-product *bc* those contributing to negative association. The difference between the two cross products (*ad* − *bc*) indicates the size and the sign of association in the table.

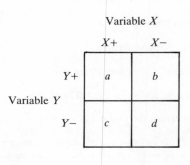

Variable *X*

Many coefficients for measuring association in two-by-two tables have terms for differences in the cross products in the numerator, e.g. **Yule's** *Q*, where

$$Q = \frac{ad - bc}{ad + bc},$$

See also RELIABILITY, **Inter-rater Reliability**

Cross-Section Analysis See under CROSS-SECTIONAL DESIGN

CROSS-SECTIONAL DESIGN
The distinguishing feature of cross-sectional design is that data are obtained once only, rather than several times as in LONGITUDINAL STUDIES. The data may, however, still cover previous time periods retrospectively — e.g. if a group of subjects were to be asked about their childhood.
Cross-sectional designs are usually adequate for describing the distribution of a variable in a **population** and for describing the relationships between **variables**. For instance, there is little difficulty in gaining valid information on the distribution of attitudes towards disarmament among white women or on the voting intentions at a forthcoming election. Describing relationships between variables may be attempted by either of two basic variants of the same method. An **experimental group** who have had a **treatment** — e.g. exposure to an advertising campaign — is compared with a **control group** who have not, on some **dependent variable** — e.g. alcohol consumption. Alternatively, the level of a particular treatment variable — e.g. hours spent watching

educational TV — is measured and correlated with the measured level of the dependent variable — e.g. I.Q. There are many variations of these designs. Control group data may sometimes be culled from other studies, or from **norms** on the dependent variable. Several **independent variables** may be tested at the same time and there may be several experimental and/or control groups.

The problems with this purely descriptive approach are mostly technical and statistical. Sufficiently large random samples from defined populations should be used and the correct statistical methods applied. The refusal rate should be kept low, the conditions of testing kept standard, and **response** and **interviewer biases** eliminated as far as possible. Extraneous influences which might affect later respondents, e.g. word of mouth reports from earlier respondents, should be kept to a minimum.

More serious problems arise when cross-sectional designs are used to infer causation. Unless the researcher is in the unlikely position of being able to assign people to groups in the manner of a true experiment, a control group may differ experimentally from the experimental group on factors other than the independent variable. These factors may account for any effects found. This problem is exacerbated when an experimental treatment is deliberately given to a particular group of people — e.g. compensatory education to all low school achievers. The direction of causation may be unclear — e.g. watching educational TV might raise IQ scores or people with high IQ might watch more TV. The inferences to be drawn may be valid for the populations or settings sampled, but may not generalize to other ones.

Various measures may be taken to overcome the problems. Possible extraneous factors may be measured and allowed for. Where this is impossible, factors thought to be related to the extraneous variables may be measured instead — social class and age are often used this way. The direction of causation may sometimes be inferred from previous theory or from common sense. It may be possible to gather certain easily remembered data retrospectively, thus introducing a longitudinal element into a cross-sectional study. However, in many situations a full-scale longitudinal study, with testing at more than one point in time, will be necessary.

Cross-validation Exact repetition of an experiment to see whether it will yield the same results. Cross-validation is particularly necessary when results are reported which were not hypothesized in advance. Also, batteries of items devised for a particular task within one sample need to be cross-validated to see if they will still perform the task in another similar sample. (For instance, one might select a series of items which distinguished good from poor sales representatives. The items selected would then need to be re-tested on a new sample, because at least some of them are likely to have discriminated by chance.)

Cross-validation is sometimes taken as synonymous with **replication**, but the latter term more properly refers to the collection of several different observations under identical experimental conditions.

C-scale See **Conservatism Scale (C-scale)**

Culture-free (fair) Test A test intended for cross-cultural comparison, where steps are taken to restrict or, if possible, to eliminate the effect of a subject's culture on his or her score. The most usual application of the term is to an intelligence test which does not rely on language. The subject may, for example, be asked to select from a number of alternatives a pattern piece which best completes a given design. Even so, culture-free tests have been attacked by some critics on the grounds that the effects of language in structuring perception are so pervasive that non-linguistic IQ tests are not really culture-free at all.

Cumulative Frequency Distribution A DISTRIBUTION obtained by starting at one end of a range of scores and, for each **class interval** in turn, adding the frequency in that class interval to all the frequencies preceding it. This enables one to see how many observations fall above or below any particular value of the variable. A plot of cumulative frequency on the Y-axis against the value of the variable on the X-axis is known as an *ogive*.
See also **Frequency Distribution**

Cumulative Relative Frequency Distribution A **cumulative frequency distribution** of the percentages of the total cases falling in each **class interval** of a DISTRIBUTION.

Cumulative Scaling The process of forming a series of items into a scale in the form of a hierarchy. This hierarchy is such that agreement with an item some stages up implies agreement with, or in some other way subsumes, all items lower down.
See also **Guttman Scale**, ATTITUDE SCALING

Curvilinear Relationship A curvilinear relationship exists between two variables when, on plotting them against each other, a curve of some kind results rather than a straight line. The curve can be of any shape but is usually smooth, and the term curvilinear is not usually applied to a plot in which there are *completely separate* groups of points which do not fall on a straight line.

D

D_{YX} See **Somer's d$_{YX}$**

Data   Observational records, test results, scores, interview records, etc. — any observed facts from which general inferences may ultimately be drawn.

Data Analysis   The processing of data in order to yield general conclusions.

Data Matrix   A display which may be notional or real, to show how each single observation in a set of data is placed on one or more classifying dimensions simultaneously. A number of *cells* are set up representing all the possible combinations of scores on the dimensions, and each cell is specified by suffixes. Thus, if there are two dimensions, the first split into two categories, the second into three, there will be $2 \times 3 = 6$ cells set out in two rows and three columns with suffixes as shown:

(11)	(12)	(13)
(21)	(22)	(23)

As an example, one might be interested in reading speed measured under three different lighting conditions (dim, medium, and strong) and two different levels of motivation (low and high). Cell (11) would then contain observations of reading speed in dim light under low motivation. There may be only one observation in each cell or there may be several. If there are several, an extra suffix is sometimes used to differentiate between them; e.g. O (124) would be the fourth observation in cell (12). However, this practice is not universal.

Data Set   A collection of observations of several different variables on the same individuals or units.
See also **Data Matrix**

Data Triangulation   See under **Triangulation**

D (Decision) Study   A study in which there is a normal application of a test, for example when an intelligence test is actually used to decide on intelligence in a group of people. A D (decis-ion) study may be distinguished from a **G (generalizability) study**, the latter being a study to discover and quantify all the possible sources of **error variance** in a test. For example, in an intelligence test a G (generalizability) study might measure errors from taking the test at different times of the day, having different people score it, changing the environment, etc.

Death-Rate   The crude death-rate is the total number of deaths in a year in a defined population (e.g. England and Wales) divided by the total population, estimated at the mid-year point.
Death-rates are conventionally given as rates per 1,000 of the population e.g. 11.8 in 1978 for England and Wales.
Age-specific death-rates are calculated in a similar way but for particular age-groups, and may be further subdivided by sex and by geographical region.
See also **Birth-Rate**

Decay   Outdating of published lists used as sampling frames, e.g. electoral rolls, phone directories.
See also **Sampling Frame**

Deciles   The values of a variable which divide a set of observations into ten subsets each containing an equal number of observed values.
See also **Frequency Distribution**

Decision Variable   Any **independent variable** which may, in principle or in practice, be manipulated or changed in value by a decision-maker attempting to obtain an optimum solution to a management or planning problem. A **dependent variable** (or effect) is not a decision variable because it is produced only indirectly by decisions on the values at which to set the independent variables.
Decision variables normally represent the independent variables in a mathematical model which has been used to simulate some real problem which is susceptible to policy choices.
See also **Optimization Models**

Deduction   See under THEORY

Deductive Argument   See under THEORY

Degrees of Freedom (df)   Mathematically, the equation expressing the DISTRIBUTION of a statistic (e.g. χ^2, t, or f) contains at least one parameter called the number of degrees of freedom. This number is always the number of cases in the sample less a few, depending on the statistic and the circumstances of its use. Thus, the equation for the t-distribution, for example, yields different results for a sample with degrees of freedom 50 from that for a sample with degrees of freedom 100. Statistical tables are therefore constructed showing **critical values** of various statistics for the various degrees of freedom from 1 up to about 120. For samples larger than this the degrees of freedom make little further difference, i.e. distribution equations with infinite degrees of freedom are, in general, very nearly the same as those with about 120 degrees of freedom.

Demographic Variable   A variable which denotes a fixed or ascribed characteristic of individuals such as gender/sex, social class, age, marital status, or race is termed a demographic variable in contrast to variables denoting attitudes, behaviour, or performance.
Demographic variables often function as background variables in analysis, that is, they are used as **independent variables** to explain differences in attitudes between individuals. The apparent immutability or permanent nature of demographic characteristics leads many analysts to give them a causal role in explanation.

Dendrogram   A diagram describing the clusters formed at each stage of a hierarchical cluster analysis. See under CLUSTER ANALYSIS

Density Function   See **Probability Density Function**

Density Search Technique   A type of CLUSTER ANALYSIS which seeks for parts of the k-dimensional space which contain a high density of individuals and other parts which contain a low density — e.g. the average density over the whole space might be computed, the space might be divided up into smaller portions, and the density within each determined. Where this is significantly higher than average, there is a cluster. This technique is usually only feasible by computer.

Dependent Variable   A variable which is to be predicted from other variables. Also known as a *criterion variable* or an *effect*. In experiments, the experimenter systematically varies some of the variables, known as **independent variables** and measures the effect on the dependent variable(s). In survey research, both sets of variables usually have to be passively observed and the distinction between independent and dependent variables is made on theoretical or other *a priori* grounds.

Depth Interview   An interview, usually unstructured, in which one tries to go deeply into some aspect of the respondent's innermost feelings, motives, attitudes, biography, etc.
See also INTERVIEW

Description   Description in social science denotes the search for and refinement of useful variables and the specification of associations between them, but stops short of *causal* explanations and rigorously tested causal models. Statistical 'explanation' is really description. Explanation proper is about the causes of phenomena, and leads to theories enabling prediction of other phenomena in a logical way.
See also CAUSATION

Descriptive Statistics   Statistical methods of summarizing large quantities of data so that patterns and relationships within the data may be seen; as distinct from statistical methods of *hypothesis testing*.
Descriptive statistics usually consist of **frequency distributions**, TABULATIONS, **measures of central tendency**, or of **dispersion**.

Descriptive Survey   A survey aimed at describing certain attributes of a population, specifying *associations* between variables or searching out **hypotheses** to be tested, but which is not primarily intended for establishing cause-and-effect relationships or actually testing hypotheses.
See also **Explanatory Survey**

Design Effect (Deff)   Samples other than a **simple random sample** (e.g. a stratified random sample or a cluster sample) are sometimes more and sometimes less efficient than a simple random sample. Design effect expresses this relative efficiency as the ratio of the **error variance** in the sample being tested to the error variance in a simple random sample of the same size.
See also SAMPLING THEORY AND METHODS, **Sampling Error**

Determinateness   See under MODEL

Deviation   The difference between an observed value or score and the average of the DISTRI-

BUTION of which it forms a part. An individual deviation is sometimes termed a deviate.

Diachronic Study An investigation which collects data on the same sample of individuals or organizations at several points in time, e.g. a **panel study** or a LONGITUDINAL STUDY.

It is to be contrasted with a *synchronic study* which collects data at only one point in time, e.g. a CROSS-SECTIONAL study.

Trend analysis, which compares samples from different time points rather than a single sample followed through time, is also diachronic.

Diagnostic and Statistical Manual of Mental Disorders (DSM) An American classification of mental disorders which is compatible with the **International Classification of Diseases (ICD)**, but more expanded. *DSM* is being continually updated and is currently in its third edition.

Diagram See under **Graphic Presentation**

Dichotomous Item An item framed to allow only two responses — e.g. yes/no or alternative *A*/alternative *B*.

Dichotomous Model A THEORY or MODEL whose variables are couched in terms of just two categories (a **dichotomy**), e.g. manual and non-manual occupations, Conservative and non-Conservative voters.

Dichotomy A true dichotomy, e.g. sex, is a variable which may take only two values. Any variable can, if necessary, be made into a dichotomy, e.g. family income might be classed as high or low although income is not naturally dichotomous.

Difference Equation See under TIME SERIES ANALYSIS

Difference Score The difference between an individual's scores on the same test or scale measured at two different points in time. Difference scores are particularly likely to be computed in **before–after studies** where a group of people are tested before and after some experimental treatment. However, some care is needed in their interpretation, because a difference score tends to be less RELIABLE than either of the components comprising it. Furthermore, where an initial score (A) is correlated against a difference score $(B - A)$ a spurious negative correlation is likely to result due to **regression to the mean** effects.

Dimension A continuous scale, conceived to underly observed behaviour. The measurement of intelligence, abilities, or attitudes, for example, is based on the researcher's model of these traits as being unitary, linear, and quantifiable, so that every person in the population could be assigned a single quantity of any of them. The attempt to measure a postulated underlying dimension empirically often suggests that it may not in fact be just one dimension (unidimensional) but be better conceived as comprising several lesser, more or less strongly related, dimensions (e.g. in the case of intelligence where various subscales seem to measure different facets).

See also **Continuous Variable**

Directional Null Hypothesis An hypothesis which states that no difference in a particular direction will be found, for instance that group *A* will not be more intelligent than group *B*.

See also **Null Hypothesis**

Disaggregation See under AGGREGATION

Discordant Ranking See under **Concordant Ranking**

Discovery-Based Approach See under PARTICIPANT OBSERVATION

Discrete Random Variable See under RANDOM VARIABLE

Discrete Variable See under **Continuous Variable**

DISCRIMINANT ANALYSIS

Analysis to determine how best to discriminate a number of groups of people from each other in terms of a number of *discriminating variables*. For example, one might try to distinguish known voters for four different political parties in terms of their income, level of education, age, sex, authoritarianism score, etc. This is achieved by weighting and combining the scores on the variables into a number of *discriminant functions* on which the groups are maximally separated. A further possible step is then to measure a new group of people of unknown group membership (i.e. voting intention) on the variables and to use the discriminant functions established to predict their most probable group membership.

A discriminant function is of the form

$$D = d_1 Z_1 + d_2 Z_2 + \dots + d_n Z_n,$$

where D is the score on the function, d_1, d_2, etc are constants (analogous to beta weights) known as *standardized discriminant function*

Discriminant Function

coefficients, and Z_1, Z_2, etc. are the *standardized scores* on the variable.

The possible number of discriminant functions which may be derived is *either* one less than the number of groups *or* equal to the number of discriminating variables, whichever is the smaller. Successive discriminant functions are **orthogonal** to each other, and contribute progressively less to the discrimination. Later discriminant functions often contribute so little that they need not be considered. One way of judging this is to derive and assess the **eigenvalue** of the function in the same way as in FACTOR ANALYSIS. Another is to view discriminant analysis as a special case of **canonical correlation analysis**, with the discriminating variables on one side being related to a set of **dummy variables** constituting group membership on the other. The discriminant functions are then identical to *canonical variates*. It can be seen whether the proportion of the total **variance** explained in one set of variables (i.e. proportion of the *total redundancy index*) is enhanced by the addition of the next discriminant function.

A *group centroid* represents the most typical location of a member of a particular group in the space defined by the discriminant functions extracted. Its co-ordinates are the mean scores of the group on each discriminant function.

Classification functions are of the form $C = C_1V_1 + C_2V_2 + ... + C_nV_n +$ constant, where C_1, C_2, ..., C_n are constants, and V_1, V_2, ..., V_n are the scores of an individual on the discriminating variables. They are used to decide group membership for a new sample of cases. There is a different classification function for each group and membership is assigned by working out all the functions for the person in question and assigning him/her to the group with the highest C value. The probability of a person belonging to each of the groups may also be calculated.

Like similar techniques (MULTIPLE REGRESSION, FACTOR ANALYSIS, **canonical correlation analysis**) discriminant analysis makes assumptions about NORMALITY OF DISTRIBUTION and homogeneity (*homoscedasticity*) of certain variances.

Discriminant Function A function used to weight and combine the scores on a number of variables in such a fashion that they discriminate maximally between different groups of people.
See under DISCRIMINANT ANALYSIS

Discrimination Index A measure of how well an item in a test of achievement or ability discriminates between high and low perfor-

mers on the test. One simple discrimination index is obtained by first dividing the sample according to total test score. Then the proportion of people in the bottom 27 per cent who get the question right is subtracted from the proportion in the top 27 per cent who get it right.

Dispersion The extent to which a set of observations is spread out over a range of values It can be measured by the **variance, standard deviation**, or **semi-interquartile range**. DISTRIBUTIONS with the same **means** may have very different dispersions.

Disproportionate Stratification A method of sampling in which the population is first divided into **strata**, e.g. men and women, different social classes, or different sizes of firms. A **random sample** from each stratum is then drawn in such a way that the strata in the final sample are not in the same proportion as in the population. Most frequently the proportions are made unequal so that strata with only few cases have a higher proportion taken. This ensures that sufficient numbers are available for the analysis of each stratum separately. If a statistic is required to summarize the total sample, then the figures for each stratum are weighted in inverse proportion to the stratum sampling fraction.
See also **Stratification**

Distributed Lag See under ESTIMATION

DISTRIBUTION
A description in the form of a graph, table, or theoretical equation of how many observations from some sample or population fall at all the different values of a variable being measured. When the observations consist of data, the distribution is termed a **frequency distribution**, the commonest kind of which is the *univariate frequency distribution*. This is obtained by dividing the range of values covered by a set of observations on a single variable into **class intervals**. These class intervals are then set down consecutively in increasing or decreasing order and the numbers of observations falling in each are tabulated. Frequency distributions are sometimes drawn up on more than one variable simultaneously. Thus, a *bivariate frequency distribution* (or *joint frequency distribution*), for instance, would demonstrate for each class interval on one variable how many people fall into the various class intervals on another variable.

Distributions observed empirically may often be descibed theoretically by mathematical functions called **probability density functions** (p.d.f.). One distribution very commonly encountered is the NORMAL DISTRIBUTION (also termed the *normal probability density function*, or the *Gaussian distribution*). This is a symmetrical bell-shaped curve and it describes many human charcteristics, at least approximately. Height, for example, shows an approximately normal distribution. most people are of medium height, while a few are short and a few are tall.

Distributions which may be viewed as departures from the normal distribution are also common. Those with too many observations at one end, but which are otherwise normal, are said to be *skewed* or, in severe cases, *J-shaped*. *Positive skewness* implies that the **mode** is less than the **median** which is in turn less than the **mean**. In *negative skewness* the reverse is the case.

Two other probability density functions often met are the **binomial distribution** and the **Poisson distribution**. The binomial distribution describes a given event which may occur with probability p or not occur with probability q equal to $1-p$, for example the event 'heads' in a large number (N) of tosses of a penny. This distribution has a mean $= Np$ and a **standard deviation** $\sqrt{Npq}$. The Poisson distribution is a better fit for the case where an event may occur but does so only occasionally with a low probability p. Both its mean and its variance $= Np$. More generally, it fits cases where the probability of occurence of a single event is proportional to the value of a continuous variable — e.g. the presence of a car within a particular length of road. The probability of this will increase with the length of road observed.

The term distribution is also applied in connection with the statistics used for hypothesis testing — e.g. the *t-distribution*, the *F-distribution*, and the *chi-square distribution*. In these cases there is a theoretical equation which describes a whole family of distribution curves — the curve to be selected being represented by a parameter in the equation which depends on sample size and is known as the **degrees of freedom**. Thus, the *t*-distribution for degrees of freedom 7 is a curve obtained by plotting the value of the *t*-ratio on the *X*-axis (with range from minus infinity to plus infinity) against the frequency of occurrence of this value by chance on the *Y*-axis. For all these distributions there are tables which show for the various degrees of freedom the values of the statistic which need to be obtained in order to reject the **null hypothesis**.

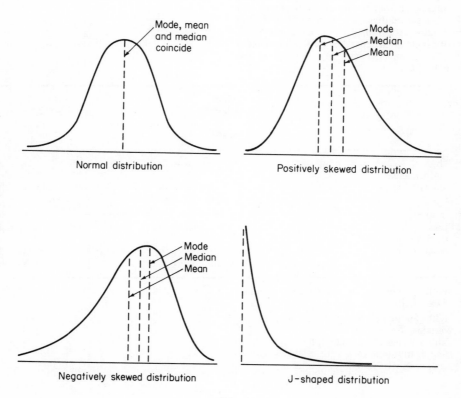

Normal distribution

Positively skewed distribution

Negatively skewed distribution

J-shaped distribution

Distribution-Free Test   See **Non-parametric Test**

Disturbance   In PATH ANALYSIS the term disturbance is sometimes used to describe a set of unmeasured causes affecting an *endogenous* (dependent) *variable*.

Don't Know Response   A response to which for whatever reason no code can be assigned.
See also **Coding**

Double Blind   An experimental procedure, used particularly in drug trials, to guard against **experimenter bias**. It is arranged that neither the subjects nor the person gathering the data are aware which treatments are being given to which subjects.

***d*-Statistic**   A measure of association useful in **two by two tables**. One of the variables is specified as the **independent variable** and the other as the **dependent variable** and for both a negative and a positive category are specified. The percentages of positive and negative scores on the *dependent* variable are determined for each category of the *independent* variable. Then in the *positive* category of the *dependent* variable the negative percentage is subtracted from the positive percentage and the result is divided by 100 to yield *d*. The *d*-statistic is asymmetric, i.e. a different value of *d* is obtained depending on which variable is taken as independent. For example in the following table:

Dummy Variable   Dummy variables are devices which make it possible to manipulate **nominal scale** data almost as if they were **interval scale** data. Each category on a nominal scale may be assigned a dummy variable which can take only two values. For instance, if one was considering Protestants, Catholics, and others, a dummy variable assigned to the category Protestant could be coded 1 for all Protestants and 0 for everyone else. Similarly, the Catholic dummy variable could score 1 for Catholics and 0 for others; and so on. Each of the dummy variables thus created may be assumed to be measured on an interval scale and manipulated accordingly, e.g. MULTIPLE REGRESSION may be performed. Only $n - 1$ dummy variables are needed to characterize n nominal categories.

Duncan Multiple Range Test   A method for making unplanned comparisons following an ANALYSIS OF VARIANCE. It is identical to the **Newman–Keuls test** except that the value of q_r is different and is read from a special table appropriate to the Duncan test. The value of W_r increases more rapidly with increasing r in the Newman–Keuls test than in the Duncan test.

	High intelligence (+)	Low intelligence (−)
High mathematical ability (+)	$n = 70$ row % = 70 column % = 58.33	$n = 30$ row % = 30 column % = 37.5
Low mathematical ability (−)	$n = 50$ row % = 50 column % = 41.67	$n = 50$ row % = 50 column % = 62.5

With intelligence as independent variable, $d = +0.208$.

With mathematical ability as independent variable, $d = +0.200$.

Though simple to calculate, there is no sampling distribution known for *d* and its significance cannot be tested.

E

Ecological Fallacy Correct conclusions may only be drawn from correlations which are based on the appropriate units of analysis. When the unit of analysis is the *proportion of people* living in a given area and a conclusion applicable to *individual people* is required, one is running the risk of the ecological fallacy. If in the nineteenth century one had found a *positive correlation* between the proportion of servants in an area and the wealth of the area, it would probably be wrong to conclude that the servants were more wealthy than the rest of the population.

Ecological Validity VALIDITY in natural settings and conditions. A research finding would have little ecological validity if it held true only in an artificial laboratory or interview setting or perhaps in one or two possibly atypical real-life settings. It would have high ecological validity if it was true under many different natural conditions.

Economic Trends Quarterly publication of the Central Statistical Office which publishes economic statistics from a number of official series such as consumers' expenditure, output, money stocks, bank lending, wage rates and earnings, balance of payments, and financial accounts for various industrial sectors. In addition, it contains current values for several economic cyclical indicators in TIME SERIES form; indicators are categorized as those which lag, coincide, or lead upturns and downturns in the business cycle and are *seasonally adjusted* or *trend-free* where appropriate.

Edwards Personal Preference Schedule (EPPS) An inventory which aims to measure fifteen basic personality variables. In order to minimise distortion due to the subjects responding in a socially approved manner they are forced to choose between alternatives which are equal in social desirability. **Norms** are available for students and for other adults.

Effect See under **Dependent Variable**

Efficiency of a Statistical Test See **Power of a Statistical Test**

Efficient Estimate See under ESTIMATION

Eigenvalue In FACTOR ANALYSIS, after the first factor extraction process, the eigenvalue for each factor may be calculated (also known as the *latent root* or *extracted variance*). This is the sum of the squares of the **factor loadings** of all the variables on that factor. The eigenvalue often serves as a criterion for retaining or discarding a factor and, from it, the proportion of the total variance explained by the factor may be obtained.

Elaboration of a Concept The splitting up of a concept into different more or less independent parts, as when intelligence is broken down into verbal and non-verbal intelligence. See also **Concept**

Elementary Linkage Analysis A method of CLUSTER ANALYSIS which, starting from a correlation matrix, provides an extremely quick way of seeing which entities cluster and how many clusters there are. However, it is not always as informative as are some of the longer methods of cluster and FACTOR ANALYSIS. From a **correlation matrix** the steps are as follows:
(1) Circle the highest correlation in each column.
(2) Cross out the highest pair of correlations and link the two variables involved, e.g. $A \rightarrow B$.
(3) Read across the rows concerning the two tests, cross out any circled correlations, and join the new variables involved into the cluster, e.g.

$$A \rightleftarrows B$$
$$| \qquad |$$
$$D \qquad C$$

(4) Repeat this reading across the rows of the newly joined in tests, and continue until no more circled correlations are found.
(5) Repeat the whole procedure starting with the next highest remaining pair of correlations. Continue until there are no more circled correlations to be crossed out.

ELEMENTARY SURVEY ANALYSIS (ESA)
A method of analysing relationships between variables from data collected by survey; it is analogous in many ways to MULTIPLE CORRE-

lation and MULTIPLE REGRESSION but unlike these forms of statistical analysis it uses only **dichotomized variables** tabulated in **contingency tables**. All variables in ESA are dichotomized no matter what their original form of measurement. **Continuous variables** are dichotomized at some convenient cutting point (e.g. the **median** value) and natural dichotomies (e.g. sex) are left in their original form.

The first stage in ESA is to examine the relationship between two variables (x and y) in a two by two contingency table and to calculate **association** using any of the numerous **contingency coefficients**;

Pupil Achievement

		High %	Low%	d
Class size	Small	50	50	0
	Large	50	50	0

Figure 1 association is calculated by the **d-statistic** which is zero in this case

(a)
School in EPA

Pupil achievement

		High %	Low %	d
Class size	Small	100	66.7	-0.33
	Large	0	33.3	$+0.33$

(b)
School not in EPA

Pupil achievement

		High %	Low %	d
Class size	Small	33.0	0	-0.33
	Large	66.7	100	$+0.33$

Figure 2 Partial contingency tables of Class Size and Pupil Achievement; Educational Priority Area controlled

All relationships must be directional in ESA and the **dependent** and **independent variables** specified at the outset. In Figure 1, class size is the independent variable. The second stage in ESA is to tabulate the relationship between x and y (xy) using a different cutting point for the dichotomy (if continuous variables were used) in order to check that any observed association is not an artefact of the particular cutting-point chosen for the first tabulation.

The third stage of the analysis is a simple form of multiple correlation; the original two-variable relationship is elaborated by the introduction of a third variable (z) which is related to both x and y. This constitutes a test of the original (xy) relationship, and the third variable is termed a *test factor* or test variable. The contingency tables for (xy) are re-calculated under the two levels of the dichotomized third variable and yield two partial contingency tables, ($xy:z+$) and ($xy:z-$), in which the relationship between x and y is displayed with z controlled. This is equivalent to calculating a **partial correlation coefficient** but using dichotomies rather than **interval** and **dummy** variables.

Figure 2 shows the partial contingency tables when a third variable, School in EPA/School not in EPA, is introduced into the relationship of Figure 1.

ESA requires a specification of the causal order of the three variables in the analysis, to be made on theoretical rather than on statistical grounds. If the test variable can be reason-

ably held to intervene or mediate causally between the original x and y variables, then it is an *intervening variable* which may reveal a hitherto suppressed relationship between the original two variables. Figures 1 and 2 represent such a case and EPA/not EPA would be termed a **suppressor variable**.

If the third variable is antecedent causally to the original two-variable relationship, then it can explain an observed association between x and y if the first association disappears when the partial contingency tables are calculated. In such a case, the association between x and y is shown to be due to the associations of x with z (xz) and y with z (yz), and the (xy) association is said to be *spurious*. Again, this has an equivalent logic in multiple correlation where it would be **spurious correlation**.

An intervening variable may change the size or even the sign (direction) of the (xy) relationship; in such a case this will be evidence of statistical **interaction** between the two-variable relationship and the test factor. The test factor is said to *specify* the relationship (xy) for the two different levels of z, the third variable. The elaboration of a two-variable relationship by the introduction of a third variable is summarized in the basic equation for ESA, which may be written as:

$$(xy) = (xy.z+) \oplus (xy.z-) \oplus (xz)\,(yz),$$

where (xy) is the direct or zero-order association between x and y; (xz) is the direct association between x and z; and similarly (yz). $(xy.z+)$ is the partial association between x and y with z held constant at the positive level of its two possible levels and $(xy.z-)$ is the partial association for the other level of z. The addition signs are circled to show that more than the simple addition of the coefficients of association is required.

ESA corresponds exactly to the logic of multiple correlation; but the computational procedures are very much simpler even though the basic coding and sorting of survey data is the same large problem whichever method of analysis is used. ESA does degrade the data to dichotomies, and this risks misleading findings. With the free availability of electronic data processing and statistical packages currently, multiple regression and correlation are invariably used.

Multiple regression and correlation retain the original scale properties of variables at **ratio** or **interval** levels of measurement and where true dichotomies (e.g. sex) are present amongst the variables they may be handled as dummy variables.

Empirical and Empirical Generalization The term empirical denotes something which has been observed. The observation may or may not have been guided by theory. In the pejorative use of the term, it refers to statistical relationships in data which have not been given a theoretical interpretation. An empirical generalization is one which has arisen out of observation, has not been deduced from a previously stated theory, and on which no satisfactory theory can be constructed.

Employment Gazette Monthly publication by the Department of Employment and it is the main source of labour market statistics in the United Kingdom. Statistical series are based on the D.o.E.'s own regular enquiries such as the Census of Employment and the **New Earnings Survey** or from other official series such as the **Census of Production.**

Series are aggregated by one or more of the following: region (nine for England and Wales), industry (the 27 orders of the **Standard Industrial Clasification**), occupation (17 **socio-economic groups**), sex, and part-time and full-time working. Regular statistical series appearing in the *Gazette* as parts of updated time series include: unemployment, job vacancies employment, normal hours of work, overtime and short-time working, wage rates and earnings, industrial disputes, and man-days lost through industrial disputes.

End Effect Synonymous with **extreme responding**

Endogenous Variable See under PATH ANALYSIS

Enumeration Counting. The British decennial census calls its temporary field interviewers 'Enumerators'.

Enumeration District See under **Census**

Epidemiology The study of the distribution of diseases and other medical conditions in a defined population. Distributions are usually expressed in terms of **prevalence** and *incidence*, the former being the total rate of occurrence (usually in cases per 1,000) in a given time period and the latter being the rate of occurrence of new cases.

Equivalent Forms When a test is constructed, two forms of it — as nearly equivalent as possible — are frequently devised. These will often have the same number of questions couched in similar terms. They are useful for testing the same respondent on different occasions, e.g. in the context of a **before–after study** or in the assessment of the RELIABILITY of the test.

ERROR

A set of observations seldom reflects reality absolutely. To the extent that it does not do so it is in error. Error stems from many sources. The *operational definition* of the variable may not correspond exactly with the concept which it is desired to measure. The collection of the data may be inadequate in various ways (see BIAS). The sampling procedure may be at fault. Inappropriate statistical manipulation may be performed. Finally, even if the research procedures are exemplary there will still be error, due to a host of uncontrolled extraneous variables (e.g. respondents having headaches or misunderstanding questions).

In statistical theory it is asumed that **measurement errors** will be *random*, i.e. there is no tendency for the errors of measurement to be predominantly in one direction. Over a large number of cases, such errors will balance out and there will be no effect on **measures of central tendency**. A person's observed score may be broken down into a **true score** and an **error score**. The variance of the error scores over the whole sample is known as the **error variance**. Equivalently, error variance is that part of the total variance which cannot be accounted for any other way. Not all measurement errors are, in fact, random. If the errors all tend to be in the same direction (e.g. if most people under- rather than over-report the amount they drink) then **systematic error** is present. This cannot be handled statistically and will bias the results of a survey.

Sampling error is distinct from measurement error, and is that part of the total error in an estimate of a **population parameter** such as the mean, which is due to a sample being unrepresentative of the population from which it is drawn. With **probability sampling** techniques this error may be estimated as a **confidence interval** in which the true value will lie with a known degree of confidence. However, with non-probability techniques (e.g. **quota sampling**) sampling error is unmeasureable. The term standard error refers to the **standard deviation** of an infinitely large set of estimates of a population parameter (mean, standard deviation, variance, etc.) obtained by randomly drawing successive samples, of the same size, with replacement from the population. The **standard error of the mean** ($\sigma_{\bar{x}}$) may be estimated from the standard deviation (S) of a single sample of size n by the formula:

$$\sigma_{\bar{x}} = \frac{S}{\sqrt{n}}$$

The square of this quantity (i.e. $\sigma_{\bar{x}}^2$) is sometimes termed the **sampling variance** but more usually (and confusingly) **error variance**. This latter term therefore has two quite different meanings, one referring to measurement error and the other to sampling error.

Error Score   In classical test theory an individual's score on an item on any given occasion is the sum of his **true score** and his error score. The true score is the average score that would have been obtained over a very large number of testings. The error score is brought about by extraneous effects which acted on that particular occasion and made the score deviate from the true score.

See also **Classical Test Theory Model**, ERROR

Error Variance   *Measurement error variance* is the variance of the error scores on a test or other measure or, equivalently, that part of the observed variance which cannot be accounted for in any other way. *Sampling error variance* refers to error introduced by sampling and is given by the square of the **standard error of the mean** or, in the case of a **stratified sample**, the sum of the squares of the standard errors of the individual strata.

See also ERROR, SAMPLING THEORY AND METHODS

ESTIMATION

The process of inferring an unknown quantity or quantities (usually **population parameters**) from sample observations.

All observations must be regarded as samples of populations and it is therefore possible that as many estimates, each differing from each other, may be made of the same unknown quantity as there are different samples from the same population.

In the case of a single sample there is a single *point estimate* (i.e. one value only) of the population parameter. The discrepancy between the point estimate and the true or population value is unknown because the latter is itself unknown. However, if the sample is a **probability sample** the possible error of estimation from sample to population may be determined subject to a stated degree of confidence in the result.

For example, in the simplest and most common case a single **random sample** is the only basis for estimation. The **mean** of a variable, $\bar{X}$, may be calculated from a sample of size N. $\bar{X}$ is the point estimate of μ_X, the true or population mean of X. The discrepancy between the point estimate and the true value ($\bar{X} - \mu_X$) is a **sampling error** which cannot be a known quantity since μ_X is unknown. But if an infinitely large number of random samples, each of size N, were drawn from the same population, then ($\bar{X} - \mu_X$) would be a RANDOM VARIABLE distributed with known characteristics, i.e. a distribution with a known mean and **variance**. Such a theoretical distribution is known as a *sampling distribution* and its properties may be used to estimate the possible error of a point estimate of a statistic such as the mean.

The sampling distributions of many statistics, such as means, standard deviations, variances, and differences between means, are normal provided the samples are random, and the properties of the normal distribution may be used to construct *interval estimates* from point estimates. The figure shows the theoretical sampling distribution of the mean:

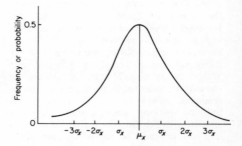

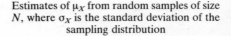

Estimates of μ_X from random samples of size N, where σ_X is the standard deviation of the sampling distribution

The point estimate of μ_X is $\bar{X}$, the mean of a single random sample. In the absence of more information $\bar{X}$ is the best available estimate of μ_X, but how good an estimate it is can only be ascertained once the possible error of estimation is known. This may be obtained from the sampling distribution which is used to transform the point estimate into an interval estimate such that a range of possible values of $\bar{X}$ may be stated within which μ_X has a known probability of lying. By convention, such *confidence intervals* are constructed to contain μ_X with a probability of 0.95 (95 per cent confidence interval) or 0.99 (99 per cent confidence interval). With normal sampling distributions the standard properties of the normal probability distribution are used to set the limits of the confidence interval. It may be shown that the standard deviation (σ_X) of the sampling distribution, more commonly termed **the standard error of the mean**, may be estimated from a single sample, and is given by $S_X/\sqrt{N}$, where S_X is the sample standard deviation and N the number of observations. The 95 per cent confidence interval then has limits ±1.96 standard errors each side of the sample mean.

In general the confidence interval for statistics whose sampling distributions are normal is:

interval estimate of statistic $=$ point estimate sample $\pm$ k. standard error,

where $k = 1.96$ for a 95 per cent confidence interval and 2.57 for a 99 per cent confidence interval.

For any given level of confidence, the width (or precision) of the interval is directly proportional to the standard error which can only be reduced for a given population by increasing the sample size so that a larger sample will give a more precise estimate than a smaller one. If more than one random sample is available from the same population, the data may be treated as a single larger sample by pooling the data from individual samples. If the subsamples are **stratified**, pooling may still be performed, but will involve weighting each stratum by the number of observations in it (see below). Interval estimates of other parameters may be made directly from point estimates once the sampling distribution is known and the standard error has been calculated. Not all sampling distributions are normal (e.g. that of the Pearson correlation coefficient for small samples) and special tables are sometimes available for calculating confidence intervals for such statistics.

The inference from sample information to population is expressed in terms of an estimator or mathematical equation which estimates the population parameters from sample information. For example, an estimator of the

population mean where the observations are from a stratified random sample is the linear equation:

$$\hat{\mu}_x = \frac{n_1\bar{X}_1 + n_2\bar{X}_2 + \dots + n_k\bar{X}_k}{N},$$

where $n_1 \dots n_k$ are the sizes of the strata and $\bar{X}_1 \dots \bar{X}_k$ are the corresponding stratum means, N is the size of the total sample and μ_X is the population mean which the equation is estimating. A large number of stratified random samples drawn from the same population would generate an equally large number of estimates of μ_X which would form a sampling distribution. Thus, any estimator can be used to generate a theoretical sampling distribution of estimates and it is the characteristics or properties of the hypothetical sampling distribution which define the type of estimator being used. The desirable properties of estimators are that they should be *unbiased, efficient*, and *consistent*. An *unbiased estimator* is one for which the mean of the sampling distribution of estimates is equal to the population mean. This means that in the case of a single random sample, the estimate formed from it by the estimator is equally likely to be above or below the true or population mean; the sampling distribution of the estimator is centred on the true value. An estimator which is more likely to overestimate or to underestimate in a consistent way is said to be *biased*.

A biased estimator may in some circumstances be preferable to an ubiased one if it satisfies some other criterion such as efficiency. The *efficiency* of an estimator is the **dispersion** or **variance** of its sampling distribution. One estimator is more efficient than another if its variance is lower than the other's. For example, $\hat{\mu}_X = \bar{X}$ is a more efficient estimator than $\hat{\mu}_X = X_i$ (the ith single value) because the variance of $\bar{X}$ is S_X^2/N and that of the single values is S_X^2. Although both estimators are unbiased, one is more efficient than the other.

A *consistent estimator* is one in which efficiency increases and bias decreases as the sample size increases. For an infinitely large sample a consistent estimator will provide a perfect point estimate of the population parameter. A biased but consistent estimator will have less and less bias as the sample size increases, so that at the limit where $N = $ infinity, the estimator becomes unbiased; this is an *asymptotically unbiased estimator*.

Estimation of **regression weights** or coefficients in simple or multiple REGRESSION ANALYSIS follows the principles above but there can be problems concerned with assumptions which are made about the error or disturbance term in regression equations (see under **Stochastic variable**.

The regression equation:

$$Y_i = \alpha + \beta X_i + e_i,$$

where e_i is an error, requires that the population parameters α and β are estimated from a set of sample observations (X_i, Y_i). The ordinary **least squares** (OLS) estimator of α and β is the most efficient or *best linear unbiased estimator (BLUE)* of the regression weights provided that the disturbance term e_i is: (i) uncorrelated with any **independent variable** in the regression equation (i.e. with X_i); (ii) uncorrelated with any other disturbance term (e.g. e_k); and (iii) the variances of all disturbance terms for all Y_i are the same (**homoscedasticity**).

If all the assumptions (i)–(iii) hold, then the OLS criterion provides *maximum likelihood estimators* (MLEs) of the regression weights. Likelihood is the probability that a population defined by the estimated parameters (α and β in regression analysis) could have generated the observations (X_i, Y_i) contained in the sample. Maximum likelihood is the mathematical criterion that the observed data (sample) have the greatest probability of constituting a random sample from a population whose parameters are the estimated regression weights α and β. If any or all of the assumptions do not hold, then OLS does not yield the maximum likelihood estimator and modifications to OLS are required in order that α and β are estimated by a maximum likelihood criterion.

If the disturbance term is correlated with an independent variable (as is common in TIME SERIES variables), then OLS will estimate coefficients which are not consistent, i.e. the bias of the estimator changes with changing sample size. This may be overcome by *two-stage least squares* (2SLS) estimation in which, first an *instrumental variable* (Z_i) which is correlated with X_i but not with e_i is substituted for X_i. The second stage is simply OLS estimation with Z_i in place of X_i. If the disturbance terms are themselves correlated, then OLS again does not yield the maximum likelihood estimator of the regression coefficients. This is common in time series variables where successive disturbance terms are often correlated and is known as *serial* or *auto-correlation*. Consider:

$$Y_t = \alpha + \beta X_t + \varepsilon_t, \quad \text{estimate of } Y \text{ at time } t,$$

$$Y_{t-1} = \alpha + \beta X_{t-1}$$
$$+ \varepsilon_{t-1}, \quad \text{estimate of } Y \text{ at time } t - 1,$$

where α and β are the regression coefficients and ε_t and ε_{t-1} are correlated errors.

The problem of serial correlation may be overcome by taking the differences between successive observations of Y and regressing them onto the differences between the corresponding X observations, so that:

$$T_t - T_{t-1} = \alpha^* + \beta^* (X_t - X_{t-1}) + \varepsilon^*,$$

where α^* and β^* denote new parameters or regression weights and ε^* is a new disturbance term which is now uncorrelated with other disturbance terms.

Any single observed Y (Y_i) may be thought of as a sample of all possible Y's at a particular point on the **regression line** or plane. The difference between Y_i and the estimated value of Y_i $(\hat{Y}_i)$ at that point is the *residual* or *error* term $(\hat{Y}_i - Y_i)$. Errors are assumed to be random variables, normally distributed, with a mean of zero (i.e. centred on the regression line) and with a variance which is the same for all points on the regression line or plane: (homoscedascity). If this assumption does not hold, then the OLS estimator will not be the maximum likelihood estimator of α and β. The MLE may be obtained when there is heteroscedascity of error variances by *weighted least squares estimation* in which the sum of squares of residuals $\Sigma (\hat{Y}_i - Y_i)^2$ is weighted for each Y_i by the reciprocal of the variance of the error term, that is:

$$\text{minimize} \quad \frac{\Sigma(\hat{Y}_i - Y_i)^2}{\sigma^2_{\epsilon_i}}, \quad \text{for all } Y_i,$$

where $\sigma_{\epsilon_i}^2$ is the variance of the error term at $\hat{Y}_i$. This is the best linear unbiased estimator of the regression coefficients which yields the maximum likelihood estimates of α and β, the regression parameters.

Estimator See under ESTIMATION

Eta (η) The correlation ratio η is an index of association for **non-linear relationships**. It is given by

$$\eta_{yx}^2 = 1 - \frac{S_{ay}^2}{S_y^2}$$

where S_{ay}^2 is the sum of the variances within arrays of Y about the array means and S_y^2 is the total variance of all Y values.

It is an asymmetric measure, so that η_{xy}^2 is different from η_{yx}^2 and is given by

$$\eta_{xy}^2 = 1 - \frac{S_{ax}^2}{S_x^2}$$

The value of η has no implications for the shape of the **joint distribution** of Y and X.

Ex Post Facto Design Research in which an attempt is made to exert control over **extraneous variables** by **matching** on them or allowing for them *after* a study has been carried out. The term is particularly applied to non-experimental situations where a group who have undergone some particular experience (e.g. teaching method, drug treatment, or natural disaster) is being compared to a **control group** who have not. The researcher may decide to look at background variables for which records exist (e.g. social class or educational level) and to try to control for these.
See also EXPERIMENT

Exhaustive A set of categories is *exhaustive* if it covers all the possible observations in a data set without exception.

Exogenous Variable A causal variable which lies outside the system being modelled and which is therefore not specified further. In PATH ANALYTIC MODELS an exogenous variable may be shown as a causal influence on one variable in the model but no path coefficients are shown to the exogenous variable.

Expectancy Chart A chart which, for each level of some given **predictor variable**, displays the chance of reaching or surpassing some criterion on another variable. For instance, for each of five CSE grades in Physics the chances of passing a City and Guilds course in Physics might be displayed.

Expected Frequency See under **Chi-square**

Expected Value The expected value of a variable is the sum of all its possible values each multiplied by their probability of occurrence.
See also RANDOM VARIABLE

EXPERIMENT
A study undertaken to test one or more hypotheses and in which the relevant variables are controlled and manipulated by the experimenter, rather than simply observed in their natural setting.

The advantage over a purely observational non-manipulative type of study is that it is easier both to control extraneous variables which might afford alternative explanations and to make causal inferences. In principle, in the simplest kind of experiment an experimental group of people is randomly chosen from a defined population and all the members of this group are given an experimental treatment. This is a systematic and carefully controlled change in their environment. A **control group** is randomly selected from the same population and treated similarly to the experimental group except that they do not get the experimental treatment. The variable being manipulated by the experimenter is known as the **independent variable**. Both groups are assessed on some outcome or **dependent variable.** (For example, the independent variable might be type of toothpaste, with the experimental group using fluoride toothpaste and the control group using non-fluoride toothpaste twice daily. The dependent variable might be some measure of tooth decay.) If the groups differ on the dependent variable, it may be concluded that the manipulation of the independent variable caused the difference. Control of alternative explanations is achieved by the randomization procedure, because, provided the groups are large enough, it is reasonable to suppose that they are equivalent in all important respects except the one being tested. Furthermore, since the experimental manipulation precedes the measurement of the outcome it is fair to infer cause.

In practice, there are still some problems, e.g. equivalence needs to be maintained throughout the experiment. Drop-out rates, for instance, should not be systematically different for the two groups. In natural settings it may be impossible to manipulate the levels of a particular independent variable without systematically changing other variables at the same time.

More sophisticated designs aim at greater efficiency. The number of subjects required may be reduced by using either a **same subjects (repeated measures)** or a **matched pairs** design. In a same subjects design each subject is made to serve as his own control, being tested on two or more different treatments, or alternatively before some experimental treatment and then again after it. This type of design reduces the number of subjects necessary to obtain a statistically significant result, because many of the extraneous factors will remain constant within the same subject from one testing to another and the **error variance** will be reduced. Much the same effect is achieved in a matched pairs design, where each experimental subject is matched with a control subject. Identical twins have often been used for this purpose. Alternatively, extraneous variables which might afford alternative explanations may be identified in advance and the subjects matched on these. Where matching has not been performed, it is sometimes possible to allow statistically (e.g. by **covariance adjustment**) for the effects of extraneous variables which might be masking a significant result.

A further step is to test several independent and/or dependent variables on the same subjects at the same time. Such designs are termed **factorial designs** and they have the further advantage that **interaction effects** between variables may be observed — e.g. variable *A* may affect outcome only in the presence of variable *B*, etc.

These more sophisticated designs have their own special drawbacks. For instance, when the same subjects are tested several times, fatigue, memory, maturation, or demoralization may affect later testings and, in addition, it may be difficult to keep the testing conditions exactly constant. This has to be met, where possible, by **counterbalancing the order** of treatments among the different subjects. Matching control and experimental subjects may lead to the final sample being unrepresentative of the population it is meant to reflect. Finally, the statistical techniques necessary for some of these complex designs may make assumptions about the data which are not valid.

Experimental Design The experimental design is intended to ensure that an experiment affords a valid, efficient, and unambiguous test of the hypotheses set up and that **extraneous variables** are controlled. Experimental designs range from the very simple to the very complex. One simple one has just two levels of a single independent variable with the effects tested on one dependent variable in two randomly chosen groups of people. Complex designs may entail having several independent variables, with matched groups and/or repeated measures and/or statistical allowance for some of the extraneous variables, etc.
See also COHORT ANALYSIS, EXPERIMENT, CROSS-SECTIONAL DESIGN, LONGITUDINAL STUDY, and **Latin Square Design**

Experimental Group A group to whom an *experimental treatment* is being given, and who will be compared with a *control group* who have not received the experimental treatment. See also EXPERIMENT

Experimental Treatment A systematic carefully controlled change made by the experimenter in the environment of the **experimental group**.
See also EXPERIMENT

Experimenter Bias If a person conducting an EXPERIMENT knows the experimental hypothesis, there is always some danger that he or she may unconsciously influence the results obtained in many small ways (tone of voice, extra encouragement, etc.) in order to confirm the hypothesis. This is the experimenter bias effect. It may be guarded against in many ways — including using experimenters who do not

know the hypothesis, simply being aware that it may happen, and using research procedures which are clear and unambiguous and less amenable to such bias.
See also BIAS

Experimenter Effect   See **experimenter bias**

Explained Variance Explained variance is that part of the **variance** of a variable which can be predicted given the values of another variable or set of variables. Unexplained variance is that part of the variance which cannot be explained in this way.

EXPLANATION

An event (or series of events) is explained if a satisfactory account can be given which shows why an event occurred rather than not, or why one event occurred rather than another. The event to be explained may be singular, e.g. one suicide, or it may be a class of similar events, e.g. suicides.

There are three modes of explanation in the social sciences: *statistical explanation, covering law explanation*, and *historical explanation*.

A variable may be regarded as an event to be explained in the sense that a particular pattern of values is observed which requires explanation as to why that pattern occurred and not another. *Statistical explanation* proceeds by explaining a pattern of values through the CORRELATION of a variable with one or more others. A high correlation may be interpreted to mean that the pattern of values in one variable is determined by the pattern of values of others. In the bivariate case the extent to which a variable is statistically explained is measured by the square of the **correlation coefficient**, which is the **variance** accounted for in one variable by its **covariation** with another. Analogous calculations of variance explained may be made for the MULTIPLE CORRELATION case where the pattern in the **dependent variable** is explained by the combined variation in the **independent variables**. Although statistical explanation is a variable quantity (ranging from 0 per cent explained to a theoretical 100 per cent) rather than a complete justification of a particular pattern the main objections to such explanation rest on other criticisms; their non-causal and untheoretical nature. Bivariate correlations are symmetrical measures; that is, if *A* is correlated with *B* then *B* is equally correlated with *A* and there is no justification in correlation as such to claim that one variable is a cause of the other. Even in multiple correlation, which statistically requires that one variable is named as the dependent or effect variable and the others as independent variables, no warrant to imply a causal relationship is contained in the statistical method. Only further considerations could make a statistical explanation become a causal one. (See CAUSATION.)

Statistical explanation is frequently dismissed as trivial because of lack of theoretical significance. The observation, for example, that suicide rates decline in time of war or national emergency becomes satisfactory as an explanation only when it is related to a wider theoretical context in which a concept of social integration is proposed as the linking variable between two variables which otherwise appear to have no necessary connection with each other. The more closely that an observed correlation can be deduced as a necessary consequence of a theory, then the more satisfactory statistical explanation becomes.

The second mode of explanation, *covering law*, is necessarily theoretical by its nature and for that reason is considered to be a more convincing paradigm than mere statistical explanation. An event is explained in this form of explanation by deducing the necessity of its occurrence from a law or law-like proposition which has been accepted after testing against empirical evidence. The scheme of explanation takes the form of an argument in logic:

Law-like proposition: If conditions $c_1 \ldots c_n$ and event a occurs, then b occurs.

Observation: Conditions $c_1 \ldots c_n$ have occurred.

Observation: a has occurred.

Conclusion: Therefore b

This is a deductive argument; if the general or law-like proposition is true and the observational statements are true, then event b must follow with logical necessity. The event b is said to be explained as an instance of the covering law. Law-like propositions are hypotheses which have been empirically tested and not refuted and since explanation is by deduction from such established hypotheses a covering law explanation is also termed a *hypothetico-deductive explanation*.

Although this type of explanation is convincing as a logical scheme there are severe difficulties in using it. Social science has few law-like propositions and at best attains only empirical regularities which are statements of relationships between events which are neither causal, invariant, nor universal. They take the form of functional propositions (e.g. suicide rates depend on the level of social integration) which are probabilistic and frequently not causal. Strict logical deductions cannot be made from statements which are not univer-

sally true and thus this form of explanation is limited.

The difficulty of finding laws of human action or even empirical regularities with a wide application has made both deductive and statistical schemes of explanation suspect in some branches of the social sciences. An alternative form of explanation is preferred which bases explanatory accounts on the specific motives and purposes of real actors rather than at best on highly abstracted 'typical' motives. If motive is taken as a sufficient cause of an action, then constructing an account by eliciting the beliefs of individuals about their situations, their calculations of means and ends, and their interaction with others, provides an intelligible sequence of causes which understandably leads to an event or outcome. The level of abstraction or conceptualization involved is low in this form of *historical explanation*; it necessarily deals with singular events rather than instances of general classes of events and therefore has a low generality and is rejected by many as fundamentally unscientific.

Explanation-by-Understanding   See **Verstehen**

Explanatory Survey   A survey aimed at elucidating cause-and-effect relationships between variables. Hypotheses will have been set up in advance, which are being tested, and special groups of people may be sampled rather than others so as to provide a quasi-experimental set-up. Such surveys are usually possible only after the field of investigation has been well described.
See also **Descriptive Survey**

Explanatory Variable   The variable which the investigator is manipulating or observing in order to predict the effect on a **dependent variable**. Often synonymous with **independent variable** or **predictor**.

Exploratory Interview   See under INTERVIEW

Exploratory Phase   A preliminary study during which possible **explanatory variables** are sought out and exact methods of measuring these variables devised and refined.

External Validity   The extent to which results may be generalized to groups of people and conditions other than those on which they were established.
See also **Internal Validity**, VALIDITY

Extraneous Variable   A variable which might explain a phenomenon just as convincingly as the **explanatory variable** under test, and which must be ruled out as a possible explanation by the use of controls.

Extrapolate   To calculate a value for a function or series of observations beyond the limits of what is already known. This is often done graphically. One might, for instance, plot the overall crime rates for the last five years. Then by joining up the five points and producing the line beyond the last point a prediction could be made of the crime rate next year.

More sophisticated methods of FORECASTING than simple extrapolation are often preferred.

Extreme Responding   A response set in which a person tends to exaggerate his responses and choose the most extreme alternative, whichever direction, on each item of a questionnaire.

See also BIAS

Extreme Value   Any value at the top or bottom end of a DISTRIBUTION. The more separated the extreme values are from the rest of the distribution the more they will affect the **mean**, the **variance**, and the **standard deviation** of the distribution.

Eysenck Personality Inventory (EPI)   A questionnaire which has been very widely used in educational, psychological, and clinical research and which measures extraversion/introversion and neuroticism/stability. There is an inbuilt 'lie scale' to detect 'faking good' and two equivalent forms are available. Both the main dimensions measured were originally obtained after extensive FACTOR ANALYTIC work and they derive considerable **construct validity** from their use as an integral part in the body of research making up the Eysenck theory of personality. There has, however, been some debate over the extent to which the neuroticism dimension measures an enduring personality trait or a more transient psychological state. The RELIABILITY of both dimensions is good and there are **norms** for several different groups in the population.

F

Facility Index   The facility index for an item in a test of ability is the percentage of individuals who pass it.

FACTOR ANALYSIS

A statistical technique aimed at describing a number of variables (or test items) in terms of a smaller number of more basic factors. In the **Eysenck Personality Inventory**, for example, ninety-six attitudinal or behavioural items are found to be describable by just three factors — introversion–extraversion, neuroticism, and social desirability (a lie scale); in the Osgood **Semantic Differential** technique the many bipolar pairs of adjectives used to describe concepts may nearly always be reduced to three factors labelled evaluation, potency, and activity.

There are several methods for factor analysis, all of which proceed through up to three stages: first, the correlation matrix is calculated; secondly, factors are extracted; and thirdly, these factors are rotated. The third stage is optional.

In the first stage a **correlation matrix** is derived in which all the items or variables being factor analysed are intercorrelated, yielding the strengths of relationship of each item to every other item.

In the next stage a smaller number of factors is derived from the correlation matrix by one of several methods (e.g. the *centroid method*, the **principal components method**, or the *principal factors method*). If the original variables (or test items) all have a great deal in common, one single factor may successfully replace them all, and a person's 'score' on this factor will be almost as informative as his scores on each of the original variables taken separately. Alternatively, there may be groups of items such that items correlate strongly with other items in a group but hardly at all with items outside it. In this situation one factor should emerge for each such group of items. Finally, if none of the original variables is related to any other variable, the factor analysis will not be successful and there will be as many factors as there are original variables so that no statistical simplification of the situation is possible. A factor which, to some extent at least, represents all the original variables or test items is often known as a **general factor**; a factor which

covers only groups of items is known as a **group factor**; and one limited to a single item is called a unique or **specific factor**. Mathematically, there is very seldom a unique solution to a factor analytic problem. It is possible by a process called **rotation** (the third stage of factor analysis) to obtain a large number of other solutions which are just as good mathematically as the original extraction solution. Where more than one factor is extracted there are many standard ways (e.g. the **varimax**, *quartimax*, or *direct oblimin* methods) of rotating the factors obtained to yield factors which are more meaningful in theoretical terms that those originally extracted.

Some of the language of factor analysis will now be decribed. The **communality** of a variable is a measure of the degree to which it is related to all the other variables, and is technically the amount of variance it has in common with the other variables. In the factor extraction stage of the analysis assumptions have to be made about the communalities of the variables. The often used principal components methods assumed all the communalities to be unity, while in other methods estimated values less than unit are supplied. Sometimes, an **iterative process** may be used in which an initial value of the communality is estimated, the factors extracted, and then a better value of the communality is derived which is used to repeat the factor extraction. The process continues until there is little change in the communality.

The **specificity** of a variable is the complement of communality and represents the proportion of its variance which is unique to that variable and cannot be represented in terms of any of the other variables.

The **factor loading** or *saturation* of a variable on a factor is a number, usually the correlation coefficient, which represents the strength of the relationship between the factor and the variable. A *bipolar factor* is one on which some of the loadings are highly positive and others highly negative. The **eigenvalue**, *latent root*, or *extracted variance* for each factor may be calculated after the factors are first extracted and before rotation. It is the sum of the squares of the factor loadings of all the variables on that factor. From the eigenvalue the proportion of the total variance which the factor explains may be readily obtained and it is often used as a criterion for retaining or discarding factors; those with eigenvalues less than one being excluded from the analysis. The *scree test* is another method frequently used for this purpose.

In the factor extraction stage, factors are extracted so as to be **orthogonal** to each other. That is, they are uncorrelated and any two such factors may be represented by two axes drawn at right angles to each other. On rotation some methods, e.g. the quartimax and varimax methods, maintain orthogonality and other methods (*oblique solutions*) do not. Orthogonal solutions are statistically simpler and easier to interpret, whilst oblique solutions may represent reality more faithfully. If an oblique solution has been adopted it is possible to perform a second factor analysis on the first set of factors and so obtain *second-order factors*. Various guidelines exist to direct the rotation of the factors. One of these is the Thurstone theory of *simple structure*. This is a set of criteria which maximizes the number of factor loadings having negligible values, leaving a small number with high values. Another guideline which has been used as Eysenck's **criterion analysis** in which the factors are rotated to distinguish maximally between two opposite groups of people — e.g. neurotics and non-neurotics. A *factor structure matrix* show the correlations between the factors and the variables. A *factor pattern matrix* shows the weights to be used in estimating variables from factors. For orthogonal solutions these two matrices are identical. A factor estimate or *factor score matrix* shows the weights to be used in estimating the factor scores from the variable scores. The factorial complexity of a variable is the number of factors on which it has significant loadings.

The technique of factor analysis has been criticized on many grounds. It is based, usually, on Pearson correlation coefficients and therefore all the appropriate assumptions about **interval scale measurement,** NORMAL DISTRIBUTIONS, and homogeneity of variances should ideally be met. What comes out after the technique has been applied can only be as good as what is put in. Factor analysis is thus no substitute for good research design. The items to be factor analysed need to be reliable, well chosen, and representative of a research domain.

The factor structure which emerges may depend on which research domains are represented. In most applications the sampling of people to answer the items also needs to be adequate. The fact that there is seldom a unique solution to a problem means that the results are dependent on the particular method used and this leaves scope for the researcher simply to confirm his own *a priori* notions about the data. Finally, the factors obtained can be difficult to name and can seem far removed from any corresponding theoretical reality.

However, provided these limitations are understood, the technique can be a useful tool. One of its main strengths is an emphasis on the quantification of variables. It has been used successfully to explore the patterning of variables, to test hypotheses about this patterning, and as a summary device to construct simpler factors which can then be tested in further experiments.

Factor Loading The factor loading of a test, item, or variable on a factor is a number, usually the CORRELATION coefficient representing the strength of relationship between the test and the factor.
See FACTOR ANALYSIS

Factor Pattern Matrix See under FACTOR ANALYSIS

Factor Score Matrix See under FACTOR ANALYSIS

Factor Structure Matrix See under FACTOR ANALYSIS

Factorial Design A number of **independent variables** are selected and split into levels and then every possible combination of these levels is considered to find out what effect the individual variables may have on some **dependent variable**. For example, a 2×3 factorial design might involve testing the effects of sex and number of good friends on psychological symptoms. Sex would be split into male and female (i.e. two levels) and good friends into many, few, or none (i.e. three levels). Psychological symptoms would then be measured for a number of men with many friends, men with few friends, men with no friends, women with many friends, etc. (usually the same number in each cell). One can then see whether psychological symptoms depend on sex, on number of friends, and/or whether there are any interactive effects between sex and friends, e.g. women with no friends having symptoms while none of the other combinations did.
See also **Interaction,** EXPERIMENT

Fallacy of Affirming the Consequent A gross error in reasoning with propositions of the form: if *a* is the case then *b* is the case. For example, the proposition: 'if unemployment rises then the crime rate also rises' may or may not be true empirically (it is certainly testable by empirical means), but the fallacy arises by arguing 'the crime rate has risen therefore unemployment has risen'. Essentially, propositions of the form 'if *a* then *b*' are causal propositions and the fallacy is one where a presumed effect is made into a cause, i.e. the causal flow of the proposition is inverted.

Family Expenditure Survey (FES) Continuous survey since 1957 of a sample of households in the United Kingdom concerning household income and expenditure. Among other things, it is the basic source for data with which to compile expenditure weights in the **Retail Price Index**.

It is conducted by the Office of Population Census and Surveys for the Department of Employment using a three-stage **stratified random sampling** technique. Three stratifying factors are used; region, type of area (e.g. rural/urban), and an economic indicator for areas based on rateable values. After stratification, areas are selected with a probability proportionate to size of population. Within each area, about 16 addresses are selected by systematic **random sampling** techniques from the electoral roll. The selection of addresses is rotated from quarter to quarter. The basic unit of analysis is the household rather than the individual and the head of household is asked to keep a diary of expenditure and income for 14 consecutive days with separate entries for all members over 15 years of age.

Response rates average about 70 per cent with higher non-response in conurbations (in contrast to rural areas) and amongst selected addresses with higher than average rateable values. **Standard error** estimates, which take account of the multistage sampling technique, are published for most of the statistics reported in the FES. Even so, the systematic bias in the statistics because of the pattern of non-response requires care when examining income and expenditure for certain groups.

Standard tabulations of the FES include average household income by region and household size. Patterns of household expenditure by type of purchase, e.g. housing, food, vehicles, and consumer durables, are also included.

Fatigue Effect Decrement in performance in a test due to tiredness or boredom.
See also **Order Effect**

Fertility The number of live births per 1,000 women in the child-bearing range of 15–44 years.
See also **Birth-Rate**

Fertility Ratio The number of children under 5

years of age per 1,000 women in the child-bearing range of 15–44 years.
See also **Birth-Rate**

F-(fascism) Scale A scale devised for measuring authoritarian attitudes. There are 29 items to which the respondent is to register agreement or disagreement on a seven-point scale. However, all are keyed so that agreement indicates fascism and the **acquiescence response set** is therefore not controlled. Factor analyses of the scale typically yield several factors such as cynicism, rigidity, and superstition. The F-scale has had wide research use in such areas as child-rearing practices, prejudice, political orientation, and criminality.
See also FACTOR ANALYSIS, **Response Bias, Conservatism Scale (C-scale)**

Field Coding Field coding is the assignment of a respondent's answer to a predetermined category by the interviewer during the interview. In **office coding** categorization is performed at a later stage.

Field Experiment In a field experiment the experimenter is able to allocate subjects to different treatment groups at random and the experiment takes place in an otherwise natural or field setting. In contrast, in a **quasi-experiment** he is restricted to using groups which occur naturally.

Field Notes Observations recorded in written form during **field-work** or very shortly after, while the data are still fresh in the observer's mind.

They constitute the primary source from which hypotheses are both generated and tested.

Field Role A researcher cannot be present in a social setting without playing some part in it. He must decide on his overall strategy or master role: for example, he could participate fully and not reveal that he is observing; he could watch without interacting socially at all; he could reveal that he is a researcher but maintain some social distance; or he could reveal his identity and try to participate fully. He should be aware of his actions and consider the possible effects these actions may have on the field he is investigating, and on the findings.
See also **Reactivity**

Field-work The observation, participant or otherwise, of groups of people in their normal everyday living, supplemented by informal, usually unstructured, interviews with people in the group.
See also **Field notes**

Fisher Exact Test A test for analysing data which may be cast into the form of a **two by two table** and where the cell frequencies are too small for valid application of a test such as **chi-square**. As a first step the exact probability of observing the particular cell frequencies, given the **marginal** totals, is computed from the formula

$$p = \frac{(A + B)!(C + D)!(A + C)!(B + D)!}{N!A!B!C!D!},$$

where N is the total number of cases, and $A, B, C,$ and D are the cell frequencies.

The same formula is then applied to any distribution of cell frequencies more extreme than the one observed, and the resulting probabilities are summed to give the probability of a distribution of cell frequencies at least as extreme as the one observed.

Fishers Z-transformation See **Z-transformation of a Correlation Coefficient**

Fixed Zero A scale has a fixed zero point if there is a clear, natural, non-arbitrary zero.

(2)   teacher praises or encourages;
(3)   teacher accepts or uses ideas of pupils;
(4)   teacher asks questions;
(5)   teacher lectures;
(6)   teacher gives directions;
(7)   teacher criticizes or justifies authority;
(8)   pupils respond to the teacher;
(9)   pupils initiate action;
(10) silence or confusion.

The percentage of the total class time spent under each category may then be computed and used in a number of ways (e.g. to measure percentage of time teacher talks against percentage of time pupils talk).

Flow Diagram A diagram showing a step-by-step progression through a complex process. Flow diagrams are frequently used to describe computer programs and causal models. In the usual convention, oblong boxes indicate steps to be taken or stages reached, arrows indicate the direction of flow, and diamonds questions to which the answer is usually yes or no. The process branches after each diamond.

As an example here is a flow diagram for climbing stairs:

CLIMBING STAIRS

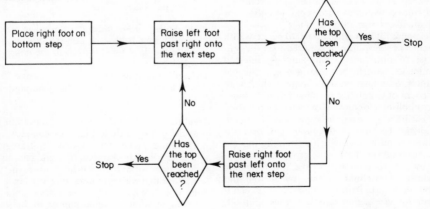

Examples are length, years of schooling, number of children.
See also **Scales of Measurement**

Flander's Interaction Analysis A method for the analysis of interaction between teacher and pupils in a classroom setting. An observer samples ongoing behaviour in the classroom, steadily, at about 3-second intervals. The behaviour is coded into one of ten categories as follows:
(1)   teacher accepts feeling;

Follow-up Study A study following-up and testing a group of people for a second (or subsequent) time. A reasonably accurate list of the original sample is needed.
See also LONGITUDINAL STUDY

FORECASTING
The prediction of future states from knowledge of current and past patterns of observations.

Forecasting methods may be divided into three general types: *delphi techniques, time series projections,* and *predictive models. Delphi technique* consists simply of the round-up of the opinions of suitable experts on the likelihoods of possible futures — usually without quantities other than subjective probabilities being assigned. Without any systematic theoretical or empirical basis to it, the Delphi technique represents little more than an aggregation of guesses, and predictions based upon it must be highly suspect if offered as well-grounded forecasts.

Time series projections are chiefly used in economic forecasting where a large number of indicators of economic activity (e.g. housing starts, retail sales, or unemployment) are regularly available from official sources. Analysis of historical economic data has revealed well-defined business cycles of an average length in the post-war period of about four years which describe the cyclical movement of the economy through expansion to contraction and vice versa. Individual or specific economic series may be used to trace the course of a current business cycle and to predict upturns or downturns in the level of general economic activity.

The first step in selecting and using specific indicators of the level of economic activity is to establish reference cycles on the basis of past data. The average time between economic peaks and between economic troughs is calculated for fundamental economic variables such as Gross National Product, for combinations of economic indicators, and for specific indicators. Business cycles are asymmetric, that is, the period of contraction (peak to trough) is only about half as long as the period of expansion (trough to peak). Indicators are classified empirically as those which lead, coincide, or lag upturns and downturns in the general cycle of business activity. The most use is made of leading indicators since they are predictors of important economic changes but coincident indicators are also important as a means of defining the lengths of the business cycle and lagging indicators are used to confirm lengths and changes of direction of the cycles. Data on current economic time series used as indicators are available in the U.K. from the monthly government publication Economic Trends.

The second stage in economic forecasting using time series is the selection of suitable indicators. The desirable properties of leading indicators are that they should:

(a) have long average leads at past upturns;
(b) be uniform both in occurring as leads and in the length of lead that they show;
(c) follow a cycle which corresponds closely to the pattern of the reference cycle; that is, have the same length of time between

peak and trough and between trough and peak and generally have the same shape of cyclical activity but displaced forward in time;
(d) have a clearly defined specific or individual cycle;
(e) have small and regular seasonal variations; and
(f) be available regularly, preferably on a monthly basis.

The third stage is to adjust the indicators in order to eliminate, as far as possible, seasonal and erratic fluctuations. Many but not all indicators have marked seasonal components, e.g. housing starts, and unemployment; some indicators, e.g. share prices and interest rates, have no seasonal variation. All indicators are liable to erratic fluctuation which must be removed in order to reveal the cyclical variation which might otherwise be obscured.

There are several methods of *seasonal adjustment,* of which the most commonly used are as follows:

(1) *The ratio-to-moving-average method* in which the ratio is calculated for each season (month or quarter) separately:

$$\frac{\text{observation in month } i,}{\text{moving average in month } i}$$

and the average value of this ratio found for all months i. A new moving average figure for the month is then divided by the corresponding adjustment factor. This has the effect of removing the seasonal variation for a particular month as a proportion. (For *moving average,* see under TIME SERIES ANALYSIS).

(2) *The constant adjustment method* adds or subtracts a constant quantity to the moving average for month i by averaging for the different months or seasons the difference between the actual observation in that month and the moving average for the same month.

(3) *The dummy variable approach* adjusts an actual moving average by representing the adjusted observation in a **regression equation** which contains two **independent** or **predictor variables,** the current moving average, and a seasonal **dummy variable** according to the appropriate month or season. Like the constant adjustment method this entails the addition or subtraction of a fixed seasonal quantity to the moving average of the actual observation. The last two methods of seasonal adjustment are defective if the indicator is a time series with a distinct trend or overall tendency to rise or fall apart from regular cyclical variations. Since many economic indicators have strong trends even when inflation has been discounted (e.g. retail sales) the addition or subtraction of a constant quantity constitutes grossly insufficient seasonal adjust-

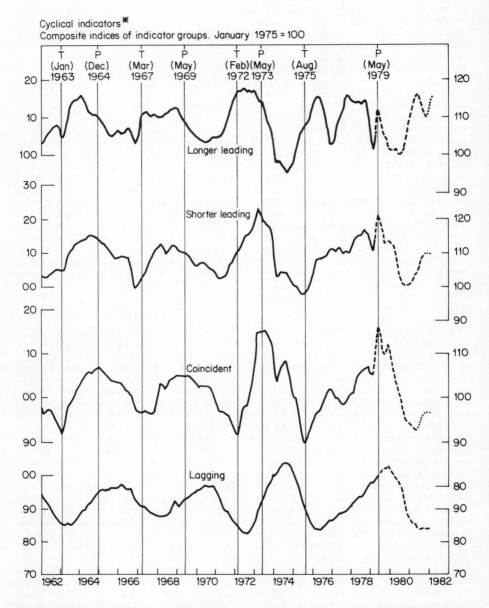

Cyclical indicators*
Composite indices of indicator groups. January 1975 = 100

*The vertical lines in the figure show the turning points of the reference cycle. Coincident indicators are selected to match these turning points exactly and should be compared to the leading and lagging ones

From *Economic Trends* March 1982.

ment when the trend is a rising one, as it usually is. The first method, using a ratio, is not subject to the limitations of constant quantity seasonal adjustment and is preferred for that reason.

Erratic rather than seasonal variations are more difficult to adjust. One method is to smooth the seasonally adjusted series itself by a moving average technique and to compute an irregular component as the difference between the smoothed seasonally adjusted series and the direct seasonally adjusted series. There is dispute, however, on whether this technique may not itself remove part of the cyclical variation, which is the main object of the analysis.

Leading indicators which have been initially chosen by the criteria above and then adjusted for seasonal and occasionally for erratic fluctuation are further evaluated in order to select those with the greater predictive power. On historical analysis, indicators may be classified by the number of times on which they give false indications of downturns (the more common case) and the frequency with which they falsely signal upturns (the rarer case) and the better performing indicators selected accordingly. A second evaluative criterion is the length of the indicator's specific cycle. By convention, three successive observations, all showing changes in the same direction, are required to signal a turning point in the business cycle. Indicators whose specific cycles are too short to allow for the possibility of four successive observations of which the last three after the suspected turning point might be in the same direction are unsuitable as leading indicators. Ideally, the longer an indicator leads on average a general upturn or downturn, then the more useful it is as a predictor.

Economic forecasting by indicators has been strongly criticized as 'measurement without theory' because the structure of relationships between variables has not been modelled; that is, there is no theory representing the working of the economy as a whole and stating the nature, size, and direction of relationships. The basis for forecasting by indicators is the empirical one of a correlation between an indicator and the general level of economic activity (measured by changes in Gross National Product). If the correlation were perfect at all times then this method of forecasting would be perfectly adequate. This is not the case and false signals from indicators are common. In addition, the occurrence of 'shock' elements in the economy — such as war, incomes policies, and international trade treaties — disturb the working of the economy in such a way as to alter existing relationships and modify the variations in the business cycle.

Prediction from econometric models differs in two important ways from time series projections: the models represent a very large number of economic relationships (a typical model for the national economy will have 200 regression equations) and these relationships hold simultaneously. Simultaneity means that the estimated value of a variable at time t will depend not on a single regression equation, no matter how complex, but on a number of other equations at time t also. In addition, the value of a variable in an econometric model typically depends on variables which are lagged. For example, personal consumption (C_t) at time t is modelled as a function of personal disposable income Y_t at time t, and of consumption at an earlier time (C_{t-1}) so that

$$C_t = kY_t + \lambda C_{t-1},$$

where k and λ are constants.

The use of lagged variables in modelling the economy and relationships between variables in it is significant because, in mathematical terms, the whole system can oscillate or move through regular cycles which may correspond to the observed business cycle if the model is constructed in a certain manner. Economists differ on whether endogenous oscillation (due only to the relationships contained in the model) is a sufficient explanation of a business cycle or whether exogenous shocks (by variables external to the model) are required to explain cyclical variation. In any case, assumptions about the state of exogenous variables (e.g. the presence or absence of an incomes policy or changes in fiscal policy) are required to make predictions using models.

Econometric models are calibrated (i.e. **regression coefficients** are estimated) from historical economic data with more weight being given to recent economic data than to earlier data. Forecasting is carried out by entering the current values of the variables in the model (including the values of lagged variables where necessary) and predicting the major **dependent variables** (e.g. unemployment, GNP) either with an assumption of no change in the state of exogenous variables or with assumptions of specific changes. The latter means that such models can be used for examining policy alternatives and comparing, for example, levels of unemployment under the assumption of an imposed incomes policy or of no incomes policy.

Forecasting from econometric models is a more powerful technique than forecasting by indicators both because it is better grounded theoretically and because it allows for alternative predictions when asumptions are made about changes in the institutional management of the economy. Both methods give increasingly unreliable forecasts the further ahead prediction is made because errors are cumulative and exogenous changes are more likely over a lengthier timespan. However, there is little to choose between the accuracy of the two types of methods for short-run predictions of a year or less and indicators continue to be used for short-term forecasting because of their simplicity.

Forecasting from models other than econometric ones is chiefly found in population projections where the **Age-cohort-survival method** is used. See under **Population projection.**

Forced Choice Technique   A technique introduced into attitude measurement to combat the tendency for the respondent to present himself in an over-favourable light. Items take the form of two or more statements, all of equal **social desirability**, measuring different traits. the respondent has to indicate which of these is most, and which least, characteristic of himself.
See also **Response bias, Attitude scale**

Foreshadowed Problem   See under PARTICIPANT OBSERVATION

Formal Sources   Any already existing, ostensibly sound and properly gathered data which may bear on the problem in hand: e.g. research articles and official statistics.
See also **Informal Sources**

Four-fold Table   Another name for a **Two by two Table.**
See also TABULATION

Frame of Reference   The basic and fundamental orientation of a social scientist to his subject matter. It includes the basic concepts, styles of analysis, and types of model to be used in explanation of phenomena. Some disciplines have generally acknowledged frames of reference (e.g. classical economics in the late nineteenth century) but competing ones are the norm in the social sciences, e.g. behaviourism and gestalt psychology, or symbolic interactionism and structural functionalism.
See also MODEL

F-ratio   A statistic used to determine whether two **variances** are significantly different. To perform an *F*-test one of the two variance estimates is divided by the other. The *F*-table is then entered with **degrees of freedom** appropriate to the numerator and the denominator and if the critical value of *F* is surpassed then the variances differ significantly. The main application of the *F*-test is in ANALYSIS OF VARIANCE

where an estimate of the **variance explained** by a variable is divided by the **residual variance**.

Free Association Technique   A PROJECTIVE TECHNIQUE which has been in use for over a hundred years. Basically, a subject is provided with a stimulus word and responds with the first word to come into his head. Various forms of the technique have found application in many fields, including clinical abnormality, verbal behaviour, personality, lie detection, intelligence, and creativity.

Frequency   The number of observations in some given category.
See also **Frequency Distribution**

Frequency Distribution   The most common kind of frequency distribution is the *univariate frequency distribution*. This is obtained by dividing the range of values covered by a set of observations on a single variable into **class intervals**. These class intervals are then set down consecutively in increasing or decreasing order and the numbers of observations falling in each are tabulated. Frequency distributions are sometimes drawn up on more than one variable simultaneously. Thus, a *bivariate frequency distribution*, for instance, would demonstrate for each class interval on one variable how many people fall into the various class intervals on another variable.
See also DISTRIBUTION

Frequency Table   A table showing the number of observations falling into each of several different categories. The categories may be points on a scale, e.g. levels of income, or simply nominal categories, such as religious affiliation. The table may be a one-way table, displaying the frequencies in the categories of just one variable, or it may be of higher order, displaying the *joint frequency distribution* on several variables simultaneously. Thus, a two-way frequency table of sex by manual/non-manual occupation would show how many people were male manual, female manual, male non-manual, and female non-manual. It could be laid out thus:

	Men	Women	Total
Manual workers			
Non-manual workers			
Total			

In this case the rows of the table and the row totals (also called row **marginals**) contain information about the manual/non-manual variable, while the columns and the column totals (column marginals) contain information about the sex variable.

See also TABULATION

F-scale   See **F-(fascism) Scale**

F-test   See under *F*-**ratio**

Funnel-Shaped Interview   See under INTER-VIEW

G

Gamma (Goodman–Kruskall's γ) A measure of association for ordinal variables. It is given by

$$\gamma = \frac{P - Q}{P + Q} \; ,$$

where P is the number of **concordant pairs** and Q the number of **discordant pairs**. It is a **symmetric measure of association** but it may sometimes be zero when there is not statistical independence, and one when there is not maximum dependence.

Gaussian Distribution Synonymous with NORMAL DISTRIBUTION

General Factor A mathematically derived variable which to some extent represents all of a number of specific variables or test items. For example, in intelligence testing a general intelligence factor is usually found to enter into all the specific abilities such as verbal ability, spatial ability, etc.
See also FACTOR ANALYSIS

General Fertility-Rate See under **Birth-Rate**

General Health Questionnaire (GHQ) A self-administered screening questionnaire for detecting psychiatric disorder in community settings. It consists of a series of items each of which has four response alternatives. The longest version contains 60 items and can usually be completed in less than 10 minutes. There are shorter versions containing 30, 28, and 20 items for use when time is very pressing and the 28-item version yields scores on four factors labelled somatic symptoms, anxiety and insomnia, social dysfunction, and severe depression.
The 60- and 30-item versions have been shown to be RELIABLE and to have good VALIDITY as measured against standardized clinical interviews and other psychiatric screening tests — the 60-item version being slightly better. All versions contain safeguards against **extreme responding** and **acquiescence**, and provided there is no motivation to fake 'good' the responses are unaffected by **social desirability**.

General Household Survey (GHS) An annual survey since 1971 of a sample of 12,000 households in Great Britain conducted by the Office of Population Census and Surveys. Sampling is by multi-stage stratified sampling using a rotation of 3,000 households from quarter to quarter. Data collection is continuous throughout the year and the sample is limited to private households, i.e. it excludes institutions such as hospitals, children's homes, and prisons. Statistics are reported for the year as a whole and by quarter so that seasonal variations may be extracted.
Although there is a year-to-year change in the survey questions (reflecting topical administrative concerns) the survey is permanently organized to obtain information in five main areas: Housing, Population, Employment, Education, and Health. Its data can be compared with the **Census** and with other official surveys such as the **Family Expenditure Survey**.
Participation in the survey is voluntary (unlike the Census) and response rates are 81–84 per cent. It is widely used by government departments and by local authorities, although to a lesser extent because of the small samples in any one locality. Researchers also make extensive use of GHS data, notably for investigations of income distribution and poverty, social mobility, and leisure activities. Because of the complex sampling scheme care is needed in calculating the **standard errors** of statistics.
See also **Design Effect**

General Universe or Population The general population is the total population to which the researcher sees his results as relevant (e.g. British schoolteachers).
See also **Working Universe or Population**

Generalizability The extent to which research findings are true for subjects or settings other than the ones which the researcher used.
See also **Replication**

Generalizability Theory A theory concerned with the extent to which a person's score on a test, under given conditions, will 'generalize' to his **universe score**, i.e. the score which would have been obtained under exactly the right

54

conditions to reflect best the behaviour of interest. The **error variance** on the test is divided into components attributable to different sources)e.g. different administrators, times of day, and test formats). These components may be separately estimated to see how best to reduce the error.

G (Generalizability) Study A study to discover and quantify all the possible sources of **error variance** in a test. For example, in an intelligence test a G-study might measure errors from taking the test at different times of day, having different people core it, changing the environment, etc. This may be distinguished from a **D (decision) study**, in which a normal application of a test is made, e.g. when an intelligence test is used to measure the intelligence of a group of people or of an individual.
A G-study is intended to specify the optimal conditions for carrying out a D-study and to predict its RELIABILITY.

Gestalt A structure, the properties of which cannot be entirely deduced from the sum of the parts which comprise it.

Gini Coefficient see **Lorenz Curve**

Goodness of Fit The extent to which two distributions match. It may be measured by the **Chi-square** test or the **Kolmogorov–Smirnov test.**

Graeco-Latin Square See under **Latin Square Design**

Grand Mean A term usually encountered in the context of ANALYSIS OF VARIANCE, denoting the mean of a set of means.

Graphic Presentation A graph is a scaled representation of how one variable relates to one or more others. Two-dimensional graphs are the most common. These have two *axes* usually, but not always, placed at right angles to each other. One of the variables to be graphed is scaled along each of the axes. In the space thus set, points are plotted for each and every observation, displaying their values on the two dimensions simultaneously. By convention any **independent variable** is placed along the horizontal axis (*X-axis*) and the **dependent variable** along the vertical axis (*Y-axis*). (Economists often reverse this convention, having price on the vertical axis and the commodity bought on the horizontal axis.) *Diagrams* are also visual summaries of data. They are not usually as detailed as graphs — not every observation is separately shown and often only one variable is displayed. Usually

there is a vertical axis representing frequency of occurrence and a horizontal one representing the variable being displayed. There are several types of diagram including **bar-charts, histograms,** and **ogives**.

Gravity Models A family of related models, based on an analogy with Newton's Inverse Square Law of Gravity, but dealing with interactions or movements between places. The general form is:

$$I_{ij} = \alpha \, \frac{M_i M_j}{d_{ij}^x} \, ,$$

where *I* is some resultant such as transport flow between points *i* and *j*, M_i and M_j are usually the populations centred at i and j, and d is the distance between the two points.
The exponent (x) of d and the constant α are fitted after empirical testing of a gravity model, x is usually 2 or greater.
See also MODEL

Grid See **Repertory Grid**

Group Centroid See under DISCRIMINANT ANALYSIS

Group Factor A mathematically derived variable which to some extent represents some of the items or variables in an item pool but not others.
See also FACTOR ANALYSIS

Group-administered Questionnaires and Tests A questionnaire completed by a group of respondents in the presence of the researcher who is on hand to give instructions, answer questions, and ensure standard conditions of testing. Many achievement and intelligence tests are designed specifically for group administration.

Grouped Frequency Distribution A **frequency distribution** in which some of the original class intervals have been **collapsed** (joined together), in order to bring out the pattern in the data more clearly.

Grouping See under CLUSTER ANALYSIS

Guttman Scale A series of items arranged in a hierarchy such that agreement with an item implies agreement with, or in some other way includes, all the items below it in the hierarchy. Selection of items is by *scalogram analysis* on a large item pool tried out on a sample population. This is basically rearrangement of the items until the best possible hierarchy is achieved. The items are usually dichotomous, and, if they are not, a cut-off point is usually established. It is not often that a perfect Guttman scale may be constructed and the **coefficient of reproducibility (R)** indicates how good the final scale is. It is given by

$$R = 1 - \left(\frac{\text{no. of errors}}{\text{no. of items} \times \text{no. of respondents}} \right).$$

An error is a deviation from the ideal pattern, e.g.

	Items					
Respondents	1	2	3	4	5	Score
1	yes	yes	yes	yes	yes	5
2	yes	yes	–	yes	yes	4
3	yes	yes	yes	–	–	3
4	yes	yes	yes	–	–	3
5	yes	yes	yes	–	–	3
6	yes	–	yes	–	–	2
7	yes	–	–	–	–	1

The five-item Guttman scale illustrated above contains the three errors ringed when tried on seven respondents. The coefficient of reproducibility is $1 - 3/35 = 0.91$.

It is desirable to establish a Guttman scale on at least one sample of 100 or more respondents and the minimum criterion for satisfactory reproducibility is usually taken as $R = 0.9$.

Guttman scales are constructed to be unidimensional and to have excellent reproducibility — a particular score is obtainable in only one way. However, this may be attainable only by severely limiting the content area covered by the scale. There is no guarantee in advance that a Guttman scale to measure a particular attitude can be constructed, and even if it can, the process of construction tends to be laborioius.

See also ATTITUDE SCALING

H

Halo Effect An effect which occurs when somebody making a judgement allows his general attitude to influence his answers to the particular items, as when the prettiest girl is rated the most intelligent and the most sociable — in other words, she is being rated on a single concept, even though three separate answers are produced.

Hamilton Rating Scale (HRS) A scale which is useful for assessing the severity of a depression after the diagnosis has been made. There are 17 variables, scored on three- to five-point scales, which are rated by a trained observer. The ratings are based on all available information, e.g. from psychiatric interviews, self-reports, and other informants' statements. The items cover all the important symptoms commonly associated with depression but lean particularly on behavioural and somatic features. The maximum score obtainable is 52, but few patients, even severely depressed ones, score above 35. The HRS has been shown to have good RELIABILITY and VALIDITY and has been widely used.

Hartley Test for Homogeneity of Variances A test of whether the **variances** of k different samples each of n cases differ significantly. The largest variance is divided by the smallest to yield the statistic F_{max}. If the value of F_{max} obtained is greater than the value in a table of the distribution of F_{max}, with **degrees of freedom** k and $n-1$, then the variances differ significantly. If the n's of the various groups differ slightly, the largest value of n may be used.

Hawthorne Effect The unwitting introduction of **extraneous variables** through the social interaction of human experimenters and human subjects. This can grossly bias the results. In the severest form, merely being an experimental subject produces BIAS

Heteroscedasticity When a number of independent groups of observations have **variances** which differ significantly the groups are said to be heteroscedastic. The converse term, describing groups of equal variance is *homoscedastic*. **Parametric techniques** such as the *t*-test,

ANALYSIS OF VARIANCE, and REGRESSION ANALYSIS assume homoscedasticity of certain variances.

In the case of the *t*-test the variances of the two groups being compared should be equal. For **analysis of variance** it is the variances of the individual cells; and for the **Pearson correlation** of Y with X it is the array variances; that is, the groups of Y observations corresponding to each particular X value (and conversely X observations for Y values).

Parametric tests are fairly robust to violations of these assumptions and there are several tests for homoscedasticity including Bartlett's test and the **Hartley test**.

Hierarchic Model (Theory) A MODEL or THEORY which is couched in terms of a set of levels which can be ordered from highest to lowest, e.g. different educational levels or degrees of moral degradation. Often the higher levels of the hierarchy will subsume the lower ones, e.g. one cannot have a third year of post-graduate education without already having had two years.

Hierarchical Regression Analysis Stepwise **regression analysis** in which the order of entry of **independent variables** into the **regression equation** is determined *a priori*.
See under REGRESSION ANALYSIS

Histogram A diagrammatic representation of a **frequency distribution**.
The **class intervals** are first marked off on the horizontal axis and rectangles are then constructed with their bases on these marked-off intervals and *areas* proportional to the numbers of individuals, observations, or cases falling in the intervals. A histogram is not a **bar-chart**. The latter is used only for representing **nominal data**.

Holding Constant the Effects If two or more variables (e.g. V, W, and X) all seem to be related to a criterion (Y) it may be that these variables all explain part of the criterion or that some of them (e.g. V and W) are important and others (e.g. X) do not add anything once the important variables have been considered.

(This may arise because X is strongly related to V and/or W and hence redundant. V might be 'father's years of education' and X 'Family income' in prediction of Y, 'son's school attainment'.) To hold constant the effects of a variable (V) is to look at the relationships between the other variables and the criterion within each level of V separately, or to allow for V by a statistical technique such as **partialling out**. Thus, it may be seen whether these variables explain any of the criterion with V taken into account.

Homoscedascity See under **Heteroscedasticity**

Horizontal Axis Synonymous with **abscissa** and *X-axis*.
See **graphic presentation**

Hypothesis An hypothesis is a conjecture about the relationships between two or more concepts. Hypotheses may be general assertions, e.g. 'man is innately aggressive', which are untestable in principle because of the imprecision of their concepts, or they may be more specific and narrow and thus testable in principle if the concepts can be empirically interpreted, e.g. 'men with an extra chromosome will be more likely to commit violent crimes than men without an extra chromosome'.

An *operational hypothesis* is one in which **indicators** have been stated for the concepts, so that it is interpreted empirically, and the procedures for testing it by observations are known.

An hypothesis which has been tested and not refuted is said to be *corroborated*.
See also THEORY

Hypothesis Testing See under STATISTICAL INFERENCE

Hypothetico-deductive Method Synonymous with **Covering Law**. See under EXPLANATION

I

Ideal Type A concept which both idealizes a particular phenomenon in the sense of focusing on its essential characteristics and typifies it at the same time by including all the important aspects of the phenomenon.

All concepts may be regarded as ideal types in that they are mental constructs for guiding the observer to those aspects of a phenomenon which are relevant but ideal types are usually considered to be complexes of concepts composed of several concepts which require connecting together in an intelligible manner, i.e. an underlying logic of interconnection is proposed in the use of an ideal type. For example, the economic ideal type of firm ignores the distinction between manufacturing and services, its form of internal structure, and its industrial sector and size as inessential to understanding its behaviour in a capitalist economy. It selects costs, level of output, and profit as essential to its typical behaviour and intelligibly reconstructs the relationships between them by the idealized rule that to maximize profit, output is varied until the marginal cost of production equals the marginal revenue.

It does not matter in ideal type analysis that no real entity conforms to its ideal type since the purpose is to obtain a useful conceptualization with which to grasp the logic of a phenomenon rather than to describe it.

Idealized Frequency Distribution An idealized **frequency distribution** represents what might be obtained with a very large (infinite) number of cases. Provided the variable is measured on a continuous scale, it would be representable as a smooth curve thus:

rather than a number of discrete steps thus:

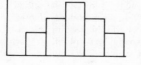

See also DISTRIBUTION

Ideographic Method See under **Nomothetic Method**

Imagery This term is used to mean a vague general idea about what attributes might make up a **concept** which a researcher is seeking to develop before using in field-work. It is an early and usually informal stage in **concept formation**.

Incidence See under **Epidemiology**

Independence (statistical) Two variables are said to be independent of each other when the values of one are in no way related to the values of the other. Independence implies *zero correlation* but zero correlation implies only that there is no **linear relationship**. There could still be a **curvilinear** one.

Independent Variable An independent variable is one which is postulated to be a cause of another (the **dependent variable**). In experimental research the independent (or **explanatory**) variable is systematically varied by the experimenter and the effect on the dependent variable studied. Manipulation of an independent variable in experiments usually establishes it as causal. Where manipulation is not possible (in non-experimental research) causality is more doubtful.

Index A single score made by combining several other scores in order to measure some given variable. The method of combination may be simple addition but is often much more complex. In particular, many indices are constructed by first **weighting** the scores to be combined and then adding.

Index Measurement Index measurement is attained when the categories of a measurement scale do not allow exact reconstruction of reality. If weights of objects are given simply as heavy, medium, and light, the exact weight of an object is not determined — the boundaries on the weight scale are not clear. If, however, a balance is used, the exact weight is determined, and this is **representational measurement**.

INDEX NUMBERS

Index numbers are relative rather than absolute measures of value and show changes without units of measurement. For example, unemployment measured absolutely was 600,000 in 1970 and 2,800,000 in 1981; in relative terms this was an increase of 4.7 as a simple ratio or 470 as a percentage or index number. 1970 = 100 and 1981 = 470 is a comparison in index numbers in which the original observations have been lost, together with the units in which they were measured, for ease of comparison. Any series of figures may be put in index number form; as a time series related to a base year which is set equal to 100, or as a comparison of groups in which one is set equal to 100 and the remainder compared as indices to it; e.g. U.K. unemployment (national average) = 100, Scotland = 180.

Although index numbers make comparisons easier, in forming them the original observations are lost and cannot be reconstructed from the index numbers alone. This is a general phenomenon of index measurement. A series of index numbers can be manipulated arithmetically, however. The base can be changed simply by dividing the whole series by the index number of a new base year or base group. If I_0, I_1, I_2 is a series in which the first number is the base, a new series can be constructed with I_1 as the base — I_0/I_1, 100, I_2/I_1.

Index numbers may be simple as in the example of the unemployment comparisons above where values of a single variable are compared, or they may be composite index numbers which combine in a single figure a number of variables and thus allow aggregates to be compared quantitatively. The **Retail Price Index (RPI)** is a composite index which combines price changes in the same time period across a large number of commodities and services. For example, if three commodities have prices p_1, p_2, p_3 in year 1 and prices P_1, P_2, P_3 in year 2, then a composite index of relative prices (year 1 compared to year 2) could be:

$$\frac{p_1 + p_2 + p_3}{P_1 + P_2 + P_3} \cdot 100.$$

In this composite index each commodity contributes equally to the index. However, most indices are weighted to reflect the proportion of expenditure which they carry in the population. If a sample typically spends twice as much on the first commodity then the index would be:

$$\frac{2p_1 + p_2 + p_3}{2P_1 + P_2 + P_3} \cdot 100.$$

Relative weights for composite indices like the Retail Price Index are continually estimated from fresh sample data. The problem becomes one in which the relative weights change from time to time. If, for the sake of comparability, the weights are fixed in the base year of a time series and not changed — a base weighted or *Laspeyres index* — then the weighting system becomes increasingly unrepresentative of true behaviour. If the weights are regularly changed according to behaviour — a currently weighted or *Paasche index* — then representativeness is retained but comparability is steadily lost. In practice, currently weighted indices are usually preferred, which means that comparison within a series of index numbers becomes risky the longer is the time span between comparisons; instead of a single comparable series there is a continuously evolving one and the use of the RPI over an extended period is no longer comparing comparable consumer price levels.

Index of Definition (ID) See under **Present State Examination**

Indicator See under **Concept**

Informal Sources Unsystematic (often unreliable) data relevant to the research in hand such as are derived from anecdotes, private conversations, etc.

Informant Analysis Analysis of interview data with a view to obtaining an accurate picture of the world in which the informants live, from the informant's perspective. This is opposed to **respondent analysis** in which the aim is to investigate the informants themselves, their ways of thinking about the world, etc. and how these depend on their social and physical environment.

Instrumental Variable See under ESTIMATION

Instrumentation The preparation of tests, questionnaires, standard interviews, and other structured forms of data collection.

Intelligence Test Intelligence tests commonly consist of a series of items to be answered within a time limit, together with **norms** against which performance may be evaluated. There may be sets of items loading on different components of intelligence such as number, verbal meaning, memory, reasoning, and spatial perception. A person's score is often expressed as an *intelligence quotient*

(IQ). This was originally defined for children as being $100 \times$ mental age $\div$ chronological age; mental age being obtained basically by comparison of a child's score on the test with those of other children the same age. For adults, tests are often constructed to yield a mean IQ of 100, with a **standard deviation** of about 15. This means that about two-thirds of the population fall in the range 85–115. Most intelligence tests have special features, e.g. they may be for children only, for academically bright people, for use across cultures, or for measuring one specific attribute of intelligence. Some require individual administration, while others may be administered to groups.

For more details of specific tests see **AH5 test, Progressive Matrices test, Stanford–Binet test, Wechsler intelligence scale for children** and **Wechsler adult intelligence scale**.

Interaction   If the various levels or categories of one **independent variable** do not affect the **dependent variable** in the same way within all levels or categories of another independent variable there is said to be an interaction effect. For example, one might be measuring boredom of children of different ages with hard or easy reading material. If the finding was that young children were more bored with difficult reading material and older children more bored with easy reading material, then it would be said that there was an interaction between age and difficulty of reading material. This useage should not be confused with the everyday meaning, as in, for example, social interaction.

Intercept   See under **Slope**

Internal Consistency   A scale is said to have internal consistency if the answers to the items comprising it tend to agree well with each other. This is a necessary condition of a good attitude or interest measure.
See also RELIABILITY

Internal Validity   The extent to which an experiment is a good test of a hypothesis under the given experimental conditions.
See also **External validity**, VALIDITY.

International Classification of Diseases (ICD)   A statistical classification of all diseases and other morbid conditions, which is being continually updated and revised. It is currently in its ninth edition. There are seventeen major sections and, within each, conditions with properties in common are grouped together. The bases for classification are pragmatic and variable and include topography, symptoms, and aetiology.

Interpolation   The placing of an observation in a **trend line** (from a graph or **scatter diagram**) where there is no actual observation and between the limits of recording observations. On the usual bivariate graph, interpolation of one observation allows the value of the other variable to be read off. This may be used as a test of the regression model which has been fixed, or as a useful prediction. Interpolation near the ends of a regression line is subject to greater errors of prediction than elsewhere.
See also **Heteroscedasticity**

Interquartile   Range   and   Interquartile Ratio   When a distribution is split into four equal parts the *quartiles* are those values below which 25, 50, and 75 per cent of the distribution lie. The distance between the '75 per cent' or upper quartile (Q3) and the '25 per cent' or lower quartile (Q1) is known as the *interquartile range*. The *quartile deviation* or *semi-interquartile range* is defined as *half* the interquartile range. The *interquartile ratio* or *quartile dispersion coefficient* is a measure of how heterogeneous the data are and is given by:

$$\text{interquartile ratio} = \frac{\text{interquartile range}}{\text{median}}.$$

Inter-rater Reliability Coefficient   The relationship between scorings of the same test or behaviour, etc. by two different raters working independently. This indicates whether a scoring system is sufficiently well developed to be applied reliably by different people. Methods of measuring inter-rater reliability include **percentage agreement**, the *RE* **coefficient,,** **kappa**, and **weighted kappa**.
See also RELIABILITY

Intersubjective Understanding   See **Verstehen**

Interval Estimate   See under ESTIMATION

Interval Scale (Interval Level of Measurement)   The measurement or scaling of a variable in such a way that the numbers assigned to points on the scale possess most of the properties of the real number system and particularly the property that the intervals between scale points are measured in a comparable way. That is, the distance between £9,000 and £6,000 on a scale of annual personal incomes is the same as the distance between £9,000 and £12,000.
If a variable is scaled at the interval level, then the arithmetic operations of addition, subtraction, and multiplication may be performed on the scale values without altering the relationships of the measured data. This means that

powerful statistical techniques, such as **Pearson correlation,** REGRESSION, and FACTOR ANALYSIS, may be legitimately used.

Although the definition of interval scale is important to social science there is, ironically, no accepted example of a variable which is so scaled. Examples such as crime rates, prices, ages, and fertility rates are, strictly speaking, ratio scales which are interval scales that have a true or non-arbitrary zero so that a price of £0 or a fertility rate of 0 births per 1,000 women aged 15–45 years is both possible and meaningful.

See also **Scale of Measurement**

Interval Variable   See under **Interval Scale**

Intervening Factor or Variable See under **Elementary survey analysis**

INTERVIEW   A method of collecting data from a subject face to face by asking questions. In a **standardized** or *structured interview* each subject is asked the same questions in exactly the same order. Such interviews require considerable pilot work and may sometimes be unattainable in practice. *Semi-structured interviews* are partly standardized but also allow the interviewer greater flexibility at the expense of possibly incurring greater bias. The same set of questions may be asked in the same order but supplementary questions (**probes**) may be allowed to clarify the responses. Alternatively, part of the interview may be standardized and part not, or the content to be covered may be exactly laid down but some or all of the exact questions may be left to the interviewer.

An *exploratory interview* is unstructured, intended to develop ideas and hypotheses, and to explore possible ways of gathering data. A **pilot interview** is somewhat more developed, but still mainly intended as an aid to the design of later research. Early pilot interviews will generally be unstructured, probing for the subjects' language and concepts, while later ones may test the suitability of standard interviews.

In a *funnel-shaped interview* a specific issue is approached, at first very generally and then more directly. For instance, if the interest was in migraine headaches the researcher might first ask about symptoms in general to see if migraine is mentioned spontaneously, and then progress through headaches to migraine directly and finally to the frequency and intensity of migraine. The questioning would be stopped as soon as it was clear that more direct questions would be inapplicable.

A **depth interview** is an unstructured interview in which the aim is to probe deeply and obtain an exhaustive account of the subject's views and experiences.

Non-directive probes are probes worded so that the answer is not suggested (e.g. 'Can you tell me more about that?').

In some interviews, particularly clinical ones, observations may be systematically made not only of the content of what is said but also of the subject's behaviour, tone of voice, manner of speech, etc.

See also **Interviewer Bias**

Interview Schedule   A predetermined list of questions and instructions intended to standardize an interview procedure. Such schedules are administered by an interviewer, as distinct from **questionnaires** which are lists of questions for self-completion by the subject.

Interview Survey   A method of collecting data in which a carefully defined sample of people are interviewed under conditions which are kept as constant as possible. The sample may or may not be a **probability sample.**

Interviewer-administered   Questionnaire A questionnaire completed in the presence of an interviewer who may also verbally ask some or all of the questions.

Interviewer Bias   See under BIAS

Intraclass Correlation   A measure of **agreement** for use with **interval scale** variables originally developed (by Fisher) to correlate values of the *same* characteristic for pairs of members of the same class or family, e.g. to correlate heights, weights, or **IQ** scores for pairs of brothers or sisters. To test the hypothesis that the IQ scores of pairs of brothers in the same family are correlated and in agreement (that is, knowledge of one brother's IQ score enables one to predict the likelihood of the other brother having the *same* IQ score) the intraclass correlation coefficient should be used:

$$r = \frac{S_b^2 - S_w^2}{S_b^2 + (k-1)S_w^2},$$

where k is the number of members in each family or class and must be the same for each, S_b^2 is the variance of the mean scores for each family or class (**between-groups variance**), S_w^2 is the *within-groups variance* representing variation of the observations within each set about the mean of the set. r is a measure of **agreement** between scores; that is, the extent to which one brother's IQ score agrees or has the *same value* as the other brother's. It is a more specific measure than correlation as such.

As well as its use for calculating measures of agreement for physical or psychological characteristics for members of the same family, this measure has also been used, for example, for calculating the agreement between management and trades unions on the importance of bargained issues in conciliation procedures.

Inverse Relationship In an inverse (or negative) relationship high values on one variable tend to be associated with low values on another.
See also CORRELATION, RELATIONSHIP

Investigator Triangulation See under **Triangulation**

IQ Test See **Intelligence Test**

Item A single question or statement on a questionnaire requiring a response of some kind.
See also **Open Question, Closed Question,** INTERVIEW, ATTITUDE SCALING

Item Analysis A broad range of techniques for determining whether a particular item in an **attitude scale** or an **achievement test** is a useful item. The main forms of item analysis include tests of the *discriminating power* of the item — the extent to which it distinguishes between subjects scoring high and subjects scoring low on the overall scale — and the extent to which the item correlates both with other items in the scale and with the total score on the scale. Items which discriminate poorly between high and low scorers or which correlate weakly with overall score should normally be discarded.

The discriminating power of an item may be calculated by (a) locating the subgroups of the sample who score above and below the first and third **quartiles** of the *overall* scale, and (b) comparing these two subgroups' scores on the item under examination. The larger the difference the better does the item discriminate.

A more sensitive method, but which is also more laborious, examines the discrimination of an item over the whole range of total scale scores, i.e. for all types of subjects. A subject's score on the item is plotted against his overall score on the scale; and over all subjects in the sample this produces an *item trace line*. Ideally, this should be approximately linear with a slope greater than unity but not more than about four. Items which are non-linear, or which have near-zero slopes for part of their range, will be detected by this method and can therefore be discarded.
See also COMPOSITE MEASUREMENT

Item Pool A large number of items written in the same format (e.g. **Likert** format) in order to tap some attitude dimension. The best can then be selected using recognized scale construction techniques.

See also COMPOSITE MEASUREMENT, ATTITUDE SCALING, **Item analysis**

Item Trace Line See under **Item Analysis**

Iterative Process A process in which the same action is repeated many times, as when one climbs stairs or solves a square root by a method of closer and closer approximation.
See also **Flow Diagram**

J

Joining See under PARTICIPANT OBSERVATION

Joint Frequency Distribution A **frequency distribution** drawn up on two or more variables simultaneously. The simplest and most common type of joint frequency distribution (the *bivariate frequency distribution*) demonstrates, for each **class interval** on one variable, how many cases fall into the various class intervals on the others.

See also TABULATION

K

Kappa (κ) A measure of **inter-rater reliability**. See under **RELIABILITY**

Kendall Coefficient of Concordance (W) A measure of the degree of agreement or concordance between several independent sets of rankings of the same individuals or objects. It would be appropriate, for example, for indicating the extent to which a panel of interviewers are using the same standards in judging the merits of a number of job applicants. W takes values between zero and one, zero meaning no agreement and one perfect agreement.

Kendall Partial Rank Correlation Coefficient A **partial correlation coefficient** which may be used on **ordinal scale** data and thus makes no assumptions about the data's **DISTRIBUTIONS** or **variances**.
For the three variables X, Y, and Z the partial rank correlation between x and y with z **partialled out** or controlled is given by:

$$\tau_{xy \cdot z} = \frac{\tau_{xz} - \tau_{zy} \cdot \tau_{xz}}{\sqrt{((1 - \tau_{zy}^2)(1 - \tau_{zx}^2))}} ,$$

where τ_{XY}, τ_{ZY}, and τ_{xz} are the Kendall rank correlations between xy, zy, and xz, respectively.

Kendall's Rank Correlation Coefficient (Tau) A correlation coefficient which requires only **ranked** data and makes no assumptions about the **DISTRIBUTIONS** or **variances** of the variables being analysed. If used on **interval scale** data its **power** efficiency at rejecting the **null hypothesis** is 91 per cent of that of the **Pearson r**. However, unlike **Spearman's** ρ, tau is not an estimate of r and its numerical values are usually less than the ρ values calculated on the same data. It contains a correction for ties, and there is a **partial Kendall rank correlation coefficient** available when a third variable is to be **partialled out**. The formula is

$$\tau = \frac{S}{\sqrt{((\frac{1}{2}N(N - 1) - \tau_X)(\frac{1}{2}N(N - 1) - \tau_Y))}}$$

S is obtained as follows, (i) Rank the pairs of observations on both variables (X and Y) and set one of the variables (X) into rank order beginning with rank 1. (ii) Beginning with rank 1 on X look at its pair Y_1 and examine the Y ranks below this, counting up those greater than Y_1 (**concordant rankings**) and subtracting those less than Y_1 (**discordant rankings**). Values equal to Y_1 are ignored. If there are ties for rank 1 on X (e.g. $X_2 = X_1$) then the corresponding Y ranks are ignored (e.g. Y_2). (iii) Repeat the above for the second rank on X and for all other ranks. (iv) Sum over all pairs to obtain S. Alternatively, S is the total sum of all the concordant rankings (P) − total sum of all the discordant rankings (Q). N is the number of pairs. $\tau_X = \frac{1}{2} \Sigma t(t-1)$, where t is the number of tied observations in each group of ties on the X variable. τ_Y is the similar quantity for the Y variable.
For the following data:

X	Y
1	1.5
2	1.5 } tie
tie { 3.5	5
3.5	4
5	3

$$\tau = \frac{(3 - 0) + (3 - 0) + (0 - 1) + (0 - 1)}{\sqrt{((\frac{1}{2}(5)(4) - 1)(\frac{1}{2}(5)(4) - 1))}}$$

$$= +0.44.$$

For small N ($\leqslant 10$) significance testing is by special tables; for $N > 10$, the quantity

$$\frac{\tau}{\frac{2(2N + S)}{N(N - 1)}}$$

is **NORMALLY DISTRIBUTED**.
See also **CORRELATION**

Kendall's Tau See **Kendall's Rank Correlation Coefficient**

Kolmogorov–Smirnov Test A test to determine whether two independent samples have been drawn from the same population (or whether a single sample fits some theoretical distribution). The test is sensitive to differences in central tendency or in shape of distribution.

Cumulative frequency distributions using the same **class intervals** are obtained for both samples. For each class interval the difference between these distributions is observed. If this difference becomes too large at any point the samples are probably drawn from different populations.

Kruskal–Wallis Analysis of Variance A one-way ANALYSIS OF VARIANCE technique which may be used on data in the form of ranks. It tests whether k independent samples are likely to be drawn from the same population and requires no assumptions about normality of distribution or homogeneity of variances (**homoscedasticity**). When used on **interval scale** data, it is about 95 per cent as **powerful** as orthodox analysis of variance.

All the observations are cast into rank order, ties being given their average rank, and the statistic H is computed, given by:

$$H = \frac{\dfrac{12}{N(N+1)} \sum_{j=1}^{k} \dfrac{R_j^2}{n_j} - 3(N+1)}{1 - \dfrac{\Sigma T}{N^3 - N}}$$

where N = total number of observations,
k = number of independent samples,

n_j = number of cases in the jth sample,
R_j = sum of the ranks in the jth sample,
T = $t^2 (t-1)$, where t is the number of tied observations in the group of ties.

For all $n_j > 5$, H is tested for significance by entering a chi-square table with $R - 1$ degrees of freedom. If any $n_j \leqslant 5$, special tables are used to determine the significance of H.

Kurtosis A characteristic especially exhibited by distributions which are symmetrical and approximately normal in shape. Such distributions may be either *leptokurtic* or *platykurtic*. The former are too peaked relative to the normal distribution and have too many observations in the tails. The latter are too flat in the middle and have too few observations in the tails.

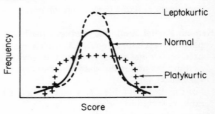

L

Lambda$_{YX}$ An **asymmetric measure of association** suitable for **nominal** data. It measures the improvement in prediction of a **dependent variable** with the addition of new information. With variable Y in the columns of a contingency table and variable X in the rows:

$$\lambda_{YX} = \frac{\Sigma \begin{array}{c} \text{maximum column} \\ \text{cell frequencies} \end{array} - \text{maximum row total}}{N - \text{maximum row total}} .$$

Lambda$_{yx}$ measures the proportional reduction in error in relying on the **modal** categories for prediction as more information is added. It may range from zero, meaning no improvement in prediction, to 1.0 meaning perfect prediction.

As an example, suppose the dependent variable (Y) is taste in music, assessed in two broad categories for a large sample of people. It is found that 50 people prefer classical music and 550 prefer other types of music. Knowing nothing else, if asked to guess a particular person's taste one would guess 'other type'. Now suppose the results are broken down by social class (X) and are as follows:

	Prefer classical	Prefer other	Total
Middle class	30	10	40
Working class	20	540	560
Total	50	550	600

The best guess is now 'classical' for middle-class people and 'other' for working-class:

$$\lambda_{YX} = \frac{(30 + 540) - 560}{600 - 560}$$
$$= 0\cdot25.$$

Lambda$_{XY}$ does not usually equal lambda$_{YX}$

and had the prediction concerned social class, given musical taste:

$$\lambda_{XY} = \frac{(30 + 540) - 550}{600 - 550}$$
$$= 0\cdot40.$$

Lambda$_{YX}$ may be applied to **contingency tables** of any size.

Langner Symptom Scale A screening questionnaire for detecting psychiatric impairment. There are 22 items which cover psychophysiological symptoms and feelings of anxiety and depression. For each item there are from four to six response alternatives, one of which scores positive. The scale is quick and easy to administer, is RELIABLE and VALID, and has wide use, particularly in the U.S.A.

Laspeyres Index see under INDEX NUMBERS

Latent Identity An identity or role possessed by an actor but which is not relevant to the setting under study in PARTICIPANT OBSERVATION. The participant observer has to manage his latent identity carefully in order that it does not affect the functioning of the group under investigation.

Latin Square Design An experimental design which is efficient at testing an **independent variable** with the effects of two **extraneous variables** controlled. It may also be used as a straightforward test of three independent variables. All three variables must have the same number of **treatment levels** and it must be reasonable to assume that there are no **interactions** between them, since the design provides no test of interaction. Where there are less than five treatment levels, there must be more than one observation per level.

The treatment levels of the three variables are counterbalanced using a latin square arrangement. This is a square made up from letters, with each letter occurring only once in each row and column e.g.

67

	Columns	
	1	2
Rows 1	A	B
2	B	A

	Columns		
	1	2	3
Rows 1	A	B	C
2	C	A	B
3	B	C	A

	Columns			
	1	2	3	4
Rows 1	A	B	C	D
2	B	C	D	A
3	C	D	A	B
4	D	A	B	C

The rows and columns represent the two extraneous variables, the letters in the main body the independent variable. For example, A, B, C, and D might be four different teaching methods applied in rotation to four classes of pupils represented by rows 1, 2, 3, and 4 and tested on four occasions, columns 1, 2, 3, and 4. Because of the counterbalancing, the effects of order of application of methods and differing ability among pupil classes are controlled. If these are indeed important variables this will allow significant results concerning teaching methods to emerge with comparatively few subjects in each cell of the square. However, if the extraneous variables do not, in fact, matter, a latin square design will tend to be less efficient than possible alternatives.

An ANALYSIS OF VARIANCE procedure is followed and this permits assessment of significant effects of the extraneous as well as the independent variables. Thus, the design can be used as a straightforward test of three independent variables.

As the number of treatment levels increases the number of possible latin square arrangements rapidly becomes very large, e.g. for a 5 × 5 arrangement there are 161,280 possible squares. There are therefore methods available for the approximate random selection of one of these for use from the population of squares available. A *graeco–latin square* design is a similar conception allowing for three extraneous variables by superimposing two latin squares upon each other so that each letter of one square occurs once with each letter of the other.

Law See under THEORY

Least Significant Difference (LSD) Test One of the first methods devised for making **unplanned comparisons** between group means following an ANALYSIS OF VARIANCE. All the possible comparisons are made and a value (LSD) is computed which any particular mean difference must exceed in order to be considered significant. Where all groups have equal n this is given by:

$$\text{LSD} = t \sqrt{\frac{2 \times \text{residual mean square}}{n}},$$

where t is the t-value required for *half* the desired significance level, with **degrees of freedom** associated with the **residual** mean square. LSD is not recommended by statisticians and is now little used.

Least Squares Criterion A criterion used in deriving linear **regression equations** of the form

$$\hat{Y} = b_1X_1 + b_2X_2 + \dots + b_nX_n + C,$$

where $\hat{Y}$ is a prediction of a person's score on a **dependent** or **criterion variable**, to be made from his scores X_1, X_2, etc. on several **independent** or **predictor variables**.
The problem is to find the best values for the constants b_1, b_2, ..., b_n and C. If the actual score on the dependent variable is Y, then the **error score** or residual $= Y - \hat{Y}$. The values of the constants are found such that the sum of the squares of the residuals over the whole sample, i.e. $\Sigma(Y - \hat{Y})^2$, shall be a minimum. This is the least squares criterion. When there is only one predictor variable, this results in the *least squares regression line*.

$$\hat{Y} = b_1X_1 + C.$$

When the **scattergram** of Y against X is plotted, this straight line will be the best fit and the sum of the squared deviations of the points from it will be a minimum.
See also MULTIPLE REGRESSION, MULTIPLE CORRELATION

Least Squares Regression Line See under **Least Squares Criterion**

Leptokurtic See under **Kurtosis**

Level of Confidence Strictly speaking, level of confidence is the degree of certainty that a particular range of values on a scale contains a **population parameter** (e.g. the mean value). It is expressed as the number of times out of 100 that the interval can be expected to contain the true parameter value, if the research were repeated a large number of times. It is often, however, taken as synonymous with *level of significance*, a term which refers to hypothesis testing. (See under STATISTICAL INFERENCE.)

Level of Significance See under STATISTICAL INFERENCE

Lie Scale   A set of items intended to detect the extent of any tendency for a respondent to bias his answers to other scales so as to leave a good impression. Lie scale items are usually mixed in at random with items comprising other scales.
See also BIAS. **Social Desirability**

Life Event   An occurrence, important in some way to an individual, which takes place at a specific point in time — e.g. an accident, a death, or a house move. This is sometimes distinguished from a *long-term difficulty* which is a chronic condition lasting over a period of time — e.g. caring for an aged relative or living in a difficult neighbourhood.

Life History   A complete biography of a single subject elicited by an investigator through repeated unstructured interviews. Depending on the research problem the interviews may be unobtrusively focused to elicit particular aspects of the subject's beliefs and perceptions.

Likelihood   See under BAYESIAN STATISTICS

Likert Scaling Method   An attitude scaling method in which respondents register their response to each item on a five- (or seven-) point scale ranging from strongly disagree to strongly agree. Their score on the whole scale is the sum of their scores for each item. Scale construction proceeds by trying a large number of items on people similar to those to whom the finished scale is to be applied. **Item analysis**, usually in the form of correlating each item with the total score, is then used to select the best items. Likert scales are relatively easy to construct but may not always be **unidimensional**. They have no **reproducibility** — the same score may be obtained in many different ways. Only **index measurement** is attained.
See also ATTITUDE SCALING

Linear Model   A model in which variables are postulated to be related in simple direct proportion. Usually a single **dependent variable** (Y) is expressed in terms of one or more **independent variables** $(X_1, X_2,$ etc.) by an equation of the form:

$$Y = aX_1 + bX_2 + cX_3 + \dots + \text{constant}.$$

A change of one unit in any X leads to a constant change in Y whatever the initial value of that X or of the other X's. When only two variables are involved, the equation is that of a straight line:

$$Y = aX_1 + \text{constant}.$$

Equations containing exponents of any variable are not linear.
See also MODEL, **Additivity**.

Linear Relationship   A relationship which may be represented by an equation of the form

$$Y = aX_1 + bX_2 + \dots + nXn.$$

See RELATIONSHIP, **Linear Model**

Linearity   See **linear model**

Logarithmic Transformation   The purpose of a logarithmic transformation of a variable (A) is usually to linearize the relationship with another variable (B). In the process a log transformation may also NORMALIZE the DISTRIBUTION of A at each level of B and/or make the **variance** of A homogeneous over different levels of B. This transformation is likely to be suitable when the **standard deviations** of A for different levels of B are proportional to the means for these levels, or when, as A changes by a constant proportion, e.g. from 10 to 100 to 1,000, B changes by a constant amount, e.g. from 1 to 2 to 3. A common formula for a log transformation is:

$$A' = \log (A + 1).$$

This avoids A' values of minus infinity when $A = 0$.
See also TRANSFORMATION

Long-Term Difficulty   See under **Life Event**

LONGITUDINAL STUDY
A study in which the same groups of subjects are approached at intervals over a period of time. Usually the term refers to large-scale longer term projects which have several different aims. Shorter, more restricted, studies, with perhaps only two or three closely spaced data collection points are often termed **panel studies**, while those with only two time points and an important treatment or event in between are known as **before–after studies**. By supplying reliable prospective data at different time points longitudinal studies are often superior to CROSS-SECTIONAL ones in clarifying the sequence of factors leading to a particular outcome. This may make causal inference easier. Much valuable descriptive material may also accrue on matters such as the **incidence** of disease, changing patterns of behaviour, or longer term outcomes. The information collected may sometimes bear on hypotheses that were never envisaged when the study commenced. Another advantage claimed is that sampling may be more complete. Individuals who die or are institutionalized during the study will not be overlooked, as

they might be in a retrospective cross-sectional study. When people drop out, much information is known about them, thus making easier the assessment of the possible biases introduced.

Some problems associated with longitudinal studies are expense, time needed to mature, possible obsolescence of the theory on which the study was originally based, systematic changes in the population (e.g. an influx of immigrants) making the sample become unrepresentative, and testing of people on several occasions perhaps affecting the findings.

Furthermore, the statistical treatment of longitudinal data is not always straightforward. In particular, allowance may need to be made for correlated errors when the same subjects are tested several times, for extraneous trends which might interfere with the hypotheses being tested, and for seasonal fluctuations. One technique which is applicable is cross-lagged *panel analysis*. At its simplest this inolves measuring two variables at two time points yielding data sets $A1$, $B1$; $A2$, and B2. The correlations $r_{A1\,A2}$, $r_{B1\,B2}$, $r_{A1\,B1}$, $r_{A2\,B2}$, $r_{A1\,B2}$, and $r_{B1\,A2}$ are calculated. The latter two are known as *cross-lagged correlations*. If one is larger than the other, e.g. $r_{A1\,B2} > r_{B1\,A2}$, then it may be possible to infer a direction of causation, in this case that A causes B rather than B causes A. This inference is strengthened if the pattern of relationships is exactly repeated when subsequent measurements are made at equal time intervals. Where this is not the case valid conclusions are more difficult.

Longitudinal Survey See LONGITUDINAL STUDY

Lorenz Curve A graphical method for representing the degree of inequality in the distribution of a variable, usually such 'goods' as income, wealth, landholdings, etc. which are measured **intervally**. It is a generalization of simple summaries of distribution such as '5 per cent of the population of income earners receive 10 per cent of the total of personal incomes'. The technique is derived from the **cumulative relative frequency distribution** where the variable is transformed from its original units to a scale running from 0 to 100 per cent of the total of income, wealth, etc. Frequency is also cumulated. A line of perfect equality is drawn joining the points (0 per cent, 0 per cent) and (100 per cent, 100 per cent) against which the Lorenz curve may be visually compared. The further the curve bows away from the line of equality the greater is the inequality of distribution of the 'good'.

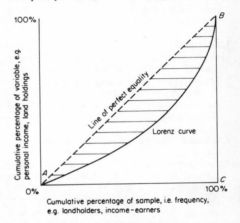

Cumulative percentage of sample, i.e. frequency, e.g. landholders, income-earners

A more exact estimate of the inequality may be calculated by the *Gini coefficient* which is the ratio of the shaded area between the curve and the line of equality to the area of the triangle ABC usually expressed as a percentage. If the Lorenz curve lay along the line of equality the Gini coefficient would be zero because the shaded area would be zero. The theoretical maximum of the Gini coefficient is 100 per cent, representing a situation where the whole of a good was concentrated in one person's ownership, or maximum inequality.

Lower Quartile See under **Interquartile Ratio**

M

Main Effect This is the overall effect an independent variable has over the whole sample. Thus, if one was considering the effects of sex, age (as a dichotomy), and height (as a dichotomy) on running speed, the main effect for sex would be the overall difference in running speed between men and women; for age it would be the overall difference between old and young; for height it would be the overall difference betwen the tall and the short.
See also ANALYSIS OF VARIANCE

Mann–Whitney *U* **Test** A **non-parametric** alternative to the *t-test* applicable to two independent samples where the data have been measured on an **ordinal scale**. The scores of the two groups combined together are ranked, the average rank being given when ties occur. Then the statistic

$$U_1 = N_1 N_2 + \frac{N_1(N_1 + 1)}{2} - T_1$$

is computed, where N_1 and N_2 are the sample sizes and T_1 is the sum of the ranks for sample 1. For $N > 20$ the quantity

$$\frac{U_1 - N_1 N_2/2}{\sqrt{\dfrac{N_1 N_2 (N_1 + N_2 + 1)}{12}}}$$

is a unit normal deviate (**Z score**). For $N < 20$ the transformation $U_2 = N_1 N_2 - U_1$ is applied and either U_1 or U_2, which ever is smaller, is compared to the values in special tables.

Marginal The total frequency in a row or a column of a **contingency table.**

Marginality In PARTICIPANT OBSERVATION, marginality is the state of being on the fringe of an observed group, thereby understanding its perspectives yet simultaneously being able to observe with detachment. Participant observers should be marginal; lack of detachment leads to over-rapport or accepting the views of the group or some part of it as obvious and without question and to be too detached may mean that the group is aware of being observed and its actions may no longer be natural.

Master Role See under **Field Role**

Matched Pairs Design A design which seeks to remove the effects of extraneous variables by having each subject in the **experimental group** matched with a subject in the **control group** on one or more of the **extraneous variables**. For example, one might be interested in a new teaching method and concerned that intelligence might obscure the issue. An experimental group of children might be taught by the new method and a control group individually matched with them on intelligence would be taught by the old method. Intelligence, being equal in both samples, would not be likely to affect the outcome.
See also EXPERIMENT

Maturation Effect A process, such as growth, within the respondent or observed social unit, producing changes as a function of the passage of time *per se*. Maturation effects need to be controlled in many LONGITUDINAL STUDIES.

Maximum Likelihood Estimator See under ESTIMATION

Maxwells' *RE* Coefficient A measure of **inter-rater reliability.**
See under RELIABILITY

Mean See **Arithmetic Mean**

Mean Deviation The sum of the absolute differences between a set of observations and their mean, divided by the number of observations. This statistic is not often used.

Mean Square See under ANALYSIS OF VARIANCE

Measurement Error The deviations of the experimental measurements from the 'true' measurements. Measurement error is always present, arising from many different sources (e.g. subjects not understanding the question, subjects not concentrating, or clerical errors) but may usually be assumed to be random.

See also BIAS, ERROR

Measures of Location or Central Tendency Measures which attempt to summarize a set of data by one single 'central' or 'most characteristic' value, thus helping in forming generalizations from the data.

The three most common measures of central tendency are the **mean**, the **median**, and the **mode**. Of these, the mode, or most frequently occurring value, is not often used. The median is that point in the distribution above and below which 50 per cent of the data lie. The mean is the arithmetic average, obtained by adding up all the data and dividing by their total number. The median has the advantages over the mean of being less affected by atypical extreme values in the distribution and of being useable on ordinal scale data. The mean, on the other hand, is amenable to more powerful statistical techniques and is the measure of choice in most cases.

See also **Positive Skewness, Negative Skewness**

Median That value of a variable above and below which 50 per cent of the observations in a distribution lie.

See also **Measures of Location or Central Tendency**

Median Test A **non-parametric test** to ascertain whether the **medians** of two independent groups differ. A **two by two table** is drawn up showing which observations in each group fall above and below the median of the two groups combined. Depending on cell numbers, the **chi-square** test or the **Fisher exact probability test** may then be used to determine whether the distribution differs from that expected if the groups had the same median.

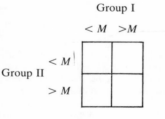

Group I

$< M$ $> M$

Group II $< M$

$> M$

M = median of all observations,
　　i.e. Groups I and II combined

Member-Identified Categories See under PARTI-
CIPANT OBSERVATION

Method Triangulation See under **Triangulation**

Minnesota Multi-phasic Personality Inventory (MMPI) An inventory consisting of 566 brief items answered 'true', 'false', or 'cannot say'. Its original purpose was assessment of traits characteristic of disabling psychological

abnormality. There are 14 scales, four being concerned with **internal consistency** and **response bias** and the other ten being labelled hypochondriasis, depression, hysteria, psychopathic deviate, masculinity–femininity, paranoia, psychasthenia, schizophrenia, hypomania, and social introversion. Eight of these scales distinguished patients with a particular diagnosis from normals. Of the remaining two, social introversion distinguished extraverts from introverts and masculinity–femininity indicated whether a person's interests were predominantly masculine or feminine. There are **norms** for the scales in the form of **standard scores** with a mean of 50 and a **standard deviation** of 10. The cut-off point for pathological deviation is usually taken as 70.

The clinical scales, however, should not be literally interpreted. A high score on any one of them, separately, does not necessarily indicate that diagnosis. Clinical judgements are more usually based on the profile of scores on all the scales. Much effort has gone into devising systems of profile interpretation and some of these are computer based.

The test may be group administered using a booklet or individually administered using a set of cards. There are shorter forms available.

Particularly in the U.S.A., the MMPI has had tremendous usage, not only clinically but also in research and there is a huge literature on it. Many other combinations of its items have been arranged into scales and it has served as a source for other inventories. It has survived some criticisms on the grounds that it is too much affected by **social desirability** and **acquiescence response sets**. However, the results do seem partly dependent on such variables as social status, age, intelligence, and race, and, in general, interpretation of MMPI profiles requires training and experience.

Mode The most frequently occurring value of a set of observations.

MODEL
The term model has a range of meanings and in some usages is indistinguishable from *theory*. It seems best described as a simplified representation of selected aspects of a phenomenon aiming to conceptualize it and allow explanations of relationships to be framed and tested.

A **gravity model** of transport flow between two cities might be

$$T = \alpha \frac{P_1 P_2}{d^2},$$

where T is the flow of transport units in both directions for a given time interval, d is the distance between city centres, P_1, P_2 are their respective populations, and α is a constant.

This model simplifies by subsuming all types of transport under 'transport units', and by assuming that populations are concentrated at the city centres. It conceptualizes a limited class of phenomena to be represented by concentrating only upon populations, distance, and transport. The equation expresses the relationship between the variables.

Usages of the term model differ in degree of emphasis placed on conceptualizing and explaining. Three may be distinguished.

(1) At its most general, model denotes a **frame of reference,** *perspective*, or *paradigm* (the three terms are used interchangeably) such as structural functionalism in sociology or behaviourism in psychology. Frames of reference define the type of concepts which are admissible (and hence the objects of study) and the scheme of EXPLANATION to be preferred. Behaviourism, for example, rules out unobservable mental states (anxiety, motive, etc.) as not capable of reliable agreement between different observers and as unnecesary for explanations of the preferred hypothetico-deductive form. *Interpretative* frames of reference take motives as the key objects of study and of explanations, and therefore conceive of the meanings which actors give to their own actions as being objects of study. Frames of reference guide in a very general way the researcher's construction of models in the next sense in which relationships between variables may be specified.

(2) More specific models contain at least one proposition or hypothesis conjecturing a relationship between concepts. These may be a set of integrated hypotheses such that deductions may be logically made. Ways of measuring the concepts may or may not be specified. If they are, it is an *operational model*. Such models are often represented as **flow diagrams,** for example:

Here the field of investigation has been conceptualized and significant variables identified. The arrows linking the variables represent unknown associations or **path coefficients** if the model is to be a causal one. The concepts in the flow diagram indicate the data to be collected and the analysis to be performed in order to estimate the coefficients for the arrows.

(3) The second type of model may be developed into one expressible in mathematical terms. The **gravity model** above is an example, as is the *regression model*:

$$\hat{Y} = b_1 X_1 + b_2 X_2 + \ldots b_n X_n + C.$$

Here $X_1, \ldots, X_n$ are **independent (predictor) variables**, $\hat{Y}$ *is the* **dependent variable (criterion** or **effect)**, $b_1, \ldots, b_n$ are constants known as **regression weights** or **regression coefficients**, and C is the regression constant. The postulated relationship is exact, a unit increase in X_1 for example is to yield precisely b_1 units of increase in $\hat{Y}$. This type of specific model may be contrasted with the more vague type (2) model of the kind 'an increase in the rate of intercommunal marriage will diminish intercommunal hostility', which, after operationalisation, may be confirmed by any **statistically significant** negative correlation.

All models simplify reality and imply a greater degree of determinateness than probably exists, particularly for social phenomena. They are essentially **heuristic** problem solving tools to be improved and refined. Such refinement, particularly from a type (2) to a type (3) model, is known as model-building. Model-building becomes model-testing when a model is **calibrated** on a sample of observations and then tested (or **cross-validated**) on a comparable independent sample. A highly specific, calibrated, and cross-validated model affords a powerful means of prediction. On the other hand, the range of application may be rather narrow, and the attempt to set up such a precise model particularly a multiple regression model may founder because underlying

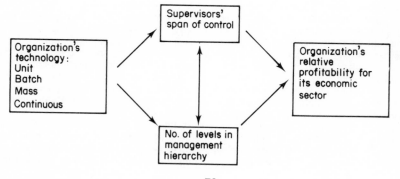

mathematical assumptions such as **additivity** and *linearity* of regression cannot be met.

Causal models may be of type (2) or type (3). They assign causal order to the variables. A **causal hierarchy** is a sequence of the variables such that ones higher up the hierarchy may cause lower ones but lower ones are unlikely to cause higher ones. Causal models are usually *non-recursive*, the causal flow being in one direction only, rather than *recursive* where cause may flow in both directions.

Moving Averages See under TIME SERIES ANALYSIS

Multicollinearity Multicollinearity arises in MULTIPLE REGRESSION when two or more of the **predictor variables** are highly correlated with each other. This can lead to severe problems.

Suppose variables A and B, which are highly correlated are being used to predict Y. First, because they are highly correlated, they are predicting much the same part of Y's **variance**. This means that if A is entered first, followed by B, B will add very little extra variance explained in Y; yet it may be incorrect to conclude that B is not important — B may almost entirely cause A. Furthermore, where there is multicollinearity, small sampling fluctuations in the values of the correlation coefficients make a large difference to the results. Hence, very large samples and/or very accurate measurement is necesssary. Finally, rounding errors in the computation of the various regression coefficients become important, and in extreme cases the calculation may be impossible.

See also REGRESSION ANALYSIS

MULTIPLE CORRELATION

The multiple correlation coefficient (R) is the correlation between the observed scores on a **dependent variable** and the scores as predicted statistically from a number of other **independent variables** combined linearly by the method of **least squares**. In several respects it has the same interpretation as the simple bivariate **Pearson correlation** (r). R^2 represents the amount of **variance** in the dependent variable which may be explained by the set of independent variables. R, however, varies only between 0 and +1. It cannot be negative. The value of R depends to some extent on the number of independent variables being combined. As the number of independent variables approaches the number of observations in the sample, R approaches unity. The *correction for shrinkage* compensates for this phenomenon. It is given by:

$$R' = \sqrt{1 - (1 - R^2)\frac{(N - 1)}{(N - n)}} \ ,$$

where R' is the corrected R, N is the total number of observations, and n is the number of independent variables.

R' is also a better estimate of what the multiple R would be in a new sample. R tends to shrink because of random error, and is particularly likely to shrink when the simple correlations between the independent and dependent variables are low.

The **standard error (SE)** of R is given approximately by

$$SE = \frac{1 - R^2}{\sqrt{N}} \ .$$

This is a good approximation only for a large N and a small number of independent variables. See also MULTIPLE REGRESSION, REGRESSION ANALYSIS

Multiple Indicators It is often the case that an abstract concept (e.g. intelligence) can be indicated in several different ways (e.g. different kinds of tests for intelligence). These different ways are said to be **multiple indicators** of the concept.

See also **Operationalization**

MULTIPLE REGRESSION (MR)

The multiple regression model has very wide applications in the social sciences. The effects of two or more **independent variables** (X_1, X_2, X_3, etc.) on a single **dependent variable** (Y) are analysed to find the amount of **variance** in Y explained or accounted for in total, and by each independent variable uniquely. A mathematical procedure is applied to a set of observations (a data set) of X_1, X_2, etc. and of Y to derive a multiple **regression equation** of the form:

$$\hat{Y} = b_1X_1 + b_2X_2 + \dots b_nX_n + \text{con-}$$
stant.

$\hat{Y}$ is a prediction (known as the best estimate of Y) of the value of the dependent variable given a knowledge of the observed values of X_1, X_2, etc. the independent or predictor variables. b_1, b_2, etc. are *regression weights* expressing how much each independent variable must be weighted in predicting $\hat{Y}$. The constant term has the same units of measurement as Y and can be positive or negative, as can the b's.

In the form shown above, the MR equation uses unstandardized variables which retain their own units of measurement. It is misleading to take the size of the b's as showing the relative importance of each independent variable to the predicted value of the dependent variable ($\hat{Y}$) because of the different units of measurement of the independent variables. An example of an MR equation from the Plowde National Survey of Primary School Children (1967) shows:

$\hat{Y}$ (pupil's attainment) = 1.1 parents attitudes + 1.9 family background + 0.16 school factors + 8.7.

This is really an 'accounting' equation used to predict an individual pupil's attainment. If the variables are all *standardized* (i.e. measured as deviations from their own **means** divided by their own **standard deviations**) the equation becomes:

$\hat{Y}$ (pupil's attainment) = 0.14 PA + 0.10 FB + 0.08 SF,

the regression coefficients are now standardized and conventionally known as *betas* (β). The constant term disappears and each β now shows the unique contribution of an independent variable after the others have been taken into account. The proportion of variance of Y explained or accounted for by each independent variable may also be given. In this example, PA accounts for 28 per cent, FB adds a further 20 per cent, SF another 17 per cent. Of the total variance of Y (pupil's attainment) 35 per cent is unexplained and may be attributed to unmeasured influences on it.

MR is a way of modelling the relationships in a data set and is frequently used particularly in educational measurement or in econometrics to predict future values of Y, the dependent variable. It may also be used to estimate the importance of the independent variables for theoretical reasons. In the first case b's are used, and in the second β's. How well the MR equation models the data is shown by R^2, the square of the MULTIPLE CORRELATION COEFFICIENT, which is the total variance explained of a dependent variable by a set of independent variables.

The discrepancy between Y observed and Y explained (the predicted value, $\hat{Y}$) is a **residual** and mathematically MR finds a regression line (or more exactly a surface) which minimizes the sum of the squares of all the residuals, thus fulfilling the ordinary **least squares criterion**. This is the same procedure as used in simple regression, although it cannot be represented diagrammatically.

Technical problems met in MR include statistical **interactions** between independent variables and **multicollinearity.** One major point about MR is that the independent variables are not necessarily the causes of the dependent variable as the language used seems to imply. β's are often called **path coefficients** when they are used in causal models where explicit attention has been given to the causal ordering of the variables.

See also MULTIPLE CORRELATION, REGRESSION ANALYSIS, PATH ANALYSIS, and MODEL

Multi-stage Cluster Sampling See under SAMPLING THEORY AND METHODS

Multivariate Analysis Analysis of several variables at the same time, elucidating their relationships to a **dependent variable** (criterion) and/or their interrelationships with each other. Examples of multivariate techniques are **partial correlation,** FACTOR ANALYSIS, MULTIPLE REGRESSION, PATH ANALYSIS, and **canonical correlation analysis.**

N

N.A.C.E. Nomenclature Générale des Activités Économiques; the European Economic Community's version of the **Standard Industrial Classification**, which it closely resembles.

Naturalism See under PARTICIPANT OBSERVATION

Negative Skewness A **unimodal** distribution is said to be negatively skewed when the **mode** occurs towards the higher end of the distribution. In this situation the mode is greater than the **median** ($\tilde{X}$), which is greater than the **mean** ($\bar{X}$), thus:

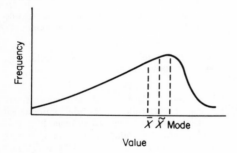

Value

New Earnings Survey Survey in April each year of a **random sample** of employees and their earnings conducted by the Department of Employment. Sampling is by reference to employees' national insurance numbers and the enquiry is made of the employer who compiles answers from administrative records. **Non-sampling error** is thought to be low because of indirect access to employers' records and the response rate is around 90 per cent — there is a legal duty to comply with the request for information.

Earnings are defined as gross earnings, before any deductions, for a specified week or month in April. Earnings from second jobs, from unearned income, of the self-employed, and from the 'hidden economy' (e.g. labour-only subcontracting in the construction industry) are excluded.

Those who are marginally employed or who otherwise avoid the official economy will be under-represented in any studies of income distribution based on the N.E.S., as will some groups who are predominantly self-employed such as many National Health Consultants. There are also problems in accurately representing earnings of those with fluctuating incomes over the course of the year since only one pay period is sampled.

Earnings series are disaggregated and reported separately for: occupational group, industry (industrial order of the **Standard Industrial Classification**), sex, and overtime inclusive and exclusive. **Means** and **medians** of earnings are reported for **quantiles** in specific earnings groups so that dispersion of income may also be assessed.

Standard errors of the mean and medians of earnings are given and are usually small for large aggregates but become large when small subgroups are concerned.

There were changes in 1970 and 1972 in the basis of classifying occupations which makes longer run comparisons of changes in earnings for different groups difficult. The N.E.S. also reports earnings by national trades union agreements, disaggregated by industry and by occupational title (note, not occupational group), and by public versus private sector employment.

Newman-Keuls Test A method for making **unplanned comparisons** between group means following an ANALYSIS OF VARIANCE. The number of observations (n) in each group has to be equal or nearly equal. All possible comparisons are made and a value W_r is computed which any particular mean difference must exceed in order to be considered significant. This is given by:

$$W_r = q_r \sqrt{\dfrac{\text{residual mean square}}{n}} \ .$$

The value of the studentized range statistic q_r varies depending on which means are being compared. The means are first ranked in order allowing the number of steps (r) between any given pair to be found — e.g. if there are five groups whose means in ascending order are $A\ B\ C\ D\ E$, there are five steps between A and E, four between A and D, etc. q_r for each comparison is found by entering a special table of q_r, with the required significance level, the **degrees of freedom** of the **residual**, and r the number of steps. A larger r always results in a larger q_r and therefore a larger W_r.

Nominal Scale A system of categorization. The categories are a set of convenient, mutually exclusive, and exhaustive labels. It is not implied that they should be in any particular order. An example would be the categorization of religious affiliation into Catholic, Church of England, Methodist, etc.
See also **Scale of Measurement.**

Nominal Variable A variable which may be placed on a **nominal scale** only, e.g. religious affiliation, eye colour.

Nomothetic Methods Methods of investigation which are aimed at establishing general laws of the relationships holding between classes of events. Ideally, law-like propositions relating events should be universal and general, i.e. they should always hold for the designated events and cover all specific events within the general class.
These ideals have not been realized in the social sciences, although some branches have been more successful than others, so that nomothetic refers more to a general approach to investigation than to the establishment of laws analogous to those of the physical sciences.
The distinguishing characteristics of a nomothetic approach are: (i) well-defined concepts with clear rules of **operationalization** — this implies a large degree of abstraction from specific behaviours in order to subsume them under broad categories, e.g. an individual's purchase of a refrigerator is an instance of 'demand for consumer durables'; (ii) a search for regularities of behaviour in which relations between specific or unique events are investigated through their membership of categories of events, which requires (iii) **correlational** measures and therefore large numbers of observations which in turn require (iv) systematic and standardized methods of data collection so that specific instances may be assigned to an observation category.
A nomothetic approach abstracts, sometimes to a very high level, from specific and concrete human actions so that the meanings and purposes of individual actors are lost, or if they remain in the scheme of explanation of an event do so only in so far as they can be subsumed under typical motives or purposes; thus, causal explanations of individual behaviour are made, in nomothetic methods, only in terms of the relationship between classes of events so that an individual act of consumption is not considered in terms of the number of personal and perhaps idiosyncratic decisions which have meaning for the individual, but only as an instance of the general principle of maximizing personal utility. Nomothetic methods are much criticized for their conceptions of adequate causal explanation of events and for the neglect of motives as sufficient causes of action as in the **verstehen** approach.
Methods of investigation which examine unique sequences of events are *ideographic* if they frame explanations without reference to general propositions but only in terms of specific antecedents and conditions in a causal narrative. **Ideal types** of particular entities may be used but these are concepts only and unless relationships are asserted in which the ideal type occurs, they are not general propositions. The origins of the First World War, for example, might be explained as the combination of a specific condition (the assassination at Sarajevo) and a general proposition of the form 'international competition for markets produces war' which is a nomothetic explanation (though not necessarily a good one); or an ideographic explanation of the same event might be couched in terms of a sequence of treaty obligations, international tension, and a precipitating event — the assassination.
See also EXPLANATION, CAUSATION

Non-directional Null Hypothesis See under **Null Hypothesis**

Non-directive Probe A supplementary question asked to clarify the meaning of a response and put in very general terms in order to avoid influencing the answer (e.g. 'Can you tell me more about that?').

Non-linear Relationships *Any* discernible relationship(s) which cannot be fitted by a **linear model** of the form:

$$Y = aX_1 + bX_2 + \ldots + nX_n + C.$$

Non-parametric Test Non-parametric statistical tests (also known as *distribution-free tests*) do not involve the estimation of a **population parameter** (e.g. the **mean** or **standard deviation**) and generally require no assumptions about how the scores in question are distributed. They may often be used when **parametric tests** are inappropriate, but they lack some of the **power** of parametric tests.

Non-probability Sampling See under SAMPLING THEORY AND METHODS

Non-recursive Model A MODEL in which cause may 'flow' in one direction only.

Non-respondent One who is sampled in a survey but who (for any reason) does not respond.

Non-sampling Error See **Measurement Error**

Normal Curve See NORMAL DISTRIBUTION

NORMAL DISTRIBUTION (GAUSSIAN DISTRIBUTION)

A bell-shaped frequency distribution curve which is often obtained when human characteristics are measured and plotted. Height, for example, shows an approximately normal distribution: most individuals are of medium height whilst a few are very short and a few very tall; thus, when height is plotted against the frequency of occurrence of particular heights in a sample the bell-shaped normal distribution curve is obtained.

A variable is likely to be normally distributed when it is determined by a large number of separate and independent causes. Height, weight, IQ scores, and errors are usually normally distributed for this reason.

One of the assumptions of the commonly-used **parametric** statistical tests (e.g. the *t*-test) is that the variables being measured are normally distributed, although in practice most of these tests are very robust to violations of this assumption.

One form of the general equation to the normal distribution is:

$$Y = \frac{N}{\sigma\sqrt{2\pi}} \exp[-(X - \mu)^2/2\sigma^2],$$

where Y is the frequency of occurrence or the probability of occurrence, σ is the population **standard deviation**, μ is the population **mean** and N is the number of observations. The three quantities N, σ, and μ are thus sufficient to define the normal distribution equation in any particular instance. In a normal distribution the highest frequency or probability occurs at the mean, and the mean, the **median**, and the **mode** all coincide. The curve is symmetrical about the mean and, in theory, the ends of the curve are asymptotic to the X-axis — that is, they come closer and closer to it the further from the mean one goes in both directions without actually touching it. The normal distribution may be thought of as either a mathematical function to which real frequency distributions more or less coincide, or as a *probability density function* which specifies the distribution of probability of occurrence of values of a variable if it is normally distributed. The Y-axis or ordinate is thus either a probability scale or a frequency scale. If probability is considered to be the frequency to be expected in a very large sample, then the two scales are the same. Any normal distribution may be transformed into the *unit normal distribution* by subtracting the mean value of X (the distributed variable) from each X-value (X_i) and dividing ($X_i - \bar{X}$) by the standard deviation of X. This yields a set of standardized scores known as *z*-scores or standard scores; and this set has a mean of zero and a standard deviation of 1.

The unit normal distribution, like all normal distributions, has certain useful properties; 68.26 per cent of the observations lie within ±1 standard deviation of the mean and 95.44 per cent lie within ±2 standard deviations of the mean. In general, all normal distributions have a constant proportion of observations or probabilities lying within a specifiable distance of the mean. This is the property which, when applied to the normal probability distribution, allows statistical inferences to be made about populations from sample statistics. (See under STATISTICAL INFERENCE.)

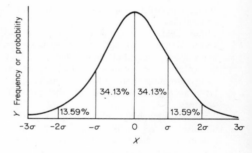

Statistical tables give, for each *z*-value, the height of the curve (i.e. the *y*-value or ordinate) at that *z*-value, the area under the curve between the *z*-value and the mean (corresponding to the total probability for that segment of the distribution), and the area or probability in the tail of the distribution between a *z*-value and the end of the curve as it asymptotically approaches the X-axis.

The area in the tail of the unit normal curve is the **one-tailed probability** of a *z*-value as high as that observed occurring by chance. An obtained *z*-value is compared against its probability value in taking a decision on whether to accept or reject the hypothesis that it is likely to have occurred by sampling fluctuations.

See also DISTRIBUTION, STATISTICAL INFERENCE

Normal Probability Density Function The equation describing the NORMAL DISTRIBUTION

Norm-referenced Test   See **Norms**

Norms   Summary descriptions of large samples of people on a psychological test. Frequently norms consist of the **means** and **standard deviations** of the scores. For some tests (particularly intelligence tests) tables of norms are provided, enabling conversion of a raw score onto a scale with a mean of 100 and a standard deviation of 15. There may be separate norms for different groups of people, e.g. men and women. In general, norms furnish a baseline against which to measure the performance of any individual, or group of individuals, undergoing that test (*norm-referenced test*).

Null Hypotheses   Before any hypothesis is tested statistically it is always stated in the form of a null hypothesis, that is, that the test will reveal no differences between the groups being tested, no relationship between the variables of interest, etc. An hypothesis which states that a difference in a particular direction will be found is known as an **alternative hypothesis**: while one which suggests that no difference in a given direction will be apparent is called a **directional null hypothesis**.

O

Oblique Solution   See under FACTOR ANALYSIS

Obtrusive Identification   See under PARTICIPANT OBSERVATION

Office Coding   See under **Field Coding**

Ogive   A diagram in which the **cumulative frequency** (or **cumulative relative frequency**) is plotted on the vertical axis (Y-axis) against the value of the variable on the horizontal axis (X-axis).

One-tailed Test   A statistical test which uses the area at only one end, or tail, of the normal (or other) distribution in order to test a **directional hypothesis**, that is, one in which the direction in which the rejection of the null hypothesis will occur can be specified.
See also STATISTICAL INFERENCE

Open Question   A question to which the respondent answers in his own way, without being restricted to a set list of alternatives.

Open-ended Interval   A **class interval** with one of its boundaries undefined. These occur at the extremes of distributions where, in order to ensure that the categories are exhaustive, the end intervals are defined as 'all those cases greater than a certain amount' or 'all those cases less than a certain amount'.

Operational Definition   See under **Concept**

Operational Hypothesis   See under **Hypothesis**

Operational Model   See under MODEL

Operationalization   The translation of an abstract concept (e.g. social status) into something which can be observed (e.g. occupation). More than one *operational definition* can usually be given for a concept, and these different *indicators* will be most unlikely to overlap completely. For instance, social status could be indicated by occupation of father, income, or highest level of education achieved. If all three were used in turn and the relationships between the resulting measures assessed, it would be found that there was considerable, but not perfect, overlap.

One philosophical position posits a division between *theoretical constructs* and *observable phenomena*. In this view, even a set of indicators will not exhaust the theoretical meaning of a concept. In contrast, *operationism* is the position that a concept is completely defined by an indicator.
See also MODEL

Optimization Models   Mathematical models which relate **decision variables** (or **independent variables**) to effects or **dependent variables** so that an optimum or best solution to a set of policy choices may be found. Optimum must first be defined as the most or least of a given consequence or effect or, in some cases, optimum means the minimum cost in terms of some undesirable effect. For a strictly mathematical model for which some numerical optimum on the dependent variable(s) may be found, the independent variables must be measured at the **interval** level and in addition some maximum and minimum values for the decision variables must be set as initial conditions. In the case of simple optimization models which involve only one decision variable, optimum solutions may be found by using the differential calculus.

If, for example, urban rents (R) are modelled as an effect of housing density (H), such that $R = f(H)$, then the function is differentiated with respect to H and the first and second derivatives are found to identify a maximum or minimum value of R. For a solution, realistic upper and lower limits of H must be set in advance as assumptions, and a policy decision taken as to whether urban rents are desirably to be minimized or maximized. For this form of analysis to have a practical usefulness one must assume that planners or others have the power to control the decision variable — housing density.

Realistic models will contain several decision variables each of which will require the setting of upper and lower limits on their values and may be soluble only by **iterative** procedures involving the use of mathematical programming.

Order Effect   An effect in which a previous test item, or the response to it, in some way influences the response to a later item. If such an effect is present and in the same direction for a whole sample of people, the test results will be biased. Two well-known order effects are the *practice effect*, in which results improve with practice, and the *fatigue effect*, which is a decrement in performance due to tiredness or boredom.

Order effects may be ruled out by **counterbalancing**. Usually this entails randomly splitting the sample into a number of equal-sized groups and giving a different possible ordering of the items to each group.
See also EXPERIMENT

Ordered Attribute   See under **Attribute**

Ordinal Scale   A scale which allows the individuals in a data set to be ranked in order, but which admits of no basis for measuring the amount of difference between ranks.
See also SCALE OF MEASUREMENT

Ordinal Variable   A variable which may be measured on an **ordinal scale**.

Ordinate   The *Y-axis* in a graph.
See also **Graphic Presentation**

Orthogonal Factors   Factors which are **independent** of each other.
See also FACTOR ANALYSIS

Overidentified Model   A path analytic model in which more than one estimate of at least one of the **path coefficients** is possible.
See under PATH ANALYSIS

Over-Rapport   See under PARTICIPANT OBSERVATION

P

Paasche Index See under INDEX NUMBERS

Panel Study A study in which a panel or sample of people is followed over a period of time with a view to assessing change in attitude or opinion. The panel may be questioned several times, often using the same questions.
See also LONGITUDINAL STUDY

Paradigm See under MODEL, THEORY

Parallel Form Synonymous with **Equivalent form**

Parameter See **Population Parameter**

Parametric Statistical Inference See **Parametric Test**

Parametric Test A parametric statistical test involves the estimation of a **population parameter** (e.g. the **mean** or **standard deviation**) and involves certain assumptions about the data. These are usually that the data are measured on at least an **interval scale**, that the populations from which the samples have been drawn are NORMALLY DISTRIBUTED, and that these populations have equal **variances**. In practice it has been shown that very considerable violations of these assumptions do not invalidate the conclusions drawn about the hypothesis being tested. The main parametric techniques are the z-test, the *t*-test, ANALYSIS OF VARIANCE, **product-moment correlation**, and MULTIPLE REGRESSION.

Partial Correlation The correlation (r) between two variables with the influence of a third variable removed. For example, if there are three variables A, B, and C, and r_{AC}, r_{BC}, and r_{AB} are all positive, A might correlate positively with C purely because it correlates positively with B and B correlates positively with C. The partial $r_{AC.B}$ measures the extent to which this is so, and is the correlation for A with C with B held constant. This is achieved theoretically by finding the **linear** regression lines for A with C and for B with C and then correlating together the *deviations* of corresponding points from these two **regression lines**. (Thus, partial correlation assumes linearity of regression.) However, deviations are not

actually calculated because it may be shown that

$$r_{AC.B} = \frac{r_{AC} - r_{AB} \cdot r_{BC}}{\sqrt{(1 - r_{AB}^2)(1 - r_{BC}^2)}}$$

So that a partial correlation coefficient may be calculated only from knowledge of the bivariate **zero-order** correlation coefficients between A, B and C.

Partial Regression Coefficients The weights (b_i) to be applied when a set of **independent variables** (X_i) are used in a **regression equation** to predict a **dependent variable** {Y},. i.e. in the equation:

$$\hat{Y} = b_1 X_1 + b_2 X_2 + \dots + b_i X_i + \text{constant}.$$

The term **partial regression coefficient** refers to an *unstandardized* weighting. The variables in the equation are measured in their original units. It is to be contrasted with **regression coefficient**, which refers to the *unstandardized* weighting of a single variable predicting another, and with **standardized partial regression coefficient** (β_i) which is a weight applied in a regression equation with the variables in STANDARDIZED form.
See also MULTIPLE REGRESSION, REGRESSION ANALYSIS

Partialling Out If several variables (e.g. V, W, and X) all seem to be related to some **criterion** or **dependent variable** (Y) it may be that V, W, and X all predict part of Y or that (say) V and W are important and X does not add anything once the other two have been considered. (If this is the case it probably arises because X is strongly related to either V or W or both and thus X is redundant.) To partial out or hold constant the effects of V and W is to allow for these effects statistically so that it may be seen whether X then predicts any of Y. The most usual techniques for partialling out involve **partial correlation** and MULTIPLE REGRESSION.

PARTICIPANT OBSERVATION
A research method which involves the investigator in becoming a participating member of a natural social group. The method is characterized by *naturalism*, low *reactivity*, discovery more than the testing of **hypotheses**, informal rather than structured methods of data collec-

tion, and an emphasis on the problems of understanding the multiple perspectives of meanings which are inherent in social interaction.

Structured methods of investigation, e.g. standardized questionnaires or EXPERIMENTS, require respondents to assume roles which are artificial and to respond to stimuli in a way which is not conditioned by normal social interaction. The generalizability of responses elicited in structured situations to natural settings has been severely questioned in the behavioural social sciences and participant observation as a tradition originating in twentieth-century anthropology is directed at a naturalistic form of investigation in which actors' meanings are discovered by unobtrusive observation. Participant observation is intended to minimize the reactivity of subjects, i.e. the effect which the knowledge of being observed by an 'outsider' may have on the behaviour and responses of subjects. Data is collected informally as part of the participation of the observer in the group's natural processes and this participation may be covert or, more rarely, open.

Reactivity is of two types: *personal* and *procedural*. The first is concerned with the impact that the behaviour or ascribed characteristics of the investigator (e.g. accent or other social class indications) may have on observed actions. In structured methods of research, personal reactivity is controlled by careful training of interviewers and is checked by replicating an experiment under equivalent conditions but with different interviewers or by comparing response-patterns for different interviewers across comparable samples of respondents in sample surveys. In participant observation, the investigator minimizes the effect of personal characteristics by *joining* or entering a group or organization by the normal method of recruitment and by conducting himself as much like an ordinary member as possible. The observer's *latent identities*, i.e. aspects of his role which are not central to the group's functioning, may disturb social interaction and bias data and have to be carefully managed. Covert participation is less reactive and less likely to raise problems of latent identities and is therefore preferred where practicably and ethically possible.

Procedural reactivity is the effect that the whole structure of a research method may have on subjects' responses; participant observation, because of its emphasis on naturalism, is less procedurally reactive than other methods, particularly if the observer's role is covert rather than open.

The methodological tradition of participant observation is more directed at exploration or the mapping of a field conceptually and the creation of hypotheses than at the testing of well-defined hypotheses, although recent developments in the theory of the method have emphasized testing as well as a *discovery-based approach*. The participant observer enters the field with a focus of interest — a *foreshadowed problem* — but otherwise without **concepts** to select and order observation. The foreshadowed problem may include *sensitizing concepts*, such as the management of death in a terminal ward, or a research idea (as opposed to an hypothesis), such as the socialization of working-class boys in middle-class schools, or a combination of both.

In the initial phases of field-work, data is collected copiously in the form of verbatim notes made unobtrusively and as close to occurrence as possible. The data is sorted for *member-identified-categories*, i.e. the meanings and concepts which are salient to the actors. Interpretation of events or meanings may be checked by the *documentary* or *prospective–retrospective method*. In this a number of alternative meanings or explanations are generated and their ability to capture a meaning is assessed by evaluating them against similar past or future events or meanings.

Throughout field-work a process of *progressive focusing* continues and the categories of analysis and the foreshadowed problem are reformulated as more data is acquired. For example, the socialization of working-class boys in middle-class schools was reformulated as the field was explored for all types of actors (teachers, pupils) as the polarization of the boys into conformist and deviant types with respect to school culture; after reformulation, observation and data collection continued with new categories.

The final phase of exploratory field-work is to theoretically sample similar settings or groups in order to further refine analytic categories arrived at after intensive study of one setting. In *theoretical sampling* no attempt is made to find a statistically representative sample of settings, roles, or individuals; instead a purposive sample is constructed in order to maximize certain relevant differences between settings or to minimize others. Observations are then carried out across the theoretical sample in order to test the applicability of analytic categories across the range of possible actors' perspectives or settings; when categories are no longer changed to accommodate new meanings, the point of *theoretical saturation* has been reached.

Hypotheses discovered in field-work may be tested comparatively by *analytic induction*; in this an attempt is made by the investigator to apply an hypothesis to new but comparable settings where there is an *a priori* expectation of their holding as an explanation. Adaptation of the hypothesis is usually required in order to increase its power of explanation by improving its generalizability. A conscious attempt should be made to find negative instances of an hypothesis in order to emphasize deficiencies in the earlier formulation and to improve it. An hypothesis which has been successively improved and which has been corroborated without the need for further reformulation is a well-grounded one. The extensive time required to carry out analytic induction means that it more frequently remains a goal rather than a practice.

Participant observation is a highly labour-intensive method of investigation because its emphasis on the discovery and mapping of multiple perspectives in social interaction necessarily requires a deep knowledge of the participant culture and a long period of observation. Although it offers distinct advantages over more structured methods of investigation (particularly in the study of deviancy) it is itself subject to potential biases. The observer may, for example, become *obtrusively identified* when by virtue of his participation he becomes identified with a particular faction in a group and is thus deprived of information from other factions. The problem of *marginality* or the maintenance of a role which is both participatory and detached or observational is frequently a difficult problem and *over-rapport* or excessive identification with the subjects may result in the observer adopting the subjects' views as obvious and beyond question and result in failure to test competing interpretations. Such problems can be assessed if the observer maintains a reflexive account simultaneously with the research notes proper. *Reflexivity* requires that the observer is continuously aware of himself as an observer and of his interactions with subjects and any reactivity he may have produced either in responses or in the functioning of the group. Reflexive accounts are ideally written up with the research or analytical report so that a careful comparison may be made between them.

PATH ANALYSIS

A method of breaking down and interpreting linear relationships between variables. The first step is to specify, *a priori*, a structural model involving all the variables of interest. Basically, a *causal hierarchy* is established such that some variables may possible cause others but definitely cannot be caused by them. For instance, sex might cause attitude to children but not the other way around, event A prior to B in time might cause B but not B cause A. A

path diagram (Figure 1) may then be drawn showing how several variables may affect each other.

Diagram 1

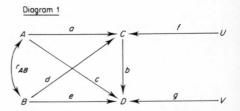

$ABCD$ are variables which have been *measured*. The arrows indicate that A and B may cause C and D and that C may cause D. To complete the picture of the causation of C and D, the *unmeasured* sets of variables, U and V, sometimes known as *disturbances*, are postulated, U causing C and V causing D. A and B are not caused by C or D and are known as *exogenous* (or sometimes **independent**) variables. C and D are known as *endogenous* (or **dependent**) variables. The double-headed arrow between A and B indicates that these variables are related but that there is no hypothesis about the direction of causation. U and V are shown as being unrelated to each other or to A and B.

The path diagram is mathematically represented by a set of *structural equations* which define the mathematical model which has been set up. The letters on the arrows in the diagram are weights or *path coefficients* in the structural equations which in this case are

$$C = aA + dB + fV$$

and

$$D = cA + eB + bC + gV.$$

(Note there is no hypothesis about the direction of causation from A to B and r_{AB} does not enter the structural equations.)

To use the model, A, B, C, and D are measured in a sample of subjects, and from the scores and the correlations between these variables all the path coefficients may be found. The model may then be tested in various ways. For instance, if c is zero, it is refuted. A does not directly cause D. However, if a and b are non-zero, A might still show a correlation with D. This would be due to A causing C which then causes D.

On paper an infinite variety of models might be envisaged. It might be unnecessary to assume that the disturbances are uncorrelated. Any number of variables might be modelled, not all of which might be measured. There is however a sharp mathematical restriction on what might be done, because although the structural equations of any model may easily be written, they cannot always be solved to obtain the path coefficients. The model is then said to be *underidentified*. It can also happen that a model is *overidentified*, in which case more than one different estimate of a path coefficient is possible. This can be turned to account in that if the different estimates are found on testing to be unequal, then the model is refuted.

A very commonly applied path analytic model is one in which it is assumed that the disturbances are uncorrelated with the exogenous variables. For this model the path coefficients are estimated by the *beta weights* or ordinary MULTIPLE REGRESSION equations, e.g. as shown in Figure 2.

Diagram 2

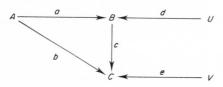

a is the beta weight for A when B is regressed on A, b and c are the beta weights of A and B when C is regressed on A and B, and d and e are estimated by $\sqrt{1 - R_{AB}^2}$ and $\sqrt{1 - R_{CAB}^2}$, where R_{AB} is the simple correlation of A with B and R_{CAB} is the MULTIPLE CORRELATION of C with A and B.

Path analysis can never prove that a particular variable is, in fact, caused in a particular way by other variables. The most that can be done is to say whether or not a particular model of causation is compatible with the data and, if it is, what the strengths of the causal effects might be, given that model.

Path Coefficient A weight in a **structural equation** indicating the degree of direct causation between two variables. Under many circumstances path coefficients are represented by *beta weights*.
See under PATH ANALYSIS

Path Diagram A diagram showing possible causal relationships between variables.
See under PATH ANALYSIS

Pearson r See **Product-Moment Correlation Coefficient**

Percentage Agreement A measure of agreement between two raters given by $100 \times$ proportion of ratings upon which they agree.
See under RELIABILITY

Percentiles Those values of a variable which divide the observations in a data set into 100

intervals each containing an equal number of observations.

Periodic Cycle A periodic cycle exists in a **sampling frame** when the list making up the frame is ordered in such a way that some important variable varies in a systematic and repetitive fashion as one reads down the list, e.g. if the frame consists of married couples arranged wife–husband, wife–husband, etc.

Periodicity See under TIME SERIES ANALYSIS

Personal Reactivity See under PARTICIPANT OBSERVATION

Personality Test A test measuring one or more enduring **personality traits** such as extraversion, dominance, or extrapunitiveness.

Personality Trait An enduring personality characteristic shared by many people and leading to a particular type of perception and/or action over a wide variety of situations.

Perspective See under MODEL, THEORY

Phi-coefficient (ϕ) An estimate of the **product-moment correlation coefficient** which may be used when both variables are dichotomous, e.g. one variable might be pass/fail in an examination and the other yes/no to a particular test item. It is given by:

$$\phi = \frac{BC - AD}{\sqrt{(A + B)(C + D)(A + C)(A + D)}},$$

where A, B, C, and D are the **joint frequencies of** occurrence on the two variables (values in the cells of the **two by two table**).
See also CORRELATION

Pi (Scott's π) A measure of **inter-rater reliability**.
See under RELIABILITY

Pilot Interview A small-scale exploratory interview undertaken to develop questionnaires and to expose and remedy hidden difficulties in a proposed piece of research work.
See under INTERVIEW

Pilot Study A small-scale preliminary study undertaken to test the feasibility of the proposed research and to improve the procedures and methods of measurement.

Placebo Effect An effect whereby a completely inactive clinical treatment (placebo) causes a patient's condition to improve or to seem to improve. The placebo effect has to be controlled when testing new drugs. See also **Hawthorne Effect**

Planned Comparison See under **Unplanned comparison**

Platykurtic See under **Kurtosis**

Point Biserial Correlation Coefficient An estimate of the product-moment correlation coefficient which may be used when one of the variables is a dichotomy and the other is measured on an interval or ratio scale. It is given by:

$$r_{\text{pb}} = \frac{(\bar{Y}_1 - \bar{Y})}{s_y} \sqrt{\frac{n_1}{n_2}},$$

where n_1 is the number of observations in category 1 of the dichotomy, n_2 is the number of observations in category 2, $\bar{Y}_1$ is the mean on the interval of variable of those cases which fall into category 1 on the dichotomy, $\bar{Y}$ is the overall mean of the interval variable, and s_y its standard deviation.
See also CORRELATION

Point Estimate See under ESTIMATION

Point Prevalence See **Prevalence**

Poisson Distribution A theoretical distribution which fits circumstances where the probability of an event is low and is proportional to a continuous variable. For instance, if the probability of seeing a car on a short piece of road is 0.2 (length of road is the continuous variable), then if a large number of experiments were carried out in each of which the road was observed ten times, the frequency of cars seen in the experiments would probably follow a Poisson distribution. Both the **mean** number seen and the **variance** would equal 2, i.e. $N \times p$, where N is the number of observations per experiment and p the probability of occurrence of a single event. In shape the Poisson distribution resembles a highly skewed NORMAL DISTRIBUTION.
See also **distribution**

Population Any group of people or observations which includes all possible members in that category, e.g. all 6-year-old children living in London.

Population Parameter A descriptive summary of some characteristic of a **population**. Examples are the **mean, median**, and **standard deviation**. The term *statistic* (or **sample statistic**) is used for the same type of entity when used to describe a **sample**.

Population Projection A forecast of the future size and composition (age and sex) of a human population — usually a national one — based on assumptions about fertility, mortality, and migration.
The projection starts from a base year (t) whose **age-specific fertility** and death-rates are applied to age **cohorts** of the population in year t in order to calculate survivors (from death-rates) and live births (fertility). Projection may continue for successive years ($t + 1$, $t + 2$, etc.) ahead of the base year allowing for cohorts ageing steadily and thus requiring new age-specific rates. Projection errors are cumulative and systematic because rates are fixed in the base year and may (and, for fertility, usually will) change. Population projections are therefore continually revised to use the most recent birth-and death-rates, and are increasingly prone to error the further ahead a projection is made.

Positive Skewness A **unimodal** distribution is said to be **positively skewed** when the **mode** occurs towards the lower end of the distribution. In this situation the mode is less than the **median** ($\tilde{X}$), which is less than the **mean** ($\bar{X}$), thus:

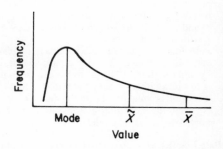

Posterior Probability See under BAYESIAN STATISTICS

Power of a Statistical Test The power of a statistical test reflects its efficiency at correctly rejecting a **null hypothesis** at a particular **significance** level. The fewer observations needed to obtain a statistically significant result, the more powerful the test. **Parametric tests**, where these are appropriate, are the most powerful. The power of other tests is usually expressed as a percentage of the power of the most appropriate parametric test — e.g. the power of the **median test** for large N is about 63 per cent compared to the *t*-test. Thus, for the situation where both tests could be applied, if the *t*-test rejects the null hypothesis with 63 observations, the median test would require 100.

Practice Effect   See under **Order Effect**

Precision   See under **Sampling Error**

Pre-coded Question   A question to which the respondent's answer is restricted to a set list of alternatives, each of which has been assigned a code in advance. Synonymous with **closed question**.

Predictive Validity   A test has predictive validity if it may be used to make accurate predictions of future performance.
See also VALIDITY

Predictor Variable   A predictor, **explanatory**, or **independent variable** is one which a researcher is varying (by experimental manipulation) or observing (in non-experimental work) in order to predict some other variable. The three terms are interchangeable in use, though not originally in theory.

Present State Examination (PSE)   A standardized clinical interview which aims to assess a person's current psychiatric symptomatology and to provide a diagnosis if appropriate. It consists of a series of questions asked in a standard form supplemented by observation of the person's behaviour during interview. When the answer to any question indicates that a symptom may be present, the examiner probes as appropriate in order to confirm this and to ascertain the severity of the symptom. Where certain profiles of symptoms of sufficient severity are present, a psychiatric diagnosis may be made. The threshold for a psychiatric diagnosis is defined by an eight-point *index of definition*. Levels one through four of this index, while reflecting increasing levels of symptomatology, indicate absence of a conventional psychiatric diagnosis. Level five provides a minimal basis for a diagnosis while levels six through eight make it increasingly certain that one can be assigned. The PSE allows classification of disorders into symptoms, independent subclasses, or overlapping syndromes and there is a computer programme, *CATEGO*, designed to perform the classification. Its RELIABILITY and VALIDITY are adequate provided that the personnel administering it have been trained in its use. There is a short form available for population surveys.

Prevalence   The *period prevalence* of a disease or condition is its rate of occurrence in a given population in a given time period. For example, the prevalence of psychoses in 'blanktown' might be 6 per 1,000 population per annum. If the time period is brief, e.g. a single day, the term *point prevalence* is applied. Prevalence is to be distinguished from **incidence** which is the rate of occurrence of new cases within a population during a specified time period.

Primary Sampling Unit   The first set of clusters in multi-stage cluster sampling.
See also, **Cluster Sampling,** SAMPLING THEORY AND METHODS, **Probability Proportional to Size**

Principal Components Analysis   A factor analytic method of deriving a smaller number of factors to represent a larger number of tests. This method assumes that all the **variance** of all the tests may be assigned to the common factors to be extracted. There is no attempt to keep either the **error variance** or the *specific variance* of the tests out of the factors. The method extracts **orthogonal factors**.
See also FACTOR ANALYSIS

Prior Probability   See under BAYESIAN STATISTICS

Probability Density Function   A mathematical equation specifying a theoretical frequency distribution such as the **normal distribution** or the **Poisson distribution.**.
See under DISTRIBUTION

Probability Distribution   The set of possible probabilities of a RANDOM VARIABLE

Probability Proportional to Size   See under SAMPLING THEORY AND METHODS

Probability Sample   Another term for **Random Sample**

Probe   A supplementary question asked to clarify the meaning of an answer. In order to avoid influencing the answers, probes may often be put in very general terms such as 'can you tell me more about that?'

Procedural Reactivity   See under PARTICIPANT OBSERVATION

Product-Moment Correlation Coefficient (*r*)   The most common index of the correlation between two variables (*X* and *Y*). It is theoretically given by the formula:

$$r = \frac{\text{cov}}{s_X s_Y},$$

where s_X and s_Y are the standard deviations of the variables *X* and *Y* and cov is their **covariance**. Both variables should be measured on an **interval** or **ratio scale**. For further details see CORRELATION.

87

Profile The significant features of an individual, group, or organization.

A common specific meaning is a graphical representation of an individual's scores on a set of tests.

Progressive Focusing See under PARTICIPANT OBSERVATION

Progressive Matrices Tests Non-verbal **intelligence tests** devised by J.C. Raven in which the subject has to select, from a number of alternatives, the item which best completes a pattern. There are versions (with **norms**) for general use, for use with very intelligent people, and for cross-cultural and other purposes.

PROJECTIVE TECHNIQUES
Personality tests which are distinctive in that the subject has to respond to an ambiguous stimulus. In doing so he is supposed to reveal aspects of his personality such as his needs, attitudes, and unconscious desires.

The two most widely known projective techniques are the *Rorschach test* and the *Thematic Apperception test (TAT)*. The stimuli in the Rorschach test consist of ten standard 'inkblots'. Five of these are printed in varying shades of grey. The other five are either partly or completely composed of other colours. The subject responds to each blot by telling the examiner what he sees in it. There are various scoring systems, mainly aiming to arrive at a global overall picture of the subject's personality (although estimates of such separate traits as intelligence and creativity may often be derived).

The stimuli for the original TAT consist of pictures. There are four different but overlapping sets of these for men, women, boys, and girls. The subject is asked to make up a story about each picture, describing what led up to it, what the characters are thinking and feeling, and what the outcome will be. These stories may then be analysed to reveal the subject's needs and the environmental forces acting on him.

There are several variants of both the Rorschach test and the TAT, and the ambiguous stimuli used in projective techniques are not confined to inkblots and pictures. Other examples of stimuli used are single words, cartoon drawings, incomplete sentences, and toys. The advantages of projective techniques lie in their flexibility as means of acquiring unusual data about subjects, in their inherent interest to most subjects, and in their non-threatening nature. The disadvantages stem mainly from their intrinsically dubious **reliability** and **validity**. For example, it is difficult to be certain a character hitting another character in a TAT story fairly represents a need for aggression on the part of the subject; that this need is not confined solely to the realm of fantasy, that it is not a stereotyped response to that picture, and is not just a passing symptom exhibited by the subject. Furthermore, it is hard to be sure the need would have been elicited, noticed, and scored in exactly the same way by any other examiner.

Many attempts, however, have been made to grapple with these basic problems. For example, in some cases scoring systems have been carefully developed and scorers thoroughly trained to reach a high level of **inter-rater reliability**. Validity has sometimes been checked by comparing responses of people known to have a certain need with those of people known not to have this need, and in some projective tests there are *parallel forms* and/or sets of **norms**.

Projective Test See PROJECTIVE TECHNIQUES

Proportionate Stratification See under SAMPLING THEORY AND METHODS

Q

Q-mode A Q-mode factor analysis aims to see if individual *people* have similarities in their **profiles** on a set of variables. This is to be contrasted with **R-mode** which assesses whether *scores* on different variables group together.

Q-technique An approach focusing on whether individuals agree with each other across a series of tests, or alternatively whether the same individual gets the same pattern of scores at different times or under different conditions. A Q-type factor analysis investigates whether there are types of *people* by seeing if different people's profiles of scores on a series of tests go together in recognizable patterns. This may be contrasted with **R-type factor analysis** where correlations between test *scores* are the focus of interest.
See also CLUSTER ANALYSIS

Qualitative and Quantitative Measurement Measurement or classification at the **nominal level** where observations are assigned to categories (e.g. boy/girl) with no implications of relative value or size is qualitative measurement. If numbers are used to code the observation categories then they have no more significance than do words although they are more convenient for data processing. A **dummy variable** in **regression** (often termed a qualitative variable) may code 1 = male, 2 = female, but the only property of numbers that is used here is their uniqueness; that is, 1 is distinct from 2 but equally distinct from 1,002. A number code may be changed arbitrarily, but as long as the categories themselves are not changed the information contained in the classification of a set of observations is the same. All that is required in qualitative measurement is that coding, whether numbers are used or not, is consistent.
Once any of the properties of numbers are used in addition to uniqueness then it is legitimate to speak of quantitative measurement. If the ordinal properties of numbers are assigned to separate observations as in an **ordinal scale**, then a variable is regarded as a single property which has different intensities of value even if it is only possible to say that the number 3 on the scale is greater than the number 2.
There are different conventions in the social sciences on the use of qualitative and quantitative. All agree that **interval measurement** is quantitative but some disciplines (notably economics) regard anything less than interval measurement as qualitative, whereas others use the term only for nominal measurement.
See also SCALE OF MEASUREMENT

Quantiles A set of values which divides the **frequency distribution** of a variable into a number of segments each of which contains an equal number of observations. The spacing of the quantile-values along the variable scale will depend upon the shape of the frequency distribution; they will not be equally spaced except in the very rare case of a rectangular distribution.
The general term quantile has specific examples such as *quartiles* — division into four segments each containing 25 per cent of the frequency — and *deciles* where the variable scale is divided into ten segments.
See also **Interquartile Range**

Quantitative See under **Qualitative and Quantitative Measurement**

Quartile Deviation See under **Interquartile Range and Interquartile Ratio**

Quartile Dispersion Coefficient See under **Interquartile Range and Interquartile Ratio**

Quartiles Those values of a variable below which lie 25, 50,, and 75 per cent of the observations in a data set, known respectively as the laver quartile (Q_1), median, and upper quartile (Q_3).

Quasi-experiment An experiment where the experimenter only has partial control and is unable to manipulate the **experimental treatments** and/or assign subjects randomly to groups. For instance, if one wished to experiment on whether broken homes produce juvenile delinquency, a number of married couples would be randomly assigned to be deliberately separated by the experimenter and another group of married couples would be kept together, whether they wished it or not. The offspring of both groups would be followed up to see whether they became delinquent. This clearly is not possible and the best that can be

Questionnaire

done is a quasi-experiment in which couples are selected who fit into the two groupings. Proper random assignment is quite impossible. The effect of such constraints on experimental manipulation is to make causal interpretations of any results much more difficult. **Extraneous variables** will not necessarily balance out over the various groups and may easily account for any effect found.

See also EXPERIMENT, COHORT ANALYSIS, CROSS-SECTIONAL DESIGN, LONGITUDINAL STUDY

Questionnaire A predetermined, written list of questions which may be answered by a subject, without supervision or explanation by an interviewer. A well-developed questionnaire has clear unambiguous instructions, but otherwise may contain both open-ended questions and questions to which the answers are to be chosen from a list of alternatives. It may cover just one topic or many.

See also **Interview Schedule, Open Question, Closed Question,** ATTITUDE SCALING, STANDARDIZATION, INTERVIEW

Quota Sampling In quota sampling the populatio is divided **a priori** into subgroups (e.g. social class) and the interviewers have to find a quota of people from each subgroup so that the subgroups are in the same proportion in the sample as they are in the population. The representativeness of a quota sample is only assured on the divisions defined at the outset. The sample may well be unrepresentative on all other variables which could be used to divide the population.

See also **Non-probability Sample, Stratified Sample**, and SAMPLING THEORY AND METHODS

R

Random Allocation People are allocated randomly to different groups in an experiment, so that it is purely a matter of chance which person ends up in which group. The aim is to make the various groups comparable on all factors except the **independent variable** which can then be assigned by the researcher.

Random Error In statistical theory random error is error of measurement which may stem from any one of a large number of uncontrolled sources. It is assumed that over a large number of cases random error will balance out, i.e. that there is no tendency for the errors to be predominantly in one direction rather than another. Thus, for large samples, **measures of central tendency** such as the arithmetic mean will be unaffected by random error. It is to be contrasted with **systematic error**, which does not cancel out over a large number of cases. Random error is sometimes referred to as 'noise', particularly in modelling.
See also SAMPLING THEORY AND METHODS

Random Error Coefficient (*RE*) A measure of **inter-rater reliability**.
See under RELIABILITY

Random Numbers Numbers generated at random but in such a way that all the numbers appear an equal number of times in the overall table. Tables of random numbers are used for the selection of **random samples**.

Random Sample A sample in which all members of the population have a known chance of selection, this chance, for any population member, being greater than zero and less than one (i.e. certainty). Also termed a **probability sample**.
See also SAMPLING THEORY AND METHODS

Random Sampling Sampling so that every element in the population has a known, non-zero probability of being selected.
See also SAMPLING THEORY AND METHODS

RANDOM VARIABLE
This is a variable which assigns numerical values to a set of events each of which may possibly occur. For instance, the toss of a penny might be specified by a random variable

taking the value 1 for heads and 0 for tails, or the weather at some given place and time might be characterized by 1 for sunny, 2 for cloudy, and 3 for raining. The numerical values assigned need have no particular significance — the values +20 and −2 for heads and tails would be just as valid as 1 and 0. However, it is often convenient to use 1 and 0, or to use numbers already implied in the events, e.g. for throwing a die it is obviously convenient to use the numbers 1 to 6 to specify the different outcomes.

Random variables which may take only two values are sometimes known as *indicator* random variables. Otherwise random variables may be *discrete* when they take only a limited number of values at certain intervals or *continuous* when they may assume any value between two extremes. The number of cakes of different sizes sold by a bakery on a given day would be discrete, while the total weight would be continuous.

To each value of a discrete random variable there corresponds a probability of occurrence. The probabilities for a whole set of values sum to one. Thus, if a coin is tossed twice and the outcomes are specified as 1 = heads twice, 2 = once heads and once tails and 3 = tails twice, the probabilities of 1 and 3 are both ¼ and that of 2 is ½. The sum of the probabilities is 1. The same holds for continuous random variables when they are divided into class intervals and the sum of the probabilities is obtained over all the class intervals. The set of possible probabilities of a random variable is known as its *probability distribution*. Some commonly encountered probability distributions are the standard NORMAL DISTRIBUTION, the **binomial distribution**, and the **Poisson distribution**.

The **mean** or *expected value* of a random variable is the sum of the possible values of the random variable each multiplied by the probability of the occurrence. In the coin-tossing example above this is $3 \times \frac{1}{4} + 2 \times \frac{1}{2} + 1 \times \frac{1}{4} = 2$. The **variance** of a random variable can also be found. That of a discrete random variable is given by $\sum_{1}^{j} (x_i - \bar{x})^2 p_{x_i}$, where x_i is the *i*th value of a random variable which can take the values 1 to *j*, $\bar{x}$ is the expected value and p_{x_i} is the probability associated with x_i. Thus, for the coin-tossing example the variance is

$$(1^2 \times \tfrac{1}{4}) + (0^2 \times \tfrac{1}{2}) + (1^2 \times \tfrac{1}{4}) = \tfrac{1}{2}.$$

The **standard deviation** is therefore $\sqrt{\tfrac{1}{2}} = 0.707$
A *standardized random variable* is one in which each value has been transformed by subtracting the mean and dividing by the standard deviation. In the coin-tossing example this yields values of $+1\cdot414$, 0, and -1.414. Standardized random variables have mean value 0 and standard deviation 1.
See also DISTRIBUTION

Randomization The balancing up of **extraneous variables** which occurs when large numbers of subjects are allocated to different groups at random. Thus, if two groups of schoolchildren are randomly selected, one to be taught by a new method the other not, if the groups are large enough and the process of selection has been truly random, extraneous variables such as social class, intelligence, and interest in the subject being taught will on average balance out and are said to be randomized across the groups.

Randomize the Order A method of controlling for the effects of the order of presentation of two or more experimental treatments given to the same subjects, used instead of **counterbalancing the order**, for instance where there are many treatments to be presented. The order is changed randomly, so that each possible order is equally likely to occur, and therefore no particular treatment occurs always at the beginning or at the end of the experimental session.
See also **Order Effect**

Range The difference between the largest and smallest values of a distribution.
See also **Measures of Dispersion**

Rank Order See **Ranking**

Rank Order Correlation Coefficient (r_s) An estimate of the **product-moment correlation coefficient** for data in the form of ranks. It is given by

$$r_s = 1 - \frac{6\Sigma d^2}{n(n^2 - 1)},$$

where n is the number of pairs of observations and d is the difference in rank between members of a given pair.
See also CORRELATION

Ranking The process of ordering a set of observations on a scale, but with no implication that the intervals between ranks are equal.
See also **Concordant Rankings**

Rate The number of events occurring in a given time period divided by the number of such events that could have occurred.

Rating A number indicating an evaluation of something along some given dimension.

Ratio Scale An **interval scale** which has a true fixed zero point. On this scale not only would 20 be as far above 15 as 15 is above 10, but 20 would represent twice as much of the quantity being measured as 10.
See also **Scale of Measurement**

Ratio Variable A variable which is measureable on a **ratio scale**.

Raw Data Observations as originally recorded, i.e. with no operations, transformations, or re-categorization performed on the numbers or values. Percentages, **index numbers, means, standard deviations, standardized scores**, etc. are not raw data since they are constructs from at least two observations and mathematical or statistical operations will have been performed in order to obtain them.

Reactivity See under PARTICIPANT OBSERVATION

Redundancy Index See under **Canonical Correlation Analysis**

Reflexivity see under PARTICIPANT OBSERVATION

Refusal Rate The refusal rate in a survey is the number of people originally sampled who refuse to take part divided by the total number *contacted*. It is usually expressed as a percentage.

Registrar-General's Classification of Occupations A classification of the population into 17 socio-economic groups intended to contain people whose social, cultural, and recreational standards and behaviour are similar. The classification is carried out on the basis of employment status and occupation. There is also a broader classification of the 17 groups into five ordered social classes, labelled: I professional occupations, II intermediate occupations, III skilled occupations, IV partly skilled occupations, and V unskilled occupations. It is this classification which is frequently used in surveys to represent an individual's social class. Social class III is often further subdivided into IIIa and IIIb, basically non-manual and manual skilled occupations.

There is an extensive index assigning many thousands of occupations to the classification system.

Registrar-General's Statistical Review Annual summary of the statistics of births, death, causes of death, and marriage and divorce collected by the local registrars of births, marriages, and death in England and Wales. Tabulations are national and regional and offer intercensal estimates of total population as well as **age- and sex-specific death-rates**, marriage rates by sex and age group, **birth-rates**, and still-birth and infant mortality rates, **standardized mortality ratios**, and **fertility-**rates.

See also CENSUS

REGRESSION ANALYSIS

The use of multiple regression techniques to test theories about how several **independent variables** may combine to predict a **dependent variable**.

In *stepwise regression analysis* the independent variables are entered into a **regression equation** (see MULTIPLE REGRESSION) one at a time. After the entry of each variable the effect is usually judged in terms of extra **variance** explained in the dependent variable. If this is not significantly different from zero, then the independent variable just entered probably has no extra predictive validity over and above the variables already entered. There is no need for the independent variables to be independent of each other. For example, suppose variables *A, B,* and *C* are entered in that order to predict a fourth variable (*Y*). When *C* is finally entered on top of *A* and *B* the effects of both *A* and *B* are statistically controlled (**partialled out**) and any *additional* effect of *C* may be seen. Any kind of variable (e.g. **nominal, interval, dichotomous, continuous**) may be used and the **interactions** between variables may also be entered and assessed separately (see below). This flexibility is a great advantage, particularly in the survey situation where experimental manipulation is usually impossible.

Some method of specifying the order in which the independent variables are to be entered is necessary. In stepwise regression this is usually determined *post hoc* by entering first the variable which explains the most variance and then following with the one which adds most after that, etc. A much better method, i.e. that of *hierarchical regression analysis*, is

to determine the order *a priori*. The interest may be in the effects of variable *C* with extraneous variables *A* and *B* controlled, in which case *A* and *B* are entered together on step 1 and *C* on step 2. If *causation* rather than just *prediction* is at issue, a *causal hierarchy* of variables will be sought such that variable *A* can cause *B* and *B* cause *C* but *C* is not likely to cause *A* or *B* and *B* is not likely to cause *A*. The variables will then be entered in the order *A,B,C*. If Some pre-established theory is to be tested such that *C* will have no effect once *A* and *B* are taken into account, the order will again be *A,B,C*.

If interest is purely in the total effect of all the independent variables, then *simultaneous regression analysis* is appropriate, all the independent variables being entered together in one single step and the total effect assessed. Three commonly encountered statistics in regression analysis are the MULTIPLE CORRELATION coefficient (*R*), the **standardized partial regression coefficient** (β), and the **partial correlation coefficient** (*p_r*). *R*, which can vary between 0 and +1, is an index of the total degree of relationship between the independent variables (X_1, X_2, etc.) and the dependent variable (*Y*). β_i is the weight to be applied to variable X_i in the regression equation with all variables in **standardized** form. P_{ri} is the partial correlation between variable X_i and *Y* with all the other independent variables partialled out. R^2, β_i^2, and P_{ri}^2 are all of interest. R^2 represents the total variance explained by all the variables. In a geometrical analogy, the variables may be represented by overlapping circles of equal size. R^2 then indicates the shaded area in Figure 1.

Figure 1

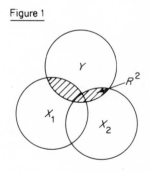

β_i^2 and P_{ri}^2 (and therefore β_i and P_{ri}) are both indicators of the unique contribution of an independent variable with the others partialled out, thus:

Figure 2

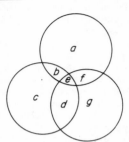

$$\beta_i^2 = \frac{f}{f + g}, \quad \text{while} \quad P_{ri}^2 = \frac{f}{f + a}$$

An independent variable (X_1) may itself have no correlation with the dependent variable but can enhance the multiple R and increase the variance explained if it correlates with another independent variable (X_2) which does relate to Y. This phenomenon is known as **suppression** because X_1 is suppressing some of the irrelevant variance in X_2 and making it a better predictor of Y.

Nominal variables (e.g. Catholic, Protestant, or neither) may be entered as sets of **dummy variables** reflecting the presence or absence of categories. In general it requires one less dummy variable than the number of nominal categories. (Catholic, Protestant, or neither would be represented by two dummy variables Catholic/not Catholic, Protestant/not Protestant. The 'neither' category is covered by the values 'not Catholic' in conjunction with 'not Protestant'.) **Interactions** between variables may be entered as products after the entry of the 'simple' variable which must be in the equation first. For example, the effect of the interaction between variable A and B is obtained by entering A and B first and then entering a new variable consisting simply of the product $A \times B$.

Two major difficulties with the technique concern the assumptions that it requires and the phenomenon of **multicollinearity**. The assumptions underlying regression analysis are (1) that the relationship between the variables is linear, (2) that the dependent variable (Y) is normally distributed, and (3) that Y has the same variance within each value of each dependent variable. In practice the technique is robust to violation of the assumptions. If they are not met then it is sometimes possible to find a TRANSFORMATION of the Y-variable

which will improve the situation. Fortunately, when the relationship is made linear, satisfying condition (1), it is usually found that the other two conditions are also fulfilled. Another way of tackling the problem of non-linearity of regression is to use several variables to represent different aspects of a relationship. Thus, for example, an independent variable might be split into three parts: a linear component, a quadratic component, and a cubic component. These parts can be entered as separate independent variables and tested for significance.

The problem of multicollinearity arises when the independent variables are highly correlated with each other and thus explaining much the same part of the variance in the dependent variable. Serious multicollinearity leads to highly unstable results from sample to sample and makes the calculation of the various regression coefficients hazardous because rounding errors become important. In very extreme cases the calculation may be impossible.

See also MULTIPLE CORRELATION, MULTIPLE REGRESSION

Regression Coefficient The weight (B) to be applied when a single **independent variable** (X) is used in a **regression equation** to predict a **dependent variable** (Y), i.e. the equation

$$Y = bX + C,$$

where C is a constant.

Regression Constant See under MULTIPLE REGRESSION

Regression Equation An equation of the form either

$$\hat{Y} = \beta_1 X_1 + \beta_2 X_2 + \dots + \beta_n X_n$$

or

$$\hat{Y} = b_1 X_1 + b_2 X_2 + \dots + b_n X_n + \text{constant,}$$

expressing the best possible linear relationship between a prediction $\hat{Y}$ and the set of independent variables $X_1, X_2, \dots, X_n$.
See under MULTIPLE REGRESSION

Regression Line The straight line of best fit to the **joint distribution** of two variables.
See also MULTIPLE REGRESSION, REGRESSION ANALYSIS, **Least Squares Criterion**

Regression Model See under MULTIPLE REGRESSION, REGRESSION ANALYSIS

Regression to the Mean The tendency for the value of a second observation made on an individual to be closer to the group mean than a first observation of the same variable. Regression to the mean arises because of error of measurement. At the extremes of a distribution it is more likely that any measurement error in an observation has been away from, rather than towards, the mean. Hence, assuming the errors are random, a second testing on the same individual tends to result in the score regressing towards the mean.

Regression Weight   A general term for a **weight** applied in a **regression equation**. The term may be loosely used to mean **regression coefficient, standardized regression coefficient, partial regression coefficient** or **standardized partial regression coefficient.**

RELATIONSHIP

Relationship and *association* are virtually synonymous. Both are used when there appears to be some connection between the values of one variable and the values of another but neither term implies causality.

The term relationship rather than association would usually be used when talking of a mathematical equation which provides a precise model of the connection between the variables. The connection may take many forms: high values on one variable may go with high values on the other (e.g. body height and body weight); high values on one might be seen with low values on the other (e.g. social class and propensity to commit detected crimes), or certain categories on one variable may be connected with certain categories on another (children of rich parents attending private schools).

Relationships are strong when knowing the values on one variable enables good predictions to be made of the values on the other, and relationships are weak when such a prediction is little better than a guess. They are positive when high values on one variable go with high values on the other (and low values with low values) and negative when high values on one variable go with low values on the other.

A *causal relationship* is one in which the occurrence of certain values on variable *A* lead directly to the occurence of certain values on variable *B* (e.g. the relationship between driving fast and having traffic accidents). Not all relationships are causal: height and intelligence are positively (though only slightly) related. Height does not cause intelligence, nor does being intelligent make one taller. Other factors, such as a better diet in childhood, underlie the relationship and operate as independent causes of both variables which therefore **covary**. A non-causal relationship of this kind is sometimes termed a **spurious**

relationship. Although the relationship itself is real, its interpretation as a causal one is spurious. A **linear relationship** between variables X and Y is one which may be reasonably (not necessarily exactly) be represented by an equation of the form:

$$Y = aX_1 + bX_2 + cX_3 + \dots + nX_n + \text{constant},$$

which is a linear equation necessarily containing no exponents of X greater than 1. For the two-variable case, a graph of Y against X (a **scattergram**) has the points tending to fall about a straight line.

The terms **curvilinear relationship** and **non-linear relationship** are used when this is not the case. The former term is often used quite generally but it implies that the **joint distribution** is in the shape of a curve of some kind — e.g. an exponential, parabolic, or quadratic curve. Such relationships must be modelled by non-linear equations or polynomials.

There are many mathematical formulae whose aim is to measure the strength of a relationship. Linear relationships are usually measured by **correlation coefficients** — a relationship between two variables being covered by a simple correlation (e.g. the **Pearson** r or **Kendall's tau**) and between one variable and several others by the MULTIPLE CORRELATION COEFFICIENT (R)..

An index of the strength of a curvilinear relationship is the **correlation ratio** η (eta). this is defined as:

$$\eta_{YX} = \sqrt{1 - \frac{S^2_{aY}}{S^2_Y}},$$

where η_{YX} is the correlation ratio for predicting Y from X, S^2_{aY} is obtained by working out the deviation of each Y score from the **array mean** of the Y scores, squaring these and summing over all the Y scores and dividing by the total N, and S^2_Y is the **variance** of the Y scores.

The correlation ratio yields no information about the shape of the relationship, it merely indicates (if significant) that there is a relationship of some sort. η always exceeds r except when there is a perfect linear relationship, in which case both η and $r = 1$. If η significantly exceeds r (significance ascertained by analysis of variance techniques) then it is reasonable to assume that the relationship between Y and X is not linear.

Unlike the Pearson r, the correlation ratio is an **asymmetric measure**. η for predicting Y from X does not have the same value as η for predicting X from Y, even on the same data. In general, an **asymmetric relationship** is one which has a clear direction; causal relationships are necessarily asymmetric in the direction of cause to effect.

For example, 'smoking causes lung cancer' but lung cancer does not cause smoking.

Other examples of asymmetric measures of relationships are **Somer's** d_{YX} for two-by-two tables, and **lambda**$_{YX}$.

See also CAUSATION

Relative Frequency Distribution In a relative frequency distribution the frequencies for each class interval are expressed as percentages of the total number of cases.

See also **Frequency Distribution**

RELIABILITY The extent to which a test would give consistent results if applied more than once to the same people under standard conditions. Reliability coefficients are indices (usually CORRELATION coefficients) assessing reliability. There are various ways of obtaining these. In the *split-half method* the scores on a randomly chosen half of the test questions are correlated with the scores on the other half. *Cronbach's alpha* is the mean value of all the possible split-half reliability coefficients. These two coefficients are examples of *internal consistency measures*: they both depend on the amount of agreement between the different items on a single administration of a test. In the *test-retest method* a correlation is obtained between scores on the test administered to the same people on separate occasions. The *alternate forms method* is similar except that a second form of the test, as nearly equivalent to the first as possible, is administered on the second occasion. Increasing the number of items in a test will normally improve its reliability, and the extent of the improvement may be assessed by the *Spearman–Brown formula*. In its most general form this is:

$$r_n = \frac{mr_0}{1 + (m - 1)r_0} ,$$

where r_n is a correlation coefficient representing the improved reliability of a test which has been lengthened m-fold and which originally had a reliability of r_0.

Reliability coefficients assume that the errors made on the various items of the test are random and uncorrelated with the item scores or with each other. Particularly for internal consistency methods, this may not be so. For instance, for a person with a headache the total scores on both halves of a test might be too low. The effect of this is to give a spuriously high reliability. On the other hand, the test–retest method suffers from memory carry-over and from changes in the characteristic being measured between the two testings. The

alternate forms method avoids memory carryover but still suffers from the latter drawback.

Inter-rater reliability refers to the extent to which two raters making the same series of judgements would get the same results. The method of measurement depends on circumstances. Among such methods are *percentage agreement*, the *phi coefficient (φ)*, *kappa (κ)*, *pi (π)*, *random error coefficient (RE)* and *weighted kappa (κ_w)*. Of these the phi coefficient is applicable only to **two by two tables** and weighted kappa to $k \times k$ tables with k greater than two. For the following table

		Rater 1		
		Category 1	Category 2	Total
	Category 1	a	b	P_1
Rater 2	Category 2	c	d	P_2
	Total	q_1	q_2	1

where a, b, c, and d are the proportions of ratings in each cell:

Percentage agreement = $100 (a + d)$

$$\phi = \frac{ad - bc}{\sqrt{P_1 P_2 q_1 q_2}}$$

$$\kappa = \frac{(a + d) - \Sigma P_i q_i}{1 - \Sigma P_i q_i} = \frac{(a + d) - (P_1 q_1 + P_2 q_2)}{1 - (P_1 q_1 + P_2 q_2)}$$

$$= \frac{2(ad - bc)}{P_1 q_2 + q_1 P_2}$$

$$\pi = \frac{(a + d) - \Sigma \left(\dfrac{P_i + q_i}{2}\right)^2}{1 - \Sigma \left(\dfrac{P_i + q_1}{2}\right)^2} ,$$

$$RE = (a + d) - (b + c).$$

Percentage agreement is the least satisfactory because it makes no allowance for agreement by chance and can therefore be spuriously high. The other four all take account of chance agreement, but in different ways.

Weighted kappa allows disagreements to be weighted according to how serious they are (For two by two tables it simplifies to kappa.) It is given by

$$\kappa_w = 1 - \frac{\Sigma V_{ij} P_{oij}}{\Sigma V_{ij} P_{cij}} ,$$

where V_{ij} is a weight assigned by the experimenter to a disagreement occurring in the ijth cell, P_{oij} is the observed proportion of ratings in this cell, and P_{cij} the proportion expected by chance.

Reliability Coefficient See under RELIABILITY

Repeated Contact Design   A design in which the same subjects are contacted on more than one occasion.
See also LONGITUDINAL STUDY

Repeated measures   The same measures assessed on the same people at different points in time.
See also LONGITUDINAL STUDY, EXPERIMENT

Repertory Grid   A two-way inventory. The object is to see to which of a number of concepts, situations, people, etc. the subject applies certain other concepts. Thus, one might want to know which people he decribes as good and bad, happy and unhappy, honest and dishonest. The subject has to decide in what important way two specific people known to him (e.g. wife, ex-girlfriend) are alike and different from a third person. This usually reveals a salient personality dimension. The procedure is continued using different sets of three people to elicit all such dimensions. The grid which results, consisting of people along the top and personality dimensions (constructs) down the side, can then be completed by the subject.

Replication   The collection of several different observations under identical experimental conditions.
See also **Cross-validation**

Representational Measurement   See under **Index Measurement**

Representative Sample   A sample, drawn from a **population**, which accurately reflects all the important characteristics of that population. This allows valid generalization of results from the sample to the whole population.
See also SAMPLING THEORY AND METHODS

Reproducibility   See **Coefficient of Reproducibility, Guttman Scale,** *and* ATTITUDE SCALING

Research Design   The overall plan of research ,intended to yield specific unambiguous answers to research questions or to allow useful new hypotheses to emerge. The design to be employed depends on many factors. For further details see entries under EXPERIMENT, CROSS-SECTIONAL DESIGN, LONGITUDINAL STUDY, COHORT ANALYSIS, INTERVIEW, BIAS, and SAMPLING THEORY AND METHODS.

Research Diagnostic Criteria (RDC)   A set of criteria for psychiatric diagnoses, applicable to patients suffering functional disorders. There are 25 major diagnostic categories, some of which may be subdivided on a number of overlapping dimensions. The necessary information for an RDC diagnosis may be gathered from any sufficiently detailed and reliable case material, but is better obtained using the **Schedule for Affective Disorders and Schizophrenia (SADS)** which was specially developed for the purpose. Both current and past episodes of illness may be diagnosed and the RDC allow each diagnosis to be designated as definitely absent, probably absent, and definitely present. The RELIABILITY and VALIDITY of diagnoses made using the RDC are good and the RDC have been widely used in research, particularly in the U.S.A.

Residual   In many statistical procedures, such as **classical test theory,** ANALYSIS OF VARIANCE, MULTIPLE REGRESSION, and FACTOR ANALYSIS, a person's score on a test or variable is broken down into a component or components which can be explained or predicted and a component which cannot. The latter is known as the residual or alternatively as the **error score**.

Residual Mean Square   See under ANALYSIS OF VARIANCE

Respondent   A person chosen to be approached in a survey (whether or not he or she finally takes part). 'Respondent' and 'subject' are often used synonymously, but subject is more appropriate for experiments rather than surveys.

Response   This can have its ordinary connotation of an answer to a question, or it can mean the proportion of the people sampled who finally reply to a questionnaire, take part in a survey, etc.

Response Bias   A systematic bias or set pervading someone's answers to a test. **Acquiescence response set** is a tendency to answer positively to questions on a questionnaire irrespective of their content. Acquiescence can be controlled by wording questions so that for half of them a 'yes' and for the other half a 'no' answer represents presence of the trait or attitude being measured. **Extreme responding** is the tendency to select extreme alternatives to items in a test. **Social desirability** is a response set in which one responds, either consciously or unconsciously, in such a way as to leave a good impression. Methods for detecting and controlling social desirability include incorporation of **lie scales** which consist of items of which one of the alternatives is 'too good to be true' and use of the **forced choice technique**. In the latter subjects have to choose between alternatives of equal social desirability.

Response Category

See also BIAS

Response Category One of a number of categories which the respondent may choose in answer to a **closed question**.

Response Rate In a survey the response rate is the percentage of the sample chosen who actually participate. There is virtually always a proportion who refuse or who cannot be found, etc. Although there are no hard-and-fast rules, 90 per cent or above of respondents would be considered a high response rate for most purposes; 70–80 per cent might be considered acceptable.
See also **Non-respondent, Refusal Rate**

Response Set Often taken as synonymous with **response bias** which is a systematic bias pervading the answers of a respondent to a test, e.g. a desire to leave a good impression or a tendency to answer yes to all the items irrespective of content. Response set is more exactly a deliberately induced tendency, e.g. if the respondent is required to answer as quickly as possible.

Retail Price Index (RPI) A continuous time series of changes in retail price levels originating in 1916; the current series dates from 1956. It is a composite index number aggregating price changes for most private households over eleven categories of consumption: food, clothes, transport, housing, etc. Many old age pensioners and very high income earners are excluded from the data collected for its compilation.
The weights to be given to different categories of expenditure are derived from the annual **Family Expenditure Survey** and are changed each year according to the value of a three-year **moving average** of the proportion of income spent under each heading. Changes in income levels, tastes, and relative prices have strongly affected the relative weightings since 1956; food, for example, had a relative weight of 350 (out of 1,000) in 1956 and 214 in 1980, whilst transport and vehicles had doubled over the same period from 68 to 151.
The RPI is fundamentally a currently weighted (or *Paasche*) index and is not, therefore, a single continuous series. Comparisons over lengthy periods, although suggestive, are invalid to the extent that the relative weights have changed. A separate retail price index is published for low income pensioners whose expenditure on food, for example, is higher and more heavily weighted than for other types of household.
See also INDEX NUMBERS

Reversible Transformation See under TRANS-FORMATION

R-mode An **R-mode** factor analysis assesses whether *scores* on different variables group together. This is to be contrasted with **Q-mode** in which the aim is to see whether individual *people* have similarities in their profiles on the variables.

Robustness The extent to which a statistical procedure, particularly a **parametric** one, can stand violation of the assumptions underlying it.

Rorschach Test See under PROJECTIVE TECHNI-QUES

Rosenzweig Picture Frustration Study A projective test of reaction to frustration in which the subject is shown a series of cartoons depicting frustrating situations. Each cartoon contains two people, one of whom is saying something which draws attention to the frustrating situation. The subject's task is to specify the reply the other person would make. The replies may be scored for 'obstacle-dominance', in which the frustrating object is emphasized, for 'ego-defense', where the attention is on minimizing damage to the frustrated individual, and for 'need-persistence', in which a constructive solution to the problem is put forward. They may also be scored for extrapunitiveness, intropunitiveness, and impunitiveness, where the subject blames the environment, blames himself, or does not assign blame. **Norms** exist for these categorizations and there is also a *group conformity rating* which shows the subject's overall tendency to give responses similar to the norm. There are separate forms of the test for adults and children.

Rotated Solution The factors first obtained in a FACTOR ANALYSIS often make better logical sense after rotating the reference axes. A rotated solution is mathematically equivalent to the original and a number of methods have been devised for performing the rotation, e.g. the **Varimax method.**

Rotter Incomplete Sentences Blank A PROJEC-TIVE TEST in which the subject completes 40 sentences to 'express his real feelings'. Each sentence is then rated on a seven-point scale for degree of adjustment or maladjustment. The sum of the individual ratings provides the total maladjustment score. Anchoring illustrations of ratings are available. Responses may also be classified as unhealthy, neutral, or healthy. There are RELIABILITY and VALIDITY data for college groups.

S

Same Subjects Design An experimental design in which the same subjects take part in all the different treatments. This design is very effective in controlling extraneous variables, but **order effects** (e.g. **fatigue** and **practice**) must be controlled, e.g. by having different groups of subjects undergo the treatments in every possible order.
See also EXPERIMENT

Sample A group selected from a larger **population** with the aim of yielding information about this population as a whole.
See also SAMPLING THEORY AND METHODS

Sample Estimate An estimate, from a sample value, of what the value would be in the **population** from which the sample is drawn; e.g. when the sample **standard deviation** is used as an estimate of the population standard deviation.
See also SAMPLING THEORY AND METHODS

Sample Statistic A descriptive summary of some characteristic of a sample, e.g. the **mean** or **variance**. The term **population parameter** is applied to the same kind of entity used to describe a **population**.

Sample Survey A survey conducted using STANDARDIZED instruments on a sample drawn from a defined population and yielding results which may be generalized to that population.
See also SAMPLING THEORY AND METHODS

Sampling Accuracy The extent to which the sample is free from errors of all kinds, including **sampling error, systematic biases**, and **measurement errors**.
See also SAMPLING THEORY AND METHODS

Sampling Distribution See under ESTIMATION

Sampling Error No sample, however carefully drawn, can be perfectly representative of the **population** from which it is drawn. Any estimate of the population value of, for example, the **mean** or **standard deviation**, made on the basis of a sample is therefore liable to be more or less wrong depending on the representativeness of the sample. Such error is known as sampling error. The *less* the sampling error the greater the **precision** of the sample. Sampling error does *not* include error due to **systematic bias** in the sample, nor does it include **measurement error**.
See also SAMPLING THEORY AND METHODS

Sampling Fraction The proportion of the total **population** which is to be included in the sample.
See also SAMPLING THEORY AND METHODS

Sampling Frame A record or set of records which sets out and identifies the population from which a sample is to be drawn, e.g. the electoral roll, the list of patients in a GP's practice, or a list of all local authority primary schools.
See also SAMPLING THEORY AND METHODS

Sampling Interval The interval between cases who will be selected in **systematic sampling**, e.g. if every fifth person is selected the sampling interval is five.
See also SAMPLING THEORY AND METHODS

SAMPLING THEORY AND METHODS
Samples are selected to yield information about the populations from which they are drawn. In particular, inferences may be made about the population DISTRIBUTIONS on a number of variables and about **population parameters** such as the **mean, standard deviation**, and **variance**. One way to ensure validity of these inferences is to have a sample which is representative of the population in all respects which might affect the variables of interest. For example, in many surveys, the ages, sex, and social class of people in the sample should be in the same proportions as in the population. To ensure representativeness a **simple random sample** may be drawn. A **sampling frame** such as an electoral roll or doctor's list is obtained and a proportion (or **sampling fraction**) of the total names from it is drawn at random. The method used should ensure that every person in the sampling frame has, at the outset, an equal chance of being chosen. This may be achieved using **random numbers** or by **systematic sampling**. The latter involves randomly selecting the first respondent and then every *n*th person after that. *n* is a number sometimes termed the **sampling interval** which

determines the sampling fraction, e.g. a sampling interval of 10 will give a sampling fraction of one-tenth. Systematic sampling requires care if there are systematic repetitions or **periodic cycles** in the sampling frame, e.g. if the list is arranged wife–husband, wife-husband, etc.

If a simple random sample is large enough the characteristics which might bias it should balance out. Nonetheless, no sample, however carefully drawn, can be perfectly representative. Any estimate of a population parameter is therefore likely to be more or less in error depending on how representative the sample is. Such error is termed **sampling error**. The less the sampling error the greater the *precision* of the sample. Sampling error does not include **measurement error** and the extent to which a sample is free from errors of all kinds including measurement error, sampling error, and systematic biases is termed **sampling accuracy**.

Sometimes a simple random sample is not sufficiently efficient to obtain reasonable precision at reasonable cost. **Stratified random sampling** increases precision for a given sample size by dividing the population into layers or **strata** (e.g. social classes) and drawing a random sample from each. For improved precision, the variables, or stratifying factors out of which the strata are formed, have to be relevant to the question at issue. In a survey on attitudes to classical music it would be useless to stratify on eye colour but probably helpful to stratify on social class. Stratification is **proportionate** when each stratum is sampled in the same proportion as in the population, **disproportionate** when this is not so. Disproportionate stratification may be to ensure sufficient numbers for analysing each stratum separately. Estimates of total population parameters may still be made using weighting procedures.

Another method of saving expense, this time involving some loss of precision, is **cluster sampling**. The population is divided into groups (e.g. classes of schoolchildren, branches of a bank) and a random sample of these is drawn. If all the members of the groups selected are then approached, this is *single stage cluster sampling*. In *multi-stage cluster sampling* the process goes further. For instance, in choosing a national sample of schoolteachers one might (1) sample local authorities, (2) sample schools within authorities, (3) sample teachers within schools. The first clusters drawn under this procedure (e.g. the local authorities) are known as *primary sampling units*. The others (e.g. the schools) are termed *secondary sampling units*. Loss of precision occurs in these procedures because the members of the chosen units might tend to be like each other but different from people in other units — five teachers from school A and five from B might not give the same results as two each from A, B, C, D, and E. To reduce this distortion the primary sampling units may be chosen with **probability proportional to size.** This may be done by systematic sampling. The sizes of the units (e.g. numbers of teachers in each school) are set down cumulatively — that is, if unit one has 50 members and unit two 100, unit one takes numbers 1–50 and unit two 51–150 and so on. A random number is chosen and the unit in which it falls selected. The appropriate sampling interval is then applied to select the correct sampling fraction.

A variant of cluster sampling, known as *area sampling*, divides the area in which the total population resides into small units and uses these as primary sampling units.

All these methods yield a **random** or **probability sample**, defined as a sample in which all members of the population have a known probability of being selected, which is neither zero nor unity. The **sample statistics** of such a sample (e.g. the mean or variance) may validly be used as estimates of underlying population parameters. Furthermore, estimates may be given of the limits of error for these parameters, usually in the form of **standard errors**. The standard error of an estimate is the standard deviation of an infinite number of such estimates obtained by drawing samples all of that same size from the population (with replacement). For a simple random sample the **standard error of the mean** ($\sigma_{\bar{x}}$) may be estimated for a single sample of size n by the formula;

$$\sigma_{\bar{x}} = \frac{S}{\sqrt{n}} .$$

The square of this ($\sigma_{\bar{x}}^2$) is the **error variance** or **sampling variance**. For a stratified sample the *total error variance* is given by the weighted sum of the squares of the standard errors of the individual strata (stratum error variances). Sometimes it may be impossible to obtain a random sample, and a **non-probability** or **purposive sample** has to be used; one in which it cannot be said that all the members had a known probability of selection. This may arise, for instance, where there is no time for a full-scale sampling procedure, as in opinion polling during elections, or where there is no available sampling frame, e.g. if the population of interest is drug takers. Three common methods of non-probability sampling are **quota, snowball,** and **volunteer sampling**. In a quota sample the population is divided into subgroups and the interviewers have to find a quota from each so that the subgroups are in the same proportion as in the population. In snowball sampling one starts with a small number of known cases (e.g. drug-takers) and is led onto others in chain letter style. Volunteer sampling involves persuading volunteers to undergo a test procedure usually because it is in some way unpleasant. A quota sample is likely to over-represent people who are co-operative and easy to contact. For situations where this is unlikely to matter much it is comparable to a stratified sample and estimates of population parameters may be attempted. However, for the other two methods and for non-probability samples in general, there is no statistically sound way of estimating population parameters.

Sometimes non-probability sampling may be improved by using a multi-stage procedure of which some of the stages satisfy probability sampling. For example, one might commence by randomly sampling areas of a town and then doing a snowball sample, or, equally, by finding a 'volunteer' group of schools and then randomly sampling within each.

The population from which a sample is drawn should be clearly defined. Strictly speaking, sampling theory only allows generalizations to be made to exactly that population.

Another practical problem concerns non-respondents. However carefully a random sample is drawn at the outset, refusals of less co-operative people and failure to trace highly mobile people may bias it. There are special techniques for replacing non-respondents in order to introduce the minimum bias. Alternatively, known characteristics of non-respondents (e.g. their sex) may be compared with those of respondents to see how and whether the sample finally obtained has been affected.

Sampling Variance The **variance** of the **means** of a large number of **samples drawn with replacement** from a **population**. It is also termed **error variance** and is given by the square of the **standard error of the mean.** See also SAMPLING THEORY AND METHODS

Scalability See under **Guttman Scale**

SCALE OF MEASUREMENT
Any convenient, predetermined, mutually exclusive, and exhaustive set of categories (including numbers) into which a set of cases may be placed. In a *nominal scale*, such as religious affiliation (Protestant, Catholic, Jew) or gender (male, female) there is no implication that the categories are ordered; any labels will do to distinguish cases as long as they are mutually exclusive.

An *ordinal scale* requires mutually exclusive categories but allows the cases to be ranked in some order. It does not allow a basis for measuring the amount of difference between ranks. Examples of ordinally-scaled measures are army ranks and social classes; the difference between higher professional and managerial workers in Class I, and Class II — lower professionals and white-collar workers — has to be treated as the same as the difference between semi-skilled and unskilled workers (Classes IV and V). Any mathematical operation which retains the rank order of the original scale may be performed but it is mathematically improper to, for example, calculate means or deviations from means for points on an ordinal scale because this implies that the intervals between points on the scale are known quantities. **Pearson correlation** and techniques based on it such as MULTIPLE REGRESSION and FACTOR ANALYSIS should not be performed on ordinal scales.

An *interval scale* is one in which the distances or intervals between scale-points have been measured. The distance between £9,000 and £6,000 on a scale of annual personal incomes is the same as the distance between £9,000 and £12,000. If a variable is scaled at interval level then the arithmetic operations of addition, subtraction, and multiplication by a constant quantity may be performed on the scale values without altering the relationships in the data or imputing relationships which have not been measured. The powerful statistical techniques which could not be performed on ordinal level data can be performed on interval level data.

Although the requirement of interval scaling is important statistically there are no accepted social science variables which are only interval level. Examples such as crime rates, prices, ages, and fertility-rates are strictly *ratio scales* which have the same properties as interval scales but also have a true or non-arbitrary zero so that a price of £0 or a fertility-rate of 0 births per 1,000 women aged 15–45 is both possible and meaningful. In an interval scale a score of 20 is ten units distance from a score of 10 but it does not necessarily represent twice as much of the variable which is being scaled. With ratio scales which have a true zero, a fertility rate of 40 births is twice a rate of 20 births.

Each scale of measurement, besides its distinctive properties, also possesses the properties of scales below it in the hierarchy so that a requirement of interval scaling will be met by a ratio scale but not by an ordinal scale.

Another aspect of scales of measurement is *index* versus *representational measurement*. *Representational measurement* scales allow the exact reconstruction of reality from the responses or measures. Measurement of height with a ruler or of commodity prices in currency units is representational. In knowing the result, the value (e.g. height) of the object measured can be reconstructed. Measurement of prices as high, medium, or low allows no such reconstruction because the information has not been obtained for it to be done. Whilst an ordering of prices has been made the boundaries of the ordered categories are unknown. This is *index measurement*.

For other aspects of measurement scales, see under ATTITUDE SCALING.

Scalogram   See under **Guttman Scale**

Scalogram Analysis   See under **Guttman Scale**

Scatter Diagram (Scattergram)   A plot of the **joint distribution** of two variables, i.e. a visual presentation of their intercorrelation. A Scattergram is an advisable preliminary to the calculation of an interval level **correlation coefficient** because it will show if the relationship is **curvilinear** — and this would not be captured by correlation calculations.

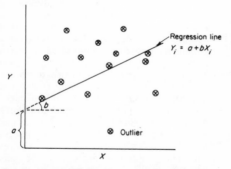

The **regression line** is fitted to the scatter of observations (⊗) but is not extended beyond the range of the observations. The dotted line projects the regression line to show the intercept where it cuts the Y-axis and the angle it makes with a line parallel to the X-axis; the tangent of this angle is b, the slope coefficient.

The approximate size, direction, and form (linear or curvilinear) of correlation can be gauged by eye from the scattergram and outliers — observations which appear to be anomalies in the general pattern — may be identified and investigated.

Scattergram   See **Scatter Diagram**

Schedule for Affective Disorders and Schizophrenia (SADS)   A standardized clinical interview designed for making a psychiatric diagnosis using the **Research Diagnostic Criteria (RDC)**. The SADS has three versions. The regular version deals in detail with current illness

episodes and also covers previous ones. The lifetime version (SADS–L) covers any episode current or past and can be used where there is no current episode. The SADS–C is suitable -for measuring change in clinical condition. The questioning proceeds via a set of general questions to establish the possible presence of a particular diagnosis, followed, if necessary, by specific probes to clarify the diagnosis precisely. Administration of the SADS requires special training, but, properly used, it is a RELIABLE and VALID instrument.

Schedule of Recent Experiences (SRE)   A questionnaire for measuring the degree of social readjustment a subject has undergone due to life changes over some specified period. The original schedule contained 43 items of the type 'pregnancy', 'gain of a new family member', to be ticked if they had occurred. A standard social readjustment score was derived for each item by having 394 judges assign it a score in comparison to 'marriage' which was given an anchor score of 50. The mean of these 394 ratings was taken as the item score. Subjects completing the scale are assigned a total life change score consisting of the sum of the scores of the items ticked. The scaling procedure has been repeated in several different cultures and has been generally found to lead to excellent agreement on the ordering and magnitude of the item scale values. Several different versions have been developed, differing slightly in item content. The scale has been used very widely, in studies relating life events to symptoms and illnesses of various kinds. It has also been the object of major criticisms, notably that it is hazy on the definition of a life event, it assumes additivity of effects for live events, assigns the same score to a life event whatever the individual circumstance, does not distinguish pleasant from unpleasant events, and does not distinguish events which cause illness from those which result from it.

Scheffé Method   A flexible method for making **unplanned comparisons** between group means following an ANALYSIS OF VARIANCE. It does not require equal numbers of observations in each group, and it may be used not only to compare single means (e.g. mean A against mean B) but also combinations (e.g. means A and B combined against C). A quantity S is computed which must be exceeded by the difference under test. The formula for comparing two single means is:

$$S = \sqrt{(K - 1)(F)(\text{residual mean square})\left(\frac{1}{n_1} + \frac{1}{n_2}\right)}$$

where K = total number of experimental groups, $F = F$ ratio needed for significance, with degrees of freedom $K - 1$ and those of the **residual** mean square, and n_1 and n_2 are the numbers in the groups being compared.

Score A number yielded by a test item, test, or series of tests, etc. The term score is sometimes distinguished from **value**, the latter having implications for the meaning of a score. The same score on a test of mental arithmetic might have a high value on the variable 'arithmetic ability' but a somewhat lower one on the variable 'general intelligence'.

Scott's π A measure of inter-rater reliability. See under RELIABILITY

Scree Test See under FACTOR ANALYSIS

Screening Test A brief test administered to a large sample with the aim of selecting for further study a smaller sample who fulfil some criterion.

Seasonal Adjustment See under TIME SERIES ANALYSIS

Secondary Sampling Unit See under **Cluster Sampling**

Secular Trend See under TIME SERIES ANALYSIS

Self-administered Questionnaire A questionnaire which contains full and clear written instructions about how to complete it and which need not be administered by an interviewer.

Self-completion Questionnaire Synonymous with **Self-administered Questionnaire**

Semantic Differential Technique A very flexible method of attitude measurement. Subjects rate the concepts in which the experimenter is interested (e.g. myself, apartheid, the British breakfast) on several bipolar scales (usually seven point), the ends of which are defined by pairs of adjectives opposite in meaning (e.g. 'good/bad', 'hard/soft', 'fast/slow'). Any concepts and any adjectival scales may be used. The bipolar scales are often FACTOR ANALYSED and comparisons of concepts are then made on the factors. Most scales may be placed with reasonable confidence on one of three main factors labelled *evaluation, potency,* and *activity,* and this is often assumed without resort to factor analysis. In the *summated ratings technique* scores on the appropriate bipolar scales are added up to give a factor score for each person on each

concept. **Profiles** of the concepts can then be obtained, if desired.

Semi-interquartile Range See under **Interquartile Range and Interquartile Ratio**

Semi-structured Interview See under INTERVIEW

Sensitizing Concepts See under **Definitive Concepts**

Serial Correlation Synonymous with autocorrelation. See under ESTIMATION

Sex Ratio The number of males in a human population compared to the number of females. By convention the ratio is expressed as males per 1,000 females, e.g. the sex ratio was 924 males (to 1,000 females) in 1951 and 949 in 1978 for England and Wales. Sex ratios for a population of all ages (as above) may be re-calculated for particular age groups and are then age-specific sex ratios.

Sign Test A test of the difference between **matched pairs**, appropriate when the only available information is that one member of each pair scores more (+) or scores less (−) than the other member on some variable. The observed distribution of + and − is compared to that expected on the **binomial distribution** assuming equal probability of + and −.

Significance The result of a statistical test is said to be significant if it can be shown that a particular value of the statistic computed in the test (e.g. t-ratio, z, F-ratio, or χ^2) is unlikely to have occurred by chance. Usually if the odds against chance are more than 19 : 1 (i.e. probability less than 0.05) the result is accepted as statistically significant, but there is no hard-and-fast rule about this. See also STATISTICAL INFERENCE

Significance Test A test of the likelihood of a particular observed result occurring by chance. See under STATISTICAL INFERENCE

Simple Random Sample In a simple random sample every member of the population has an equal chance of being selected. This is not necessarily the case in all random samples. See also SAMPLING THEORY AND METHODS

Simple Random Sample with Replacement In this type of sampling, when a case has been randomly sampled from a population it is replaced in the population ('put back into the hat') so that it may be sampled again. Seldom, if ever, used in social science research.

Simple Random Sample without Replacement In this type of sampling, cases are selected by a random method, and once selected are not eligible for selection a second time.

Simple Structure See under FACTOR ANALYSIS

Simultaneous Regression Analysis REGRESSION ANALYSIS in which all the **independent variables** are entered into a **regression equation** in one single step, in order to test the overall effect upon the **dependent variable**.

Single Stage Cluster Sample See under **Cluster Sampling**

Sixteen Personality Factor Questionnaire (16PF) A test of sixteen different personality factors. It is suitable for persons aged 16 or over and is based on careful factor analytic research to validate sixteen separate dimensions of personality. There are norms for undergraduates and for other adult samples.

Skewness of Distribution A distribution is said to be skewed if it resembles a NORMAL DISTRIBUTION but departs markedly from it in some way.
See under DISTRIBUTION

Slope The angle or gradient at which a **regression line**, or plane in the case of multiple regression, meets the X-axis or X-plane. In the **regression equation**:

$$\hat{Y}_i = a + bX_i,$$

where a and b are constants or coefficients, the slope coefficient is b and it models the rate at which the predicted **dependent variable** $\hat{Y}_i$ increases for a unit increase in X_i, the **independent variable**. Y_i will increase in value by b units for every unit increase in X_i.
The term a is the constant term and is the value of Y_i when X_i is zero. Geometrically, it is the value at which the regression line intercepts the X-axis and is sometimes known as the *intercept*.
See also *Scatter Diagram*

Snowball Sampling The researcher starts with a small number of known cases (e.g. drug-takers) and is referred by these to other cases in 'chain letter' style. A snowball sample is not representative of any definite population and STATISTICAL INTERFERENCE is therefore impossible;
See also SAMPLING THEORY AND METHODS.

Social Class See under **Registrar-General's Classification of Occupations**

Social Desirability Subjects exhibiting this trait feel it important to leave the best possible impression on others. This may lead to a **response bias** in questionnaires.
Controlling for social desirability may involve setting items for which some of the response alternatives are too good to be true, or setting **forced choice items** where a choice must be made between responses of equal social desirability. The latter technique is more difficult to achieve in practice, but may be somewhat more effective.
See also BIAS

Social Desirability Responding Responding in a manner calculated to leave the best possible impression on others.
See also BIAS, **Social Desirability**

Socio-Economic Group See under **Registrar-General's Classification of Occupations**

Sociogram A diagram showing the social relationships existing within a particular group, as revealed in the privately recorded preferences of group members.

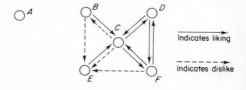

The sociogram illustrated is of a six-person group. A is a social isolate who neither gives nor receives choices of any kind. C is a star, being chosen four times out of five. E is a rejectee, receiving three negative choices. There is a clique of mutual friends C, D, and F.
Sociograms may also be drawn in the form of 'targets' showing the more popular group members in the middle and the less popular on the outside.

Somer's d_{YX} An asymmetric measure of association which may be used on data in the form of ranks. It has much in common with the **Kendall rank order correlation** and the first steps in computing it are to calculate P, Q, T_X, and T_Y. (See under Kendall rank order correlation.) With Y as the dependent variable:

$$d_{YX} = \frac{P - Q}{P + Q + T_Y}$$

With X as the dependent variable:

$$d_{XY} = \frac{P - Q}{P + Q + T_X}$$

There is a symmetric version which takes no account of which variable is dependent and this is given by:

$$d = \frac{P - Q}{P + Q + \frac{1}{2}(T_X + T_Y)} .$$

Spearman–Brown Formula A formula for assessing the extent to which the RELIABILITY of a test would improve if it was lengthened m-fold. It is given by:

$$r_{\text{new}} = \frac{m \cdot r_{\text{old}}}{1 + (m - 1)r_{\text{old}}} ,$$

where r_{new} = new reliability, and r_{old} = old reliability.

Spearman's Rank Correlation Coefficient (r_s) An estimate of the Pearson **product-moment correlation coefficient** appropriate to the situation where both variables being correlated are in the form of ranks. It is given by the formula:

$$r_s = 1 - \frac{6\Sigma D_i^2}{n(n^2 - 1)} ,$$

where D_i is the difference in rank between members of a given pair and n = number of pairs.
See also CORRELATION

Specific Factor A factor loaded on by only one test out of a group of tests.
See FACTOR ANALYSIS

Specific Variance When a group of variables are being FACTOR ANALYSED, the **variance** of any one of them may be split up into three parts. These are the *common variance* which may be represented in terms of the other variables, the specific variance unique to the variable, and the **error variance**.

Specificity That part of the **variance** of a test or variable which is specific to it and is therefore neither **error variance** nor shared with other variables being analysed. (See **Communality**, FACTOR ANALYSIS.)
Specificity may also refer to diagnosis. A diagnostic test is said to be specific if it gives a positive diagnosis on only a small proportion of people who do *not* have the condition under test. It is said to be sensitive if it does diagnose most of the people who *have* got the condition.

Split Half Method See **Split Half Reliability**

Split Half Reliability A measure of RELIABILITY in which the test items are randomly divided into two equal sets and the correlation coefficient between the total scores on the two sets is used as the estimate of reliability.

Spurious Correlation A correlation is spurious when there is in fact no direct causal link between the two variables being correlated. Height and intelligence are positively (although only slightly) correlated. Height would not seem to cause intelligence, nor would being intelligent make one taller. Other factors, such as better diet, probably underlie the correlation.

Spurious Relationship An observed relationship between two variables which may be entirely accounted for by other variables or by **artefacts** of the design of the study.
See also RELATIONSHIP, **Regression to the Mean**

Square Root Transformation The purpose of a square root transformation of a variable (A) is usually to **linearize** the **relationship** with another variable (B). In the process, the transformation may also NORMALIZE the DISTRIBUTION of A for different levels of B and/or make the **variance** of A homogeneous over different levels of B. A square root transformation is likely to be suitable when the variances of A are proportional to the means of A within ascending levels of B. Formulae often used are
$$A' = \sqrt{A + 0.5}$$
or
$$A' = \sqrt{A} + \sqrt{A + 1}.$$
See also TRANSFORMATION

Standard Deviation A measure of the spread or **dispersion** of a set of scores. It is the square root of the **variance** and is given by:

$$s = \sqrt{\frac{\Sigma x^2}{n}} ,$$

where Σx^2 = the sum of the squares of the

deviations from the mean, and n is the number of observations.

When the standard deviation of a **sample** is being used to estimate the standard deviation ($\hat{\sigma}$) of the **population** from which the sample was drawn, the above formula gives a good estimate only for large n. For small values of n a better estimate is given by:

$$\hat{\sigma} = \sqrt{\frac{\Sigma x^2}{n-1}} \cdot$$

Standard Error If an infinite number of samples all the same size are drawn (with replacement) from a **population**, the **means, standard deviations, variances**, etc. of these samples will vary. The standard error of such a **sample estimate** is simply the **standard deviation** of the whole set of estimates, e.g. the **standard error of the mean** is the standard deviation of an infinite set of means of samples all of the same size drawn randomly with replacement from the same population. The standard error of the mean ($\sigma_{\bar{x}}$) may be estimated from the standard deviation of a single sample (s) of size n by the formula:

$$\sigma_{\bar{x}} = \frac{s}{\sqrt{n}} \cdot$$

The *standard error (σ_p) of a proportion (p)* is approximately given by

$$\sigma_p = \sqrt{\frac{pq}{n}} ,$$

where n is the sample size and $q = 1 - p$.

Standard Error of a Proportion See under **Standard Error**

Standard Error of The Mean See under **Standard Error**

Standard Industrial Classification (SIC) An exhaustive classification of industry by type, originally designed for compiling output statistics for National Accounts, but now also widely used for a variety of purposes such as assessing strike-rates in different industries and even rates of industrial accidents.

All industrial enterprises are classifiable by the SIC without regard to size of organization or form of ownership. It is not co-terminous with occupational classification, and the same job may be found in a number of separate headings of the SIC.

The complete SIC consists of 181 Minimum List Headings which are usually grouped into homologous types or Orders of which there are 27, e.g. Order II, Mining and Quarrying; Order III, Food, Drink, and Tobacco. Most statistics of output, employment, and labour disputes are given for Orders rather than for the specific industries in the Minimum List Headings.

The defect of the SIC from the researcher's point of view is that Orders (and even Minimum List Headings) contain a wide range of firms differing grossly in size, technology, and ownership and the analytical use of statistics compiled on this base is therefore limited.

See also AGGREGATION, NACE

Standard Unit When interval or ratio scaling has been achieved the units of measurement (intervals between the scale points) are of one fixed size and therefore may be termed standard units.

STANDARDIZATION

The term 'standardize' can be applied to conditions of testing, to subjects, and to observations.

Standardization of conditions of testing covers the whole process of exactly specifying the questions to be asked, the manner of asking them, how the replies are to be scored, etc. A **standardized interview** is one that has been constructed in this rigorous way, has been tried out, and is ready for use in the population to be studied. A *standardized test* is similar but is constructed to measure some definite variable such as intelligence and additionally is **norm-referenced** . That is it has norms of performance available so that any individual who takes the test can be assessed relative to other people in the population. (A *criterion-referenced test* purports to demonstrate whether mastery of a particular skill or sphere of knowledge has been achieved, such as a driving test or an accountancy examination.)

Standardization of subjects refers to the exclusion of extraneous variables by restricting the sample to only certain types of people, such as men or old people or those with low income.

Standardization of observations means making two sets of observations directly comparable. The problem arises when samples of different sizes are to be compared, possibly on different variables, for example when one wishes to know whether a person's mark of 75 in French represents as great an achievement as another person's mark of 80 in Chemistry, or whether having two million illiterate adults in country A is worse than two million in country B. Common methods of standardization include transforming both sets of data into **Z-scores** or into **percentiles**.

Standardized Birth-Rate   See under **Birth-rate**

Standardized Discriminant Function Coefficient   See under **Discriminant Analysis**

Standardized Interview   An interview which has been carefully constructed and tried out, and where the exact questions to be asked, the order and manner of asking them, and the scoring of the replies have all been rigorously specified.
See also INTERVIEW

Standardized Mortality Ratio (SMR)   The actual number of deaths occurring in a given subgroup of the population expressed as a percentage of the number that would be expected to occur if that subgroup had been exactly typical of the population as a whole.
The subgroups may be social classes, regions, occupations, etc. The SMR, unlike crude **death-rates**, removes the effect of differences in age structure or the **sex ratio** from the comparison between subgroup and population. Such differences are known to have marked effects on death-rates with males and older and very young age groups having a higher probability of death. An SMR is derived by (a) multiplying the **age-specific death-rate** for each age and sex classification by the number of people so classified within the subgroup, (b) summing the *expected* deaths so obtained across all classifications, and (c) expressing actual deaths as a ratio or percentage of these expected deaths.
The further from 100 per cent the SMR departs, the greater or lesser is the expectation of death in the subgroup compared to the population when differences of age structure or sex ratio have been accounted for. SMRs are usually calculated for each sex separately and differences in social class composition may also be accounted for if class specific death-rates are also used.

Standardized Partial Regression Coefficient   The weight (β) by which an **independent variable** (X) in STANDARDIZED form must be multiplied in the **regression equation** specifying the best prediction of a (standardized) **dependent variable** (Y) from a set of independent variables. Other terms for the standardized partial regression coefficient are *beta, beta coefficient*, and *beta weight*.
See also MULTIPLE REGRESSION, REGRESSION ANALYSIS

Standardized Question   A question in which the

wording, manner of asking, and scoring of the replies have all been rigorously specified.
See also STANDARDIZATION

Standardized Questionnaire   A questionnaire which has been carefully constructed so that the order and wording of the questions and the scoring of the replies are rigorously specified.

Standardized Random Variable   A RANDOM VARIABLE in which each value has been transformed by subtracting the **mean** and dividing by the **standard deviation.**

Standardized Regression Coefficient   The weight (β) to be applied when a single **independent variable** (X) in STANDARDIZED form is used in the **regression equation** to predict a **dependent variable** (Y) also in standardized form, thus:

$$Y = \beta X.$$

In this case β = **product-moment correlation** (r) between X and Y.

Standardized Score   See **Z-score**

Standardized Test   See under STANDARDIZATION

Stanford-Binet Test   An intelligence test which may be applied to children from age 2 upwards and also to adults. There are separate forms of the test for each age group, at half-yearly intervals from ages 2 to 5, yearly from 5 to 14, and three forms for adults of varying intelligence. There is an alternative version available for each age group. There is no **group administered** form and testing requires skill and training. Testing of an individual commences at a year level where he can pass all the items (the basal level) and finishes at a year level where he fails them all (the ceiling level). By a system in which partial credits are added onto the basal level the individual's mental age is worked out. Using the mental age and the chronological age the IQ may be found from tables. The RELIABILITY of the test is excellent and the **construct** and **criterion-related validity** satisfactory.
See also **Intelligence Test**

Stannine Scale   The stannine scaling method transforms a NORMAL DISTRIBUTION into a nine-point scale by dividing it into units of half a **standard deviation**. Those cases which fall ±¼ of a standard deviation from the mean are given the middle scale value, i.e. five. Those to either side are scaled according to their position. Given that a distribution is normal there will be approximately 4 per cent of the cases in each of categories 1 and 9, 6.6. per cent in categories 2 and 8, 12.1 per cent in categories 3 and 7, 17.5 per cent in categories 4 and 6, and 19.7 per cent in category 5.

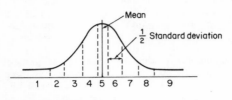

See also **Sten Scale**

Statistic A number which summarizes and describes some particular aspect of a set of observations, e.g. the **arithmetic mean** describes the central position of the observations, the **standard deviation** their spread, or, at a more complex level, the *t*-statistic describes the numerical value which results when a **t-test** is performed.

Statistical Control Statistical control attempts to unravel the affects of the **independent** and the **extraneous variables** at the analysis stage of a survey. There are various methods, including seeing if a result holds across all groups in a sample (e.g. if the result holds good for boys and girls then the extraneous variable, sex, can have no effect), matching out an extraneous variable at the analysis stage, and making allowance for the effects of an extraneous variable by techniques such as **covariance adjustment**.

Statistical Explanation An explanation couched in terms of the extent to which a set of observations may be predicted from another set. There need be no logical or causal connection between the two sets.

STATISTICAL INFERENCE
The use of statistical techniques to draw conclusions from a set of data. Statistical inference is mainly concerned with hypothe-

sis-testing, but conclusions may also be drawn about the likely size of **population parameters** such as the **mean** or **standard deviation**. The first step in hypothesis-testing is to state the hypothesis in the form of a **null hypothesis**, that is, that there are no differences between the groups being tested, no relationships between the variables of interest, etc. A statistical test is then performed to ascertain the chances that the null hypothesis is true. If the chances of this are sufficiently low, for instance as little as five chances in 100, the null hypothesis is rejected. Before commencing, the level of odds at which the null hypothesis will be rejected is specified. This is the **level of significance** designated α (alpha) and usually stated as a probability, e.g. 0.05 or 0.01 (respectively five chances and one chance in 100 that the null hypothesis is true). The region of probability from zero up to and including α is often termed the *rejection region* or *critical region*.

The value which should be assigned to α is not obvious. If α is set too high, the error, known as **type I error**, may be committed. This involves rejecting the null hypothesis when it is true. Conversely, if α is too low, the null hypothesis may be accepted when false — a **type II error**. Commonly encountered values of α are α = 0.05 and α = 0.01. The probability of making a type I error is simply α, and the probability of making a type II error, designated, β, is $1 - \alpha$.

Another choice to be made concerns the use of a **one-tailed** or a **two-tailed test** of significance. When the investigator is only interested in a result in a particular direction, e.g. $B > A$ and not $A > B$, a one-tailed test is appropriate. The area at only one end of the statistical distribution is considered, and the null hypothesis, termed a *directional null hypothesis*, is that there is no difference in a given direction. When no direction is specified, a two-tailed test is appropriate and the area under both tails of the distribution is considered. With α = 0.05 and a normal distribution the one- and two-tailed situations are as shown.

The statistical test to be used depends on

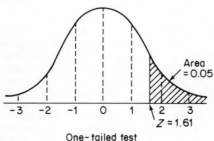

One-tailed test

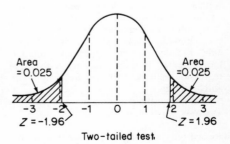

Two-tailed test

108

circumstances. The main classification is into **parametric** and **non-parametric tests**. Parametric tests involve the estimation of a population parameter such as the mean or standard deviation. They assume that the data are measured on at least an **interval scale** and that the populations from which the samples have been drawn are NORMALLY DISTRIBUTED and have equal **variances**. In practice, however, it has been shown that very considerable violations of these assumptions do not invalidate the conclusions drawn. The main parametric tests are the **Z-test**, the **t-test** and the **F-test**. Non-parametric tests (also known as *distribution-free tests*) do not involve the estimation of a population parameter, require only **nominal** or **ordinal scale** measurement, and make no assumptions about how scores are distributed. They can be useful where parametric tests are inappropriate but they are less **powerful**, i.e. they require a greater number of observations to reject the null hypothesis at a given level of significance.

Statistical inferences may also be drawn about the likely size of a population parameter given a sample of observations, and a **confidence interval** may be found. This is a range of values within which a population parameter has a specified probability of lying. The **standard error** of a parameter may also be estimated. This is the standard deviation that would be obtained for the parameter values if an infinite set of samples of the same size were drawn with replacement from the population.

See also ESTIMATION

Statistical Interaction   See **Interaction**

Statistically Significant   See **Significance**

Sten Scale   The sten scaling method transforms a NORMAL DISTRIBUTION into 10 divisions by dividing it into units of half a **standard deviation**. The mean of the distribution falls between categories 5 and 6 which comprise half a standard deviation to either side of it.

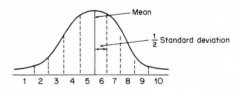

The rest of the cases are scaled according to their position.

Given that a distribution is normal there will be approximately 2.3 per cent of cases in each of categories 1 and 10, 4.4 per cent in categories 2 and 9, 9.2 per cent in categories 3 and 8, 15.0 per cent in categories 4 and 7, and 19.2 per cent in categories 5 and 6.

The sten scale is thus a simple and easily interpreted approximation to a normal distribution.

See also **Stannine Scale**

Stepwise Regression   A REGRESSION ANALYSIS in which the **independent variables** are entered into the **regression equation** in steps, either one at a time or a group at a time. The improvement in prediction is assessed after each step.

Stochastic Models   See **Stochastic Variable**

Stochastic Variable   A stochastic variable is one whose value is never fully determined by its relationship to other variables and an error is found between its value as predicted by a model and its observed value. All relationships based on human behaviour are intrinsically stochastic or subject to random fluctuations and the estimated value of a variable X_i should strictly be written $X_i + e_i$, where e_i is the *residual, disturbance,* or *error* term.

It is an assumption in maximum likelihood estimation that stochastic error is a random variable with a **mean** of zero (i.e. the distribution of possible values of X_i is centred on the true or population value of X_i) and with a **variance** which is the same for the whole range of values of X which may be estimated from a particular model. However, the residual term e_i is composed of measurement error, exogenous variables (those whose effects on X_i are not accounted for in a model) and strictly stochastic error. The first two types of error are often systematic or cumulative rather than self-cancelling over a sample of observations so that assumptions about random errors with equal variances and a mean of zero break down. Even if measurement error and error due to exogenous variables could be completely eliminated, stochastic error would remain, but because of its random nature the possible errors of inference from samples of observations could be known.

See also RANDOM VARIABLE, ERROR

Stratification   The division of a population into layers or strata (e.g. men and women, social classes) so as to be able to draw a random sample from each layer and thereby increase the *precision* of the sample without having to increase its size. The variables or *stratifying factors* out of which the strata are formed must

be relevant to the question at issue, if precision is to be improved, e.g. in a survey on attitudes to classical music it would be of no help to stratify the sample on the colour of their eyes, but it might be of considerable help to stratify it on social class.
See also SAMPLING THEORY AND METHODS

Stratified Sample A sample obtained by first dividing the population into layers or *strata* (e.g. men and women, social classes) and then drawing a **random sample** from each stratum.
See also **Stratification,** SAMPLING THEORY AND METHODS

Stratifying Factor See under **Stratification**

Stratum A layer or level of a population, which has been separately sampled, e.g. those people in the sample who are over 60, or those people of Social Class 1, or those people with incomes less than £3,000 p.a.
See also **Stratification,** SAMPLING THEORY AND METHODS

Stratum Error Variance The **error variance** within a particular **stratum**.
See also SAMPLING THEORY AND METHODS

Structural Equation An equation describing possible causal relationships between variables.
See under PATH ANALYSIS

Structure Coefficient See under **Canonical Correlation Analysis**

Structured Interview See under INTERVIEW

Student's 't' Test See *t*-test

Sum of Squares See under ANALYSIS OF VARIANCE

Summary Statistic A summary description of a set of observations, e.g. the **mean, variance**, or **standard deviation**

Suppressor Variable A variable which indirectly helps in prediction because it enhances the relationship between a criterion and a third variable. A written test to predict mathematical ability might be of limited use in a group containing some people of poor eyesight. In this situation eyesight would be a suppressor variable. Those with poor eyesight might not necessarily be bad at mathematics but would do badly on the written test. Hence, when both the test and eyesight are taken into account a better prediction of mathematical ability results — some of the irrelevant variance in the test has been 'suppressed'. A suppressor variable does not necessarily have to be itself unrelated to the criterion. To be a suppressor it must enhance some third variable, but it may also contribute to the prediction directly.
See also REGRESSION ANALYSIS, ELEMENTARY SURVEY ANALYSIS

Symmetric Measure of Association A symmetric measure of association (e.g. the *Pearson r*) gives the same numerical result no matter which variable is chosen as the **independent variable**. For **asymmetric measures of association** (e.g. **eta**) this is not the case.

Symmetrical Distribution If a symmetrical distribution is divided at its mean value, each half is the mirror image of the other. The NORMAL DISTRIBUTION is an example.

Symptom Any evidence of disease. A psychological symptom is less enduring than a **personality trait**, is usually distressing to the individual experiencing it, and has a more or less distinct time of onset.

Synchronic Study See under **Diachronic Study**

Systematic Error If a measurement is made on a sample of people and the ERRORS in this measurement all tend to be in the same direction then **systematic error** is present. Thus, in a doorstep survey of drinking behaviour many people may under-report the amount they drink while only a few may over-report it. Such a systematic error will BIAS the results of the survey in a way in which **random error** will not.

Systematic Random Sample See **Systematic Sample**

Systematic Sample A sample chosen by randomly selecting a unit or individual to start off with and then at a fixed interval after that (e.g. every tenth person or every twelfth person on the Electoral Roll). Properly: *systematic random sample*.
See also SAMPLING THEORY AND METHODS

T

TABULATION

Tabulation aims to display the numbers and/or proportions of observations falling simultaneously into various categories on one or more variables. The categories may be points on a scale, e.g. number of correct answers to three exam questions. They may be **class intervals** covering a span of values, e.g. incomes zero to £4,999, £5,000 to £9,999, and £10,000 upwards. They may be simply **nominal categories** such as religious affiliation.

Division of a **continuous variable** into class intervals sometimes leads to problems about the size and the number to be selected. When only two categories are needed (e.g. tall and short) it is usual, unless there is some other external criterion, to divide a sample at the **median** scale value (median height). Otherwise the selection of class intervals depends largely on sample size. Division into 20 intervals is sufficient for most purposes and in practice the number is often much fewer. If there are too many intervals there is little gain in information and the numbers of observations falling into some may be insufficient for statistical testing. If there are too few, important information about the distribution of the variable may be lost.

A table may be *one-way*, displaying the frequencies in the categories of just one variable, or it may be *two-way*, displaying the **joint frequency distribution** on two variables simultaneously. As an example, a two-way frequency table of sex by manual/non-manual occupation would show how many people were male manual, female manual, male non-manual, and female non-manual. This kind of frequency table is often termed a **contingency table**. It would be laid out thus:

	Men	Women	Total
Manual workers			
Non-manual workers			
Total			

The rows of the table and the row totals (sometimes called row *marginals*) contain information about the manual/non-manual variable while the columns and column totals (column marginals) contain information about the sex variable. Such tables may also show the proportions or the percentages of people falling into each category.

The table just described has two categories on each of the two variables and is accordingly termed a **two by two table**. A two by three table has two categories one one variable and three on the other, and in general a $k \times l$ table has k on one and l on the other.

In principle it is possible to classify on any number of variables simultaneously — e.g. the four-way classification $k \times l \times m \times n$. The results then require several tables for their display. This may be achieved by a series of two-way tables showing the *joint frequencies* of two variables at a time, with the values of the other variables held constant.

Tau See **Kendall's tau**

Test Factor See under **Elementary Survey Analysis**

Test–retest Method A method for assessing the RELIABILITY of a test in which a sample of people is tested on two separate occasions by the same test and the reliability taken as the correlation between the scores on these testings.

Tetrachoric Correlation Coefficient Like the **phi coefficient** this is an estimate of the **product-moment correlation coefficient** appropriate when both the variables are **dichotomous**. It is the most appropriate correlation coefficient where it may be assumed that a **continuous** and NORMALLY DISTRIBUTED VARIABLE underlies both dichotomies, but its calculation involves approximating the solution of a difficult mathematical equation. In practice the phi coefficient is sufficiently accurate for most purposes and is the correlation actually observed, whereas the tetrachoric correlation represents the correlation which might have been observed had both variables been measured on an interval scale.

Thematic Apperception Test

See also CORRELATION

Thematic Apperception Test See under PROJEC-
TIVE TECHNIQUES

Theoretical Probability Distribution The distribution of a **sample statistic** when a very large
number of samples is drawn. For example, if a
sample of 100 cases is repeatedly drawn (with
replacement) from a large population whose
mean value is 10 the **frequency distribution** of
the sample **means** is likely to follow the
bell-shaped NORMAL PROBABILITY DISTRIBU-
TION. The largest number of sample means will
fall at 10 and the further one moves from the
value 10 the lower will the frequencies be. The
normal distribution (z-*distribution*) is the most
common theoretical probability distribution.
Some others are the t-distribution, the F-distri-
bution, and the **chi-square** distribution.
Theoretical equations exist defining each of
these (and other) distributions. Theoretical
probability distributions are used to determine
whether a particular sample statistic is likely to
have cropped up just by pure chance. If the
sample statistic lies outside particular critical
values (for the normal curve usually ± 1.96, the
0.05 **level of significance**) the hypothesis of 'just
pure chance' is rejected.
See also DISTRIBUTION, RANDOM VARIABLE

Theoretical Sampling See under PARTICIPANT
OBSERVATION

Theoretical Saturation See under PARTICIPANT
OBSERVATION

THEORY
A set of integrated hypotheses designed to
explain particular classes of events. Theories
vary widely (i) in their explanatory scope and
power, i.e. in the number of classes of events
which a theory covers; (ii) in the amount of
empirical corroboration which a theory has
received; and (iii) in the extent to which they
are formalized as deductive systems.
The structure of a theory is composed of two
elements: a vocabulary of *concepts* and the
propositions expressing the relationship
between concepts. Concepts are unobservable
mental constructs which select, order, and
classify an aspect of the observable world. For
a theoretical statement to be tested against
observation its concepts must be empirically
interpretable, that is, an *operational definition*
can be given which specifies the observable
indicator which will represent an instance of
the concept and the statement of relationship
between concepts must be formulated in such a
way that it is capable of refutation. For
example, the proposition 'the history of all

hitherto existing societies is the history of class
struggles' is not a testable proposition since it is
impossible to imagine the conditions under
which some class struggle is not detectable
given the lack in the associated literature of an
operational definition of class struggle which is
unambiguous. On the other hand, 'crime-rates
vary inversely with distance from the city
centre' is in a testable form since operational
definitions of both crime-rate and distance can
be given and the relationship is stated precisely
enough so that any pattern which did not show
a diminution of crime-rates as distance from
the city centre increased would refute the
postulated relationship. Testability is a function of both the precision of the stated
relationship and the possibility of empirical
interpretation of the concepts.
A single hypothesis may be framed after
investigation of a limited number of cases and
if it remains true after testing on new cases then
it has the status of an *empirical generalization*;
that is, a relationship between concepts which
hold true for a limited number of instances. To
become a law-like proposition or theory an
empirical generalization must be asserted as
universally true. This is acceptable if it has
been tested widely and not refuted, although it
may be modified from observations before
reaching a final form. The distinction between
an empirical generalization and a law-like
proposition is not always maintained in
research practice and both types of proposition
are often claimed as theory.
Theories vary in explanatory power according
to the number of classes of events which they
cover. At the minimum a theory may consist of
a singular statement relating two event classes
and the explanation of a particular pattern of
observation, e.g. the crime-rate in city centre
X is higher than the crime-rate in the suburb of
Y, is made by claiming the observation as an
instance of the general relationship 'crime-
rates vary inversely with distance from the city
centre'. More powerful explanations are possible when two or more singular theoretical
statements are integrated into a theoretical
system and the term 'theory' is correctly used
only of sets of integrated hypotheses, although
in practice the term is also used of singular
statements.
The integration of sets of singular statements
(*corroborated hypotheses*) allows logical deductions to be made which are new in the sense
that they are not explicitly expressed in any of
the singular statements. The empirical test of a
logically deduced statement (or *corollary*) is
also a test of the theory as a whole. For
example, the two singular statements: 'The
greater the similarity among the
members of a community the greater their

social cohesion', and 'The greater the social cohesion among the members of a community, the greater their resistance to deviant behavior', allows the deduction to be made that: 'The greater the similarity among members of a community, the greater their resistance to deviant behaviour.'

If operational definitions are given for similarity (e.g. proportion in a single social class) and for deviant behaviour (e.g. crimes notified to the police per 100,000 population), then the deduced statement can be tested. If confirmed then both the original statements of the theory must be confirmed also; thus, the test of a theory consisting of a set of integrated hypotheses is more efficient than tests of both statements separately.

If the deduced statement is not confirmed, then either or both of the original statements may be false and this ambiguity of testing is a problem when large numbers of hypotheses are integrated into a system.

See also **MODEL**, **EXPLANATION**

Thurstone Scale An attitude scale consisting of items to which the respondents have to agree or disagree. Only those items with which they agree are scored. Score values for the items are determined by asking a large number of judges to rate them on a scale (usually an eleven-point scale). The median value of these opinions serves as the score for the item. A respondent's score for the whole scale is taken as the median score of the items to which he agrees.

See also **ATTITUDE SCALING**

Tied Ranking In many ranking situations it is not possible to distinguish between two or more of the people or objects being ranked. When this happens the average rank is assigned to each of the tied observations, e.g. if four people come in equal first in a race they would all be ranked 2½, i.e. the sum of the ranks 1, 2 ,3, and 4 divided by four.

TIME SERIES ANALYSIS

Observations of a variable made over time and for which there are values for each time period form a time series. The intervals are usually equal ones — months, quarters, years — and time series are typically plotted as continuous traces of the variable against time, which is conventionally plotted along the horizontal axis (Figure 1).

Some time series are not single variables but composite ones formed from the combination of several variables (e.g. the **Retail Price Index**). The analysis of both single variable time series and composite time series is the same in principle and will not be further distinguished.

Time series data may be contrasted to cross-sectional data, e.g. the **frequency distribution** of a variable where the observations have all

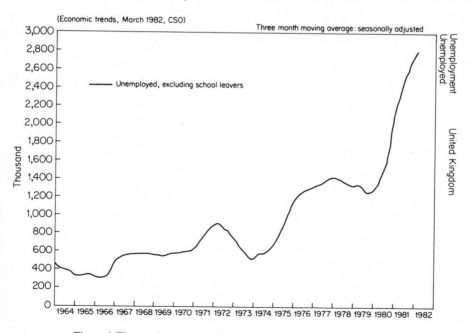

Figure 1 Time series analysis, (Economic Trends, March 1982, CSO)

been made at the same point in time and form a cross-section of a population.

The analysis of time series may be treated in two broad ways: (a) as **univariate analysis** of a single variable analogously to the analysis of a frequency distribution but requiring different techniques, and (b) as **multivariate analysis** in which one time series variable is regressed onto or correlated with other time series.

Analysis of a single time series rests on determining the pattern of observations through time and this requires the decomposition of the series trace-line into four components.

(i) *Seasonal or short-cycle variation* with a period (i.e. peak to peak or trough to trough) usually of one year in most social and economic time series. The classic seasonal variation is a monthly one in which the pattern repeats annually.

(ii) *Longer cyclical variation* with a period usually greater than a year of which the best known example is the business cycle which has had a period of about four years in the post-war economy and which many economic time series follow, reflecting variation in the level of general economic activity (see under FORECASTING). Long cycle fluctuations require long continuous time series data if they are to be detected and analysed.

(iii) *Trend*, or the overall tendency of a time series to progress upwards or downwards irrespective of the seasonal or long cycle variations. Most time series of economic variables in the post-war period show distinct upward trends since they are mainly correlated with Gross National Product which has risen continuously, if not steadily, since the Second World War.

(iv) *Error*, which is composed of both **stochastic** error in which the observed value of a variable is subject to random error as well as to determinate effects, and irregular fluctuations in which the variables which produce the time series are subject to occasional shocks of a non-random error, e.g. where purposive government action raises unemployment at time t above its expected value or where there is a patterned combination of regular seasonal and business cycle variations.

Figure 2 shows a time series in which a quarterly seasonal cycle and an upward trend are easily distinguishable. Each of the first three components into which a time series may be separated can be isolated for analytical purposes although any particular time series may lack (though usually does not) any of the three. The isolation of the seasonal variation removes short-cycle variation in order to reveal a combination of trend and long-cycle variation, Isolation of both trend and seasonal components reveals the long-cycle variations and most economic indicators are plotted in a trend-eliminated and seasonally adjusted form in order to reveal the business cycle stage of current observations for forecasting purposes.

Cyclical variations, whether short or long, may be isolated and removed by the use of *moving averages*; these rest on the assumption that over a defined period variation above and below the trend line will average to zero so that if these regular variations can be eliminated the trend of the series will be isolated. The length of the regular period must first be detected by eye and if there are two superimposed cycles only one period can be chosen to begin with. For example, retail sales follow a marked seasonal pattern corresponding to the

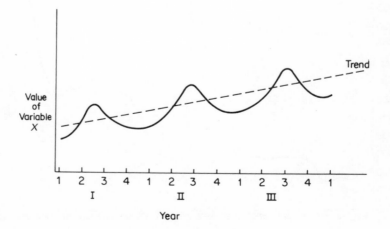

Figure 2 Time series analysis

four seasons of the year and they also fluctuate regularly according to the business cycle. If it is desired to remove the seasonal variations then a four-quarterly moving average is fitted to the series (for quarterly observations). The first four successive quarterly observations $(m_1, ..., m_4)$ are averaged as $(m_1 + m_2 + m_3 + m_4)/4$ and the new derived observation m_1^* is the first trend value. The average moves along the series by repeating the four-quarterly averaging but by dropping the first observation and adding the next so that $m_2^* = (m_2 + m_3 + m_4 + m_5)/4$ becomes the second trend value.

This has the effect of smoothing a fluctuating time series and rendering visible the trend and any longer cycle variation which may be removed in turn by fitting a second moving average to the already smoothed data whose period is equal to the length of the second longer cycle. Smoothing by moving averages, and particularly double smoothing, loses observations at the begining and end of the time series so that long series are needed for moving average techniques; the longer the moving average the more observations are needed. The essence of the technique is the assumption that the trend value at time t is an average of the observations at time t together with those before and after it. If an odd-number of observations are taken in the moving average, then the trend value is plotted on the time point m_t, that is, at the centre of the average. An even-number moving average (e.g. the common four-quarterly one) will be centred midway between actual observations and this is overcome by taking one more observation to make an odd number with an identifiable centre point but weighting the end observations by half to give the equivalent of one less observation (i.e. an even number) in the moving average. This is a centred n-period moving average, where n is the number of observations in each moving average and is an even number. Short-term forecasting by the projection of a time series beyond current observations is always done after the series has been smoothed, that is, only the trend is projected not the whole series. Recent observations are often weighted at the expense of earlier ones when projecting trends and in smoothing by moving averages a weighted average is used if this is required. The technique of *exponentially weighted moving averages* uses a series of weights which increase rapidly along the moving average, i.e.

$$m_t^* = m_t + e \cdot m_{t+1} + e^2 \cdot m_{t+2} + ...,$$

where $e = 2.7$, the base of natural logarithms.

For time series which are continuously produced, as many economic indicators are, rapid methods of seasonal adjustment are used in which a set of seasonal weights is calculated from the known pattern of the series and used to adjust current observations to the trend values, sometimes with long-cycle variation left intact and sometimes eliminated.

The best method of seasonal adjustment is the ratio-to-trend technique. First, the trend values of a series are found by moving average techniques or by regression analysis (see below), and secondly, the ratio

$$\frac{\text{observed value at } t}{\text{trend value at } t}$$

is calculated for each month by grouping corresponding months together and averaging. This forms a set of seasonal ratios which are, thirdly, standardized by dividing them by the overall average ratio-to-trend of the whole series. The reciprocal of the standardized seasonal index is used to multiply a current observation (using the appropriate seasonal index) to yield the seasonally adjusted or trend value which is the value usually reported in official statistics.

Trend values are frequently found by regresion analysis; a linear trend is modelled by a regression equation of the form:

$$\hat{m}_t = \beta m_t + e_t,$$

where m_t is the observation, $\hat{m}_t$ the fitted trend value at the same time point, e_t is the **residual** or error term, and β is a **standardized regression coefficient**. A trend which has been modelled mathematically is easily used to adjust a real observation, although a linear regression will remove all cyclical variation and may overadjust the series from the analyst's point of view.

More complex regression models which attempt to match both trend and long-cycle variation are used in various forms of curvilinear regression which isolate both irregular or error fluctuations as well as seasonal variations.

A model which fits a trend line or curve may also be used to eliminate the trend component in a series. The ratio formed by dividing the observation at time t by the fitted trend value at time t is a derived observation which has had the trend eliminated. Such a series may be further adjusted seasonally and most indicators of the business cycle are reported in such a trend-free and seasonally adjusted form so that the long cycle of the economy may be clearly seen.

Time series variables may be used in combination in multivariate analysis, for example in econometric models. These require the regression of a time series variable on one or more other variables which are also time series. It is usually the case that the prediction of a dependent time series variable depends not only on the value of the independent variable at the corresponding time but also on the values of the independent variable at earlier time periods so that Y_t is regressed not only on X_t but on X_{t-1}, X_{t-2}, etc. The regression of one time series on another takes the form:

$$Y_t = \alpha + \beta X_t + \beta_1 X_{t-1} + \beta_2 X_{t-2} \\ + \beta_3 X_{t-3} \\ + \dots + \beta_n X_{t-n} + e_t,$$

where $t - 1$ and $t - 2$ represent successively earlier time periods before t. Such a relationship between variables is said to be one where Y (dependent variable) depends on the lagged values of X (the independent variable). Such an equation is a system of *distributed lags*. The effect of X on Y is usually modelled such that its effects decay with time, that is, the remoter X is in comparison to the observation point t, then the less is its influence on Y at time t. The regression coefficients in a distributed lag model decline from β to β_n and the pattern of weights fitted to the regression coefficients is usually one of exponential decay:

$$Y_t = \alpha + \beta X_t + \lambda \beta_1 X_{t-1} \\ + \lambda^2 \beta_2 X_{t-2} \dots + \dots \lambda^n \beta_n X_{t-n} \\ + e_t,$$

where λ is a constant lying between 0 and 1. The estimation of the regression coefficients in a system of distributed lags is difficult and a simplification is made by regressing differences in successive values of Y_t on X_t. Coefficients are estimated from *difference equations* of the form:

$$Y_t - \lambda Y_{t-1} = \alpha(1 - \lambda) + \beta X_t \\ + (e_t - \lambda e_{t-1}),$$

where Y_t and Y_{t-1} are successive observations and e_t and e_{t-1} are successive error terms or residuals.

The use of difference equations to estimate coefficients in time series regression also overcomes the problem of **multicollinearity** (intercorrelation between the independent variables) which naturally occurs in most regressions involving time series variables with distributed lags since successive values of a time series variable will be obviously correlated if the time series trace is a smoothly fluctuating one, as most time series variables are.

Torrance Tests of Creative Thinking A set of ten tests of creative thinking grouped into a pictorial and a verbal battery, and suitable for both children and adults. In a relaxed and stimulating atmosphere the subject has to:

(1) Write the questions he would need to ask to find out what is happening in a situation pictured for him.
(2) List the possible causes of this situation.
(3) List its consequences.
(4) Improve a toy so that children will have more fun with it.
(5) List unusual uses for a common object.
(6) List unusual questions which could be asked about the same object.
(7) List all the unusual consequences if a given situation were true.
(8) Starting with a coloured curved shape, draw an unusual picture.
(9) Complete a picture given a few lines as a start.
(10) Produce as many pictures as possible from parallel lines or from circles.

These tests may be scored for fluency, flexibility, originality, and elaboration. There are **norms** for samples of children and of college graduates.

Total Error Variance The weighted sum of the stratum error variances.

See also SAMPLING THEORY AND METHODS

Trait An enduring personality characteristic leading to a particular type of perception and/or action over a wide variety of situations.

TRANSFORMATION

A systematic manipulation applied to all the observations in a set of data. Transformations may be *reversible* or *irreversible*. An *irreversible transformation*, such as reducing scaled data to **ranks** or **dichotomies**, involves loss of information. Once it is performed there is no logical way of going back to the original. A *reversible transformation* involves no such loss. The original data may be restored by performing a reverse operation.

Reversible transformations may be either *linear* or *non-linear*. A *linear transformation*, e.g. adding a constant or multiplying by a constant, has a uniform effect on the scores, stretching or contracting each one in the same way and/or moving it up or down a scale. Such transformations are usually made simply to give a more convenient scale, e.g. to eliminate negative values or to express proportions as percentages. There is no important effect on the relationships between the variable (A) being transformed and some second variable (B). The correlation coefficient is unaffected, as is the shape of the graph plot of the two variables.

When there is good theoretical reason for believing that the relationship between variable A and variable B is not linear, or it is empirically found to be non-linear, then a *non-linear transformation* may sometimes be successfully applied. There are three main aims for such a transformation:

(1) to make the relationship between A and B linear,

(2) to make the **variances** of variable B homogeneous at each level of variable A (or vice versa), and

(3) to make the DISTRIBUTIONS of variable B roughly NORMAL at each level of variable A (or vice versa).

Successful achievement of these aims may be necessary for the valid application of **parametric** statistical techniques such as CORRELATION, MULTIPLE REGRESSION, and ANALYSIS OF VARIANCE. Fortunately, the achievement of one of the three aims usually implies achievement of the other two.

There are several non-linear transformations which may be useful according to circumstances. Examples are the *log transformation*, the *square root transformation*, the *reciprocal transformation*, and the *arcsine transformation*.

The log transformation is appropriate when (1) as A changes by a constant proportion B changes by a constant amount, or (2) the **standard deviation** of A increases and is proportional to the mean of A within ascending levels of B. In either case B is a linear function of log A. However, the usual formula is:

$$A' = \log_{10}(A + 1),$$

as this avoids the value minus infinity should A be zero. The square root transformation is best when the variance of A increases and is proportional to the mean of A within ascending levels of B. (This situation is likely to arise when A follows a **Poisson distribution**.) One formula is simply

$$A' = \sqrt{A},$$

but it has been shown that if any A is less than about 10 then either

$$A' = \sqrt{A + 0.5}$$

or

$$A' = \sqrt{A} + \sqrt{A + 1}$$

are more appropriate.

The reciprocal transformation is useful when the square of the mean level of A is proportional to the standard deviation of A within each level of B. The formula

$$A' = \frac{1}{A + 1}$$

is used.

When variable A is a proportion (fraction, percentage, number of cases per thousand, etc.) the arcsine transformation is appropriate. The distribution of a proportion (p) tends to be bunched at extreme values, and its variance, i.e. $p(1 - p)$, depends on the value of p. The arcsine transformation spreads out the extreme values and usually renders the variance of p constant for different mean levels of p. The arcsine transformation is given by

$$A = 2 \arcsin \sqrt{p},$$

i.e. twice the angle (measured in radians) whose trigonometric sine is the square root of the proportion being measured.

Treatment A term often used in experimental research, and having the same meaning as **independent variable**. Treatments may be divided into *treatment levels*, i.e. different amounts or values of the variable being manipulated (e.g. different levels of illumination, different training programs).

Treatment Level See under **Treatment**

Trend See under **Time Series Analysis**

Trend Lines by Least Squares Method See under FORECASTING

Triangulation The use of different research methods or sources of data to examine the same problem. If the same conclusions can be reached using different methods or sources, then no peculiarity of method or source has produced a particular conclusion and one's confidence in their validity increases.
Data triangulation refers to the collection of varied data on the same phenomena, e.g. from different participants or different phases of field-work. *Investigator triangulation*, similarly, involves collection of data by more than one researcher (preferably through the adoption of different roles in the field) and *method triangulation* involves the collection of data by different methods, thus ruling out different possible sources of design artefact.

True Score See under **Classical Test Theory Model**

True Variance That part of the variance of a test which may be attributed to *common factors* plus *specific factors*, i.e. all the variance which is not **error variance**.
See also FACTOR ANALYSIS

t-**Test** A test used for determining whether the means of two small samples differ so much that the samples are unlikely to be drawn from the same population. It is given by the ratio of the difference between the means to the **standard error** of this difference. (The exact formula varies with circumstances.) It assumes **interval measurement**, approximately NORMAL DISTRIBUTION of the underlying variable, and approximately equal variances in the two populations being compared. However, in practice the t-test is extremely robust and will not usually lead to false conclusions, despite some violation of these assumptions.

Tukey Test A method for making **unplanned comparisons** between group means following an ANALYSIS OF VARIANCE. The number of observations (n) in each group has to be equal or nearly equal. All possible comparisons are made and an 'honestly significant difference' (HSD) is computed which any particular mean difference must exceed in order to be considered significant. This is given by

$$\text{HSD} = q \sqrt{\frac{\text{residual mean square}}{n}}$$

The value of q, the studentized range statistic, for the required significance level is obtained from a special table.

Two by Two Table A table displaying the joint frequencies on two **dichotomous** variables. Also known as a *four-fold table*.
See under TABULATION

Two-Stage Least Squares See under ESTIMATION

Two-tailed Test A statistical test which uses the areas at both ends, or tails, of the appropriate distribution to test a non-directional hypothesis, that is, one which does not specify the direction in which the rejection of the **null hypothesis** will occur.
See under STATISTICAL INFERENCE

Type I Error To commit a **type I error** is to reject the **null hypothesis** when it is true. The probability (designated α) of his making a type I error is specified by a researcher before he tests his hypothesis.
See under STATISTICAL INFERENCE

Type II Error To commit a **type II error** is to accept the **null hypothesis** when it is false. The probability (designated β) of his making a type II error is specified by the researcher before he tests his hypothesis. $\beta = 1 - \alpha$, where α = probability of committing a type I error.
See under STATISTICAL INFERENCE

U

Unbiased Estimator   See under ESTIMATION

Underidentified Model   A path analytic model for which the **structural equations** may be written but in which there is no way of solving these to obtain the **path coefficients**.
See under PATH ANALYSIS

Unexplained Variance   See under **Explained Variance**

Unidimensionality   A test or concept is unidimensional if it refers to a single specific attribute. Length is a unidimensional concept, referring solely to linear extension in space. Beauty is multidimensional because it is the result of a large number of different attributes interacting together, and there are clearly several quite different kinds.

Unimodal   Unimodal distributions have one distinct value around which observations tend to cluster. When plotted they exhibit a single hump, e.g.

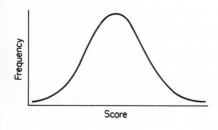

Unique Factor   In FACTOR ANALYSIS a unique factor is one which is measured (loaded on) by only one variable.

Unit normal Curve   The NORMAL DISTRIBUTION curve with zero **mean** and unit **standard deviation.**

Unit Normal Deviate   Synonymous with **Z-score**

Univariate Analysis   Any analysis performed on a single variable — e.g. plotting its **frequency distribution**, finding its **mean**, or **standard deviation**.

Univariate Frequency Distribution   See under **Frequency Distribution**

Universe   See **General Universe or Population**

Universe Score   See under **Generalizability theory**

Unplanned Comparison   After an ANALYSIS OF VARIANCE has demonstrated that the mean values (e.g. *A, B,* and *C*) of several groups of subjects differ significantly overall, the next step is to investigate exactly where the differences lie (e.g. is $A > B = C$ or is $A > B > C$, etc.) A *planned comparison* is a comparison between two or more means which was *planned in advance of doing the experiment*. A modified version of the *t*-**test** is usually appropriate for such a comparison since there is only one specific hypothesis being tested and therefore little danger of capitalizing on chance. Where a comparison is **unplanned**, i.e. not envisaged prior to the experiment it might turn up a spuriously significant difference simply because many comparisons could be made — e.g. if there are six group means, 15 different pairs of means could be compared. In this case a specially conservative statistical procedure such as the **Scheffé method** should be used. Other tests for following up an analysis of variance are the **least significant difference test**, the **Tukey test**, the **Newman–Keuls test**, and the **Duncan Multiple Range test.**

Upper Quartile (Q₃)   The value of a distributed variable above which 25 per cent of the observations lie.
See also **Interquartile ratio**

V

VALIDITY

Traditionally the extent to which a test, questionnaire, or other operationalization is really measuring what the researcher intends to measure. The modern emphasis is more on the extent to which the measure bears out the properties assigned to it by the theory in which it plays a part. A test has *face validity* if it contains items which intuitively appear to be valid, *concurrent validity* if it correlates well with other measures of the same concept, *content validity* when it samples adequately the domain which it is supposed to measure, and *predictive validity* if it may be used to make accurate predictions of future performance. Concurrent validity and predictive validity may be classified as *criterion-related validity* since they both evaluate the test against some criterion assumed to be valid. *Construct validity* refers to the extent to which the test appears to conform to predictions about it from theory, or other relevant observations. *Convergent validity* is achieved when several dissimilar methods of measurement of the same concept correlate well with the test; and *discriminant validity* is present when the test does not correlate with measures of other concepts. *Internal validity* (of experiments) is the extent to which an experiment is a good test of a hypothesis under the given experimental conditions; *external validity* refers to the extent to which the results may be generalized to other groups of people and conditions.

Value   See under **Score**

Variable   A single unidimensional property which may vary along a scale. A *continuous variable* (e.g. age) may do so in infinitely small steps. A *discrete variable* (e.g. family size) takes values only at certain points. Some properties may be measured more easily than others. The term variable is appropriately applied to properties which may be measured on an **interval**, a **ratio**, or even an **ordinal scale**. A property which may be described only on a

nominal scale is not strictly a variable, and is better termed an **attribute**.

Variance   A measure of the spread or **dispersion** of a set of scores given by:

$$s^2 = \frac{1}{n} \Sigma_i (x_i - \bar{x})^2,$$

where x_i is an individual score, $\bar{x}$ is the mean score, and n is the number of scores.

Variate   An observation which has been measured on a scale and is therefore a specific value of a **variable**.

Varimax Rotation   A widely used method of rotating factors after their first extraction. The factors are kept **orthogonal** to each other and the method maximizes the squared **variance** of the *factor loadings* on each factor. This results in factors which tend to have a few of the tests loading highly on them and the rest loading near zero.
See also **FACTOR ANALYSIS**

Verstehen (Intersubjective Understanding)   A form of investigation and of explanation of events which takes account of individual and group perspectives, motives, feelings, and purposes and which attempts to demonstrate how these and other factors may interact to produce the event under investigation. Because of the importance placed upon a full understanding of actors' meanings and purposes, verstehen investigations are ethnographic (e.g. **PARTICIPANT OBSERVATION**) rather than **nomothetic methods**
See also **EXPLANATION**

Volunteer Sample   A sample recruited by asking for volunteers. It is not representative of any defined population because the characteristics which prompted people to volunteer may be less frequent in the population than in the sample.
See also **SAMPLING THEORY AND METHODS**

W

Watts Vernon Reading Test A test of reading comprehension used in several national surveys of children's reading ability from 1948 to 1964. There are 35 questions from which the right answers are to be selected from five alternatives, the child's score being the number right in a 10-minute time limit. The questions become progressively more difficult, ranging from those that can be answered by intelligent children in infant school, to those that require the vocabulary used in leading articles of good newspapers.

Wechsler Adult Intelligence Scale (WAIS) An intelligence test for adults made up of eleven subscales. Six of these measure verbal and mathematical ability, the other five being performance tests. The WAIS is suitable for people aged 16 years and upwards and there are **norms** for different age groups.

Wechsler Intelligence Scale for Children (WISC) An **intelligence test** for children, made up of ten subscales. Five of these subscales measure verbal and mathematical ability, and five are performance tests. The WISC is suitable for children from 6½ to 16½ years old and **norms** are available for each age group.

Weighted Kappa (κ_w) A measure of **inter-rater reliability** which allows disagreements between raters to be weighted according to how serious they are.
See under RELIABILITY

Weighted Least Squares See under ESTIMATION

Weights Numbers which measure the relative significance of the scores on two or more variables for predicting scores on another variable — e.g. for predicting test C, test A might have a weight of 2 and test B a weight of 3, meaning that the best (linear) prediction of C is $(2 \times A) + (3 \times B) = C$.

Wilcoxon Test A **non-parametric test** for use with **matched pairs**. It must be possible to form a difference score (d) for each pair such that some differences are greater than others. The steps in the Wilcoxon test are as follows:
(1) Calculate the difference scores for each pair ignoring the signs of the differences.
(2) Rank these differences, dropping from the analysis any pair in which $d = 0$ and assigning the averge rank to tied ranks.
(3) Affix the sign of the difference to each.
(4) Set $T = $ sum of the positive ranks or the sum of the negative ranks, whichever is the smaller.
(5) For $N \leqslant 25$ enter special tables to see if the value of N is significant.
(6) For $N > 25$, the quantity

$$\frac{T - \frac{N(N + 1)}{4}}{\sqrt{\frac{N(N + 1)(2N + 1)}{24}}}$$

is a **Z-score**, and the significance of T is determined by entering a table of the NORMAL DISTRIBUTION
The Wilcoxon test is about 95 per cent as **powerful** as the *t*-test when used on data for which the *t*-test would be appropriate.

Within-Groups Variance See under **Between-Groups Variance**

Working Universe or Population The working population is the population from which the researcher actually draws his sample (e.g. schoolteachers in Birmingham).
See also **General Universe or Population**

X

X-axis   See under **Graphic Presentation**

Y

$\hat{Y}$ See under MULTIPLE REGRESSION

Yates Correction for Continuity A correction to be applied to the computation of the χ^2 statistic for **two by two tables** with small numbers in the cells. One recommendation is that the χ^2 test should not be used at all if the *expected frequency* in any cell is less than five and that the correction should be applied if any expected frequency is greater than five but less than ten. The usual formula for χ^2 for a two by two table with A, B, C, and D observations in the cells and N observations altogether is

$$\chi^2 = \frac{(AD - BC)^2 N}{(A + B)(C + D)(A + C)(B + D)}.$$

Incorporating the Yates' correction the formula is

$$\chi^2 = \frac{(|AD - BC| - N/2)^2 N}{(A + B)(C + D)(A + C)(B + D)}.$$

The appropriate use of the Yates' correction therefore reduces the observed value of χ^2 and makes it less likely that a **type I error** will be committed, that is, that the **null hypothesis** will be rejected when it is true.

Y-axis See under **Graphic Presentation**

Yule's Q One of the first measures of association to be devised. It applies to **two by two tables.** When the frequencies in the cells are as shown:

variable 1

		−	+
variable 2	−	a	b
	+	c	d

$$Q = \frac{ad - bc}{ad + bc}$$

Q may range from -1 for high negative association through zero for no relationship, to $+1$ for high positive association. However, values of -1 and $+1$ do not necessarily mean that all the cases fall on a diagonal.
Q is identical to Kruskall–Wallis's **gamma** when the latter is applied to a two by two table.

Z

Z-distribution See NORMAL DISTRIBUTION

Zero Order Correlation A term which frequently crops up in the context of MULTIPLE REGRESSION and which refers to the simple correlation between two variables, with no other variables **partialled out** of it.
See also **Partial Correlation**

Z-score A score obtained by expressing a raw score (x_i) as a deviation from the mean score $(\bar{x})$ and dividing by the standard deviation of the score(s):

$$Z = \frac{x_i - \bar{x}}{s}.$$

This transformation allows a comparison of scores measured in different scale units; Z-scores have a mean of 0 and a standard deviation of 1 and being pure ratios have no units.

Z-test Where the **mean** value (*MP*) of a NORMALLY DISTRIBUTED population is known, the Z-test may be used to determine whether the mean value (*MS*) of a **sample** is likely to be the same as that for the **population** (and hence whether the sample is likely to

have come from, or to be similar to, the population):

$$Z = \frac{MP - MS}{S_{ms}},$$

where S_{ms} is the **standard error of the mean** for the sample. The value of Z is computed and compared with those in a table of normal curve functions. If this value exceeds a critical value the **null hypothesis** is rejected, and it is concluded that the sample mean differs from the population mean.
See also STATISTICAL INFERENCE

Z-transformation (of a Correlation Coefficient) The DISTRIBUTION of successive samples of the **Pearson product moment correlation** (*r*) is not normal, being particularly skewed at high values of *r*. This means that statistical tests such as those for the significance of the difference between two *r*'s would not be valid if performed directly.
The **Z-transformation (Fisher's Z)** is applied to *r* and thereby renders its distribution virtually NORMAL. The transformation allows the statistical tests to be validly performed. Standard tables of the Z-transformation are widely available; alternatively Z is given by

$$Z = \tfrac{1}{2}\ln(1 + r) - \tfrac{1}{2}\ln(1 - r).$$